HOUSING
MARKET
DISCRIMINATION

HOUSING MARKET DISCRIMINATION

Causes and Effects of Slum Formation

Diane E. Gold

PRAEGER

PRAEGER SPECIAL STUDIES • PRAEGER SCIENTIFIC

Library of Congress Cataloging in Publication Data

Gold, Diane E
    Housing market discrimination.

    Bibliography: p.
    Includes index.
    1. Discrimination in housing--New York (City)
2. Slums--New York (City) I. Title.
HD7304.N5G64   363.5'1   80-11568
ISBN 0-03-052456-3

Published in 1980 by Praeger Publishers
CBS Educational and Professional Publishing
A Division of CBS, Inc.
521 Fifth Avenue, New York, New York 10017 U.S.A.

0123456789 145 987654321

Printed in the United States of America

ACKNOWLEDGMENTS

I would like to take this opportunity to thank many people who were helpful in the preparation of this book.

Dr. Thomas Vietorisz and Dr. David Gordon, of the New School for Social Research, were extremely helpful throughout the beginning stages of this book.

The cooperation of community members from Brownsville, Crown Heights, East New York, Southeast Queens, and the Rockaways was greatly appreciated.

I would also like to thank the employees of the various departments of the City of New York for their aid and cooperation in securing necessary data on housing and neighborhood quality.

Finally, I would like to thank Benedette Knopik of Praeger Publishers for her editorial assistance and Mrs. Eveline Gold for the typing and retyping of the manuscript.

Any errors found in the book are, of course, mine.

CONTENTS

LIST OF TABLES

HOUSING
MARKET
DISCRIMINATION

1
AN ANALYSIS OF THE CAUSES AND EFFECTS OF SLUM FORMATION

1
INTRODUCTORY OVERVIEW

PURPOSE

> The city is a crucible into which we pour the most
> disparate elements in our modern industrial society,
> vaguely expecting that given time they will one day
> fuse into an acceptable amalgam. But it is becoming
> increasingly clear that the prevailing shortage of
> housing and the measures taken to meet this shortage
> are turning the city into a breeding ground for ten-
> sions which may disturb the balance of society. [1]

Given the scale and ubiquity of the housing problem, it is not
surprising that people have tried to build a framework of knowledge
of urban areas in order to make it easier to control, or even con-
quer the problem. The slum, a characteristic habitat of millions,
has an extensive written past. Yet the realization by many authors
that a problem exists does not imply that it is understood. This is
certainly true of urban housing problems as witnessed by the failure of public programs to alleviate the problem of slum formation
and maintenance.

The experience of this problem in the United States and abroad
has shown that government programs have had consequences that
have been harmful to the interests of those whom housing policies
were designed to serve. This process was noted in London as
early as 1883. The Artizans Dwelling Act made matters worse for
the poor. While large areas were cleared of fever-breeding rook-
eries to make way for new construction, the rents in these new
buildings were beyond the means of the poor.

3

> They are driven to crowd more closely together in the
> few stifling places still left to them: and so Dives
> makes a richer harvest out of their misery, buying up
> property condemned as unfit for habitation, and turn-
> ing it into a goldmine because the poor must have shel-
> ter somewhere, even though it be the shelter of a living
> tomb. [2]

The problem of slum formation and maintenance in London
remains unchanged. The Greater London Council has recently been
cited for similar acts:

> The Council knocks down more houses than it replaces.
> Particularly hard hit is the private rental sector as
> many houses are taken over by the Council and others
> are converted to more profitable furnished lettings.
> The Council has considerable control over displaced
> tenants and, therefore, can successfully manipulate
> them. [3]

In the United States, attempts at slum clearance fall under
the category of urban renewal and public housing. The results of
these programs have been similar:

> The federal urban renewal program allows those in
> control of the program to change one kind of neighbor-
> hood into another kind by destroying the old buildings
> and replacing them with new ones. Naturally, the new
> ones they choose are desirable from what their view is
> of the public good. [4]

Public housing and urban renewal have actually tended to displace the poor into surrounding areas, increasing overcrowdedness,
and causing slum formation. Rents have risen considerably, since
this displacement of the poor has resulted in increased pressure on
a limited housing supply.

In this study, the process of slum formation is viewed as an
effect of the interaction of political economic forces. In order to
develop that view, the book focuses on eight neighborhoods in New
York City over the period 1950-75. For purposes of this study, a
neighborhood is defined as a section of the city lived in by people
having distinguishing characteristics.

Neighborhoods within a metropolitan area can be identified by
housing submarket type, which are derivative of the policies of
financial and governmental institutions. Geographically distinct

housing submarkets—within which identifiable community groups live—are created as a result. The geographic structure of the metropolitan housing market contributes to the potential for landlords to realize a class-monopoly rent that is set by the outcome of landlord-tenant conflict. A metropolitan housing market is divided into six submarkets, the main features of which are as follows:

1. The inner city submarket is characterized by a low-income black population. There is much conflict between landlords and tenants.

2. White ethnic areas are characterized by a lower-income white population. Rents in these areas are low and housing quality is good.

3. Black residential neighborhoods are characterized by moderate-income blacks. There is a predominance of homeowners in these areas.

4. Areas of high turnover are characterized by low-income blacks. Although much of the housing in these areas is single-family housing, the quality of these areas is poor. Many attribute the decline of these areas to corruption of FHA (Federal Housing Administration) housing programs.

5. Middle-income submarkets are generally stable neighborhoods, with a mixture of rental and owner-occupied housing.

6. Upper-income submarkets are stable, flourishing areas where rents are high, mainly because of status considerations.

In this study, eight neighborhoods are examined, five of which had experienced racial change and reflected submarkets 1, 3, and 4. The other three neighborhoods, selected as control areas, reflected submarket 2. Relying on econometric analysis and extensive field research, the process of slum formation was analyzed by examining the interdependence of rent determination, neighborhood quality, and public programs.

OBJECTIVE

The objective of this study is to analyze the process of slum formation and maintenance and its effects on urban housing submarkets. Within this general objective, more specific aims were as follows:

To study how policies of financial and governmental institutions have had racially based effects on urban neighborhoods through public housing and FHA housing

To study how the actions of speculator real estate interests
in black neighborhoods have promoted slum formation
To study the determinants of rents in different neighborhoods
To study how the city's changing allocation of services has
promoted slum formation.

METHODOLOGY

The nature and operation of urban housing markets have been
analyzed by conventional economists to show the influence of racial
composition of a neighborhood on rents. Books and articles by John
Kain and John Quigley, Richard Muth, Arthur Bailey, and Anthony
Downs represent the traditional literature on the urban housing market.[5] These authors tend to treat rent determination, neighborhood
quality, and public programs as separable. They tend to view the
housing market as a uniform market, where housing price is determined by housing and neighborhood quality. This study argues that
neither strand of conventional analysis is adequate for the analysis
of slum formation. For our purposes, three main methodological
departures have proved necessary.

The first feature of the methodology involved a literature
search for the purpose of establishing a theoretical/historical
framework for this study. This framework enables an examination
of the mechanisms that produce and reproduce slums. Books and
articles by David Harvey, Frederick Engels, and Karl Marx have
laid the foundation for a theoretical base in their analyses of the
meaning of rent in capitalist society and the structure of housing
submarkets (classes) in a metropolitan area.[6]

In order to pay proper respect to the theoretical framework,
it was necessary to apply the framework to the development of New
York City. Books on the historical development of London—H. J.
Dyos, Dyos and Reeder, Gareth S. Jones, David Weinberg, and
Rex and Moore were used as a basis for the study of New York
City.[7] Supportive materials on the United States by Robert Caro,
John Legget, and Martin Anderson were documented where ap-
plicable.[8]

The second feature of the methodology involved extensive field
research. A useful method for obtaining information on housing
submarket structure, neighborhood quality, and public programs
was to conduct a neighborhood study. This approach offered insight
into the interrelationships of these factors and helped to identify
many forces that interact in the process of slum formation and
maintenance. The field research served the purpose of gathering
descriptive historical data on selected New York City neighborhoods.

An effort was made to view the political economic history of a
neighborhood in terms of residents who inherited a historic situation and whose personalities were being constantly affected by the
neighborhood in which they lived. A substantial portion of the
material that could not be presented in a traditional format was
presented as verbatim transcription of interviews. This brought
out the actual character of the neighborhoods, because the interviews expressed the true feelings of the residents and the meaning
that the neighborhood had for them.

The third facet of the methodology involved the use of certain
quantitative techniques, like factor analysis, that permitted consideration of the interrelationships among several neighborhood quality
variables. One objective of this evaluation was to examine the different mechanisms that determine rents in different housing submarkets. Data on housing, population, and neighborhood (crime,
juvenile delinquency, fires, and health) for the eight New York City
neighborhoods were analyzed to demonstrate that rents in slum
areas are affected by different mechanisms than rents in nonslum
areas.

ORGANIZATION OF THE STUDY

Chapter 2 develops an analytical framework that permits an
examination of interdependence consistent with the assumption that
rent determination mechanisms differ across neighborhoods. This
framework focuses on the mechanisms that produce and reproduce
slums.

Chapter 3 applies that framework to the historic development
of neighborhoods in New York, reviewing the development of neighborhood structure. The choice of neighborhoods for study reflects
the historic development of the city as the institutions that have reproduced these neighborhood characteristics are analyzed.

Chapter 4 is designed to analyze, in general, the results of
the field research. It includes a presentation of the research method
employed and a discussion of the types of materials collected. The
extent to which this field research supports the hypotheses is presented.

Chapter 5 reviews some econometric tests of the main hypotheses. In that chapter, there are tests for interdependence among
neighborhood quality characteristics and for the existence of different rent determination mechanisms.

Chapter 6, the conclusion, includes a discussion of the results of this study.

The theoretic/historic approach developed in Chapters 2 and 3 leads to discussion of characteristics of individual neighborhoods in relation to other areas of the city. The New York City neighborhood analyses were structured to examine the forces that gave rise to slum conditions. As such, Chapters 7 through 11 shed light on the following issues:

> How have the policies and actions of financial and government institutions shaped neighborhood quality by public housing construction and FHA homeownership programs?
>
> How have speculator real estate interests affected the quality of private housing? Has the city encouraged these speculators by exiling welfare clients to substandard housing in slum areas?
>
> How has the city's allocation of services affected neighborhood quality? Have certain neighborhoods been allowed to deteriorate at the expense of others?

Since the development of each neighborhood differs, the emphasis in each of these chapters is different.

Chapter 7 analyzes the history of Brownsville's population, private housing, public housing, and neighborhood quality. The effects of the shift in population (both political and economic) were of particular importance.

Chapter 8 explores the history of Crown Heights population, housing, and neighborhood quality. The racial character of Crown Heights necessitated, in addition, a separate analysis of racial tension.

Chapter 9 examines the history of East New York with particular focus on the effects that FHA housing programs have had on housing and neighborhood quality.

Chapter 10 investigates the history of Southeast Queens, focusing on the relationships between South Jamaica and St. Albans/Addesleigh Park. The history of housing and neighborhood characteristics of each area was analyzed.

Chapter 11 analyzes the history of the Rockaways housing and neighborhoods, with particular emphasis on the effects of the change from a summer resort area to one inundated with public housing.

Chapter 12 defines the control areas and briefly analyzes their neighborhood structures. These areas are not analyzed in any detail since they are used solely as controls in the empirical testing.

NOTES

1. From the Foreword in John Rex and Robert Moore, Race, Community and Conflict: A Study of Sparkbrook (London: Oxford University Press for Oxford Institute of Race Relations, 1967).

2. Quoted in Henry Mayhew, Labour and the London Poor (London: G. Allen & Unwin, 1883).

3. This is the thesis of two studies on London, England, by M. Harloe, R. Issacharoff, and R. Minns, The Organization of Housing (London: Sage Publications, 1974), and J. English, R. Madigan, and J. Norman, Slum Clearance: The Social and Administrative Context in England and Wales (London: Holmes and Meier, 1976).

4. This is the general thesis of Martin Anderson's The Federal Bulldozer (Cambridge, Mass.: MIT Press, 1966).

5. See John Kain and John Quigley, "Housing Market Discrimination, Home Ownership and Savings Behavior," American Economic Review, March 1972; Richard Muth, Cities and Housing (Chicago: University of Chicago Press, 1969); Martin Bailey, "Note on the Economics of Residential Zoning and Urban Renewal," Land Economics, August 1959, pp. 288-90; Martin Bailey, "Effects of Race and Other Demographic Features on the Values of Single Family Houses," Land Economics, May 1966, pp. 215-20; Anthony Downs, "An Economic Analysis of Property Values and Race," Land Economics, May 1960, pp. 181-88.

6. See David Harvey, Social Justice and the City (Baltimore: Johns Hopkins University Press, 1973); David Harvey, "Class Monopoly Rent, Finance Capital and the Urban Revolution," Regional Studies 8 (1974): 240; David Harvey, "Class Structure and the Theory of Residential Differentiation," in Bristol Essays in Geography, ed. M. Chisolm (London: Heineman, 1974); Frederick Engels, The Condition of the Working Class in England in 1844 (London: G. Allen and Unwin, 1950); Frederick Engels, The Housing Question (New York: International Publishers, 1935); Karl Marx, Capital, 3 vols. (New York: International Publishers, 1967).

7. H. J. Dyos, The Study of Urban History (London: St. Martin's Press, 1968); H. J. Dyos and H. Reeder, in Victorian City, ed. H. Dyos and M. Wolf (London: Routledge and Kegan Paul, 1973); Gareth Stedman Jones, Outcast London (London: Oxford University Press, 1971); David Weinberg, "The Dialectics of Urban Living," unpublished Ph.D. dissertation, Massachusetts Institute of Technology, 1974; Rex and Moore, op. cit.

8. See Robert Caro, The Powerbroker (New York: Alfred Knopf, 1974); John Legget, Class, Race and Labor: Workers' Consciousness in Detroit (New York: Oxford University Press, 1968); Anderson, op. cit.

2
RESIDENTIAL DIFFERENTIATION AND SLUM FORMATION: TOWARD AN ANALYTICAL FRAMEWORK

The aim of this chapter is to develop an analytical framework for evaluating urban housing problems by using economic and political economic literature. This framework is designed to permit an examination of interdependence consistent with hypotheses of different rent determination mechanisms in different neighborhoods, while focusing on the endogenous mechanisms that produce and reproduce neighborhood transition.

The chapter is divided into two sections. The first section briefly reviews the conventional literature on urban land use and racial discrimination. In order to lay the basis for an approach that transcends the limitations of this literature, I used materials from political economy. While the diversity of theories and techniques complicates the problem, I relied heavily on the works of David Harvey, an urban geographer. Harvey's work synthesizes much of the material written by Engels and Marx on urbanization, rent problems, and housing. In the second section, using these materials I developed an alternative framework that was adopted for this study.

PRESENT THEORETICAL FRAMEWORKS

The slum is attracting increasing attention as a major social problem of American cities. The most obvious body of theory that calls for examination is that of urban land use. One large segment of this theory draws its inspiration from the Chicago school of sociologists. Park, Burgess, and McKenzie wrote on the city and elaborated an interpretation of urban form in ecological terms.[1] They noted the concentration of low-income groups and various ethnic groups within particular sections of the city. They also discovered a regularity of spatial form in the city. The concentric zone theory of the city emerged from this analysis. Park and Burgess appeared to regard the city as a sort of man-produced, ecological complex within which the processes of social adaptation, specialization of function and life style, competition for living space, and so on, acted to produce a coherent spatial structure, the whole being held together by "the moral order." The main focus of interest was to find out who ended up where and what conditions were like when they got there. The main thrust of the Chicago school was descriptive. Park and Burgess did not pay much attention to the kind of social solidarity generated through the workings of the economic system nor to the social and economic relationships that derive from economic considerations. As a result, the urban land-use theory they developed has a critical flaw when it is used as an explanation of the slum.

The common spatial structure of the city noted by Park and Burgess can be analyzed from an economic point of view. The possibility of using neoclassic economic principles to explain this phenomenon was initially indicated by von Thunen.[2] This laid the basis for an economic theory of the urban land-market in the work of William Alonso and Richard Muth.

Alonso and Muth presume utility maximizing behavior on the part of individuals In the housing market, individuals trade off the quantity of housing (space), accessibility (cost of transport to place of employment), and the need for all other goods and services, within an overall budget constraint. It is presumed that consumers are indifferent with respect to certain combinations of space and accessibility. Furthermore, individuals bid for housing at a location up to a point where the extra amount of "satisfaction" gained from a move is exactly equal to the marginal utility of spending an extra quantity of money. From this conceptualization it is possible to derive equilibrium conditions in the urban housing market—conditions that are Pareto optimal.

Urban land use is determined through a process of competitive bidding, which proceeds so that land rents are higher nearer the center of activity. In considering the residential choice open to two groups in the population (one high-income and one low-income) with respect to an employment center, we can predict where each must live by examining the structure of their bid rent curves. For the low-income group, the bid rent curve is characteristically steep since the poor have very little money to spend on transportation; and therefore their ability to bid for land declines rapidly with distance from place of employment. The high-income group has a shallow bid rent curve since its ability to bid is not greatly affected by transportation costs. When put in competition with each other, we find the low-income group forced to live in the center of the city, and the high-income group living outside. This means that the low-income group is forced to live on high-rent land. The only way they can adjust to this is to save on the quantity of space they consume by crowding into a small area. The logic of the model indicates that poor groups will be concentrated in high-rent areas close to the city center in overcrowded conditions. The rich group can always enforce its preferences over a poor group because it has more resources to apply either to transport costs or to obtaining land in whatever location it chooses.

The assumptions built into the economic approach are obviously unrealistic. There are numerous and diverse actors in the housing market and each group has a distinctive way of determining utility (use value) and exchange value.[3] These groups consist of the occupiers of housing, real estate agents, landlords, developers, financial institutions, and governmental institutions. The operations of all these groups in the housing market cannot easily be brought together into one comprehensive framework for analysis. The same house can take on a different meaning depending upon the social relationship that individuals, organizations, and institutions express in it. A model of the housing market that presumes all housing stock to be allocated among users (whose differentiating characteristics are income and housing preferences) through utility-maximizing behavior appears restricted in its applicability.

Another line of criticism of the economic approach to urban land-use theory stems from the fact that it is formulated in a static equilibrium framework.[4] The urban land-use system rarely approaches anything like an equilibrium posture and Pareto optimality will never be achieved. Differential disequilibrium is evident and there are too many imperfections, rigidities, and immobilities for the market to work well as a coordinating device. The urban area is built up over time, and activities and people take up their position in the urban system sequentially. Once located, activities and people tend to be particularly difficult to move. The simultaneity presupposed in the economic models runs counter to what is in fact a very strong process. This indicates a flaw in the economic formulations: their inability to handle the absolute quality of space, which makes land and improvements such peculiar commodities. Most writers either ignore this issue or dismiss it.

In a sequential allocation of a fixed housing stock in order of competitive bidding power, the poorest group, because it enters the housing market last, has to face producers of housing services who are in a quasi-monopolistic position. Lack of choice makes the poor vulnerable to being squeezed by quasi-monopolistic policies.

In this manner, realtor exploitation (excessively high rents) in the poorest areas will persist. This condition arises when producers compete over space for the custom of consumers trapped in space; in other words we are dealing with a class monopoly of landlords with respect to housing provision for a class of low-income tenants. There is a class of housing consumers who have no credit rating and who have no choice but to rent wherever they can. A class of land-lords emerges to provide for the needs of those consumers, but since the consumers have no choice, the landlord class has monop-oly power. Landlords will withdraw housing from the market if their rate of return falls below a certain level. The main conclu-sion to be drawn is that in a capitalist market exchange economy it is possible to realize more gains as the result of the inherent monop-olistic quality of space in some situations than it is in others. The rich, who have plenty of economic choice, are more able to escape such consequences of monopoly than are the poor, whose choices are exceedingly limited. We therefore arrive at the fundamental conclusion that the rich can command space whereas the poor are trapped in it.

TOWARD A NEW FRAMEWORK FOR
THE STUDY OF SLUM FORMATION

The phenomenon of concentric zoning in the city was noted by Engels some 80 years earlier than the writings of the Chicago soci-ologists. His interpretation of this phenomenon, however, was much more thorough, paying a great deal of attention to the workings of the economic system and the social and economic relationships that derive from economic considerations.

Manchester's central area, which is half a mile long and broad, consists of offices and warehouses. The area is deserted at night. Shops and stores line the ground floor of the main streets here. The upper floors of these buildings are occupied by the work-ing class. Beyond this central area, the middle and upper classes reside—the upper class in more remote, wholesome areas. Mem-bers of the money aristocracy, by taking the shortest road into town, never see the regions of misery where the working class resides. The thoroughfares leading into town are lined with a series of stores that are maintained by the middle and lower bourgeoisie "[that] they suffice to conceal from the eyes of the wealthy men and women of strong stomachs and weak nerves the misery and grime from which is formed the complement of their wealth."[5]

Engels's approach is far more consistent with hard economic and social realities than was the approach of Park, Burgess, and

McKenzie. With certain modifications, Engels's description could be made to fit the contemporary American city (concentric zoning with adequate transport facilities for the affluent who live in suburbs, sheltering the commuters into the city from seeing the grime and misery that is the complement of their wealth, and so on). The miseries of the city were an inevitable concomitant to a capitalist system. Social solidarity was enforced through the operation of the market exchange system.

There are some curious features about ghetto housing. One paradox is that the areas of greatest overcrowding are also the areas with the highest vacancy rates. The same areas are characterized by a large proportion of houses let go in lieu of property taxes.[6] Contrary to the general impression, landlords in the inner city housing market are not making huge profits.[7] In fact, evidence suggests that they are making less than they would elsewhere in the market, yet the rents such landlords charge are very high relative to the quality of the accommodations, while properties, if they do change hands, do so at negligible prices. The banks, needless to say, have rational business reasons for refusing to finance mortgages in inner city areas, given the drive to maximize profits. After all, banks feel that there is a greater uncertainty in the inner city. Consequently, it seems possible not to find a policy within the existing economic and institutional framework that is capable of rectifying these conditions. Federal subsidies to private housing fail; rent subsidies are quickly absorbed by market adjustments; and public housing has little impact because it is limited in quantity, too congested and localized in distribution (in those areas where the poor are forced to live anyway), and devised for use only by a particular class in society. Urban renewal merely relocates the problem and, in most cases, does more harm than good.

Engels, in a set of essays entitled The Housing Question, published in 1872, predicted that this was the impasse into which any capitalist solutions to housing problems would inevitably lead.[8] Although he was referring to nineteenth-century London, his thesis holds true for the contemporary American city. Although all serious analysts concede the seriousness of the slum problem, few call into question the forces that rule the heart of our economic system. Thus we discuss everything except the basic characteristics of a capitalist market economy. We devise all manner of solutions except those that might challenge the continuance of that economy. Such discussions eventually lead us to discover what Engels was aware of in 1872: that capitalist solutions provide no foundation for dealing with deteriorated social conditions. Engels, in The Housing Question, pointed to the consequences that flowed from the competitive market process:

The growth of the big modern cities gives the land in
certain areas, particularly in those which are centrally situated, an artificial and colossally increasing
value; the buildings erected on these areas depress
this value, instead of increasing it, because they no
longer correspond to the changed circumstances.
They are pulled down and replaced by others. This
takes place above all with workers' houses which are
situated centrally and whose rents, even with the
greatest overcrowding, can never, or only very slowly, increase above a certain maximum. They are
pulled down and in their stead shops, warehouses and
public buildings are erected. [9]

Today it is drugs and crime that are important, but the solutions
devised still have the same characteristics.

Engels pointed out that the bourgeoisie has one method of solving the housing problem. This method consists of demolishing
working-class housing in central areas. At the same time this displacement of the working class is accomplished, areas are cleared
for business or, owing to traffic requirements, for railway construction. The result of this displacement is that the housing problem of the working class is shifted elsewhere. Engels continues:

The breeding places of disease, the infamous holes
and cellars in which the capitalist mode of production
confines workers are not abolished; they are merely
shifted elsewhere! The same economic necessity
which produced them in the first place, produces them
in the next place also. As long as the capitalist mode
of production continues to exist, it is folly to hope for
an isolated solution of the housing question. [10]

The experience gained from implementing urban policies in
American cities indicates that this inherent contradiction in the
capitalist market mechanism contributes to the process of slum
formation and maintenance. If we urban renew, we relocate the
poverty; if we don't, we witness decay. If we prevent blockbusting,
blacks are prevented from obtaining housing. The poor can be
blamed for conditions and policies can be instituted based on benign
neglect or degeneration, a process that will not provoke the kinds
of questions that policy failures inevitably raise.

In order to model the real processes that produce these patterns, it is necessary to investigate the meaning and role of rent as
an allocative device in the urban system. For payments to be made,

certain basic institutions are required. Private property arrangements are crucial; rent is a transfer payment realized through the monopoly power over land and resources conferred by the institution of private property.[11] Consequently, any examination of how rent originates and is realized cannot proceed without evaluating the performance of these supportive institutions. It is useful to turn to classical political economics to elucidate the nature of rent, for the neoclassical achievement succeeds in burying some of the relevant technical issues that attach to rent as it functions in the urban land market.[12] Marx provides a lengthy generalization and synthesis of the argument surrounding the rental concept in Capital and in Theories of Surplus Value. Marx regards rent as something that can emerge in a variety of ways out of all manner of initial conditions. The feature common to all cases is the institution of private property in land. Harvey asserts that

> landed property is based on the monopoly by certain persons over definite portions of the globe, as exclusive spheres of their private will to the exclusion of others. With this in mind, the problem is to ascertain the economic value, that is, the realization of this monopoly on the basis of capitalist production.[13]

Landowners thus possess a class monopoly over land use. Marx shows in Capital how rent can arise in a variety of ways depending on the dominant mode of production and he assembles evidence in support of his argument. Marx is primarily interested in the manifestations of rent in a competitive market economy. He lists three basic kinds of rent that typically arise under the capitalist mode of production:

> Monopoly Rent arises because it is possible to charge a monopoly price "determined by the purchaser's eagerness to buy and ability to pay, independent of the price determined by the general price of production as well as by the value of the product." . . . The opportunity to charge a monopoly price creates the opportunity for the landowner to reap a monopoly rent.
>   Differential Rents arise out of the difference between "the individual production price of a particular capital and the general production price of the total capital invested in the sphere of production concerned." . . . Relative locational advantage is explicitly built into the picture. Differential rent takes on its meaning in a relative space which is structured by differentials

in productive capacity at different locations and which
is integrated spatially through transport cost relationships.

    Absolute Rent is distinguished from monopoly
rent in that it gives rise to monopoly price, whereas
an independently determined monopoly price allows
monopoly rent to be gained. Capitalist production cannot afford to destroy the institution of private property
because its own existence is predicated on the private
ownership of the means of production. Capitalism is
therefore prepared to pay a tax on production (rent) as
the price for perpetuating the legal basis for its own
existence. Such a tax must enter into the costs of production and in this regard absolute rent (and monopoly
rent) are to be distinguished from differential rent.
The distinction between monopoly and absolute rent
can be rescued by regarding the former as operating
at the individual level and the latter as something which
arises out of the general conditions of production in
some sector (it is a class monopoly phenomenon which
affects the condition of all owners of low income housing).[14]

This chapter will be concerned with what Harvey calls "class-
monopoly rents." Whether this form of rent should be included in
Marx's categories of absolute or monopoly rent is unclear. The
resolution of this question depends upon the solution of the "transformation problem," which arises out of the relationship between
values and prices in the Marxian schema.[15] Harvey's opinion is
that class-monopoly rent is best treated as a form of absolute rent.
Class-monopoly rents arise because there exists a class of owners
of "resource units"—the land and the improvements incorporated in
it—who are willing to release the units under their command only if
they receive a positive return above some arbitrary level.[16] As a
class, these owners have the power to achieve some minimum rate
of return. The key concept here is class power. If landlords could
not or would not behave in accordance with a well-defined class interest, then class-monopoly rents would not be realized. Landlords gain their class power in part since individually they can survive quite well without releasing all their resources.

    This form of rent appears inevitable in capitalistically or-
ganized land and housing markets. In addition, the transfer payments that result from class-monopoly rents are structured in certain important respects. Harvey considers the example of a landlord who lives in suburbia and gives up a class-monopoly rent to the

speculator-developer: "Notice, that the rent realized from a low income tenant has been passed on to the speculator-developer via the landlord. It is unlikely, bordering on the impossible, for rent realized by the speculator-developer to be passed on to the low-income tenant."[17] Harvey thus postulates that there is a hierarchic structure through which class-monopoly rents percolate upward, but not downward. At the top of this hierarchy sit the financial institutions.

Harvey begins by stating a proposition: A hierarchic institutional structure through which class-monopoly rents are realized is a necessity if housing market activity is to be coordinated in a way that helps to avoid economic crisis.[18] All capitalist economies must possess elaborate devices to integrate national and local aspects of economies, to integrate individual decisions with the needs of society. Harvey argues that these devices are manifest in a structure of financial and government institutions that create the basis for class-monopoly power in the land and property markets.

National institutions of government and finance operate with the intention of directing policy toward the orderly accumulation of capital, economic growth, and the reproduction of the basic social and political relationships of a capitalist society. In the housing market these general concerns are translated into three concerns for national housing policy:

> to ensure orderly relationships between construction, economic growth and new household formation.
> to ensure short-run stability and iron out cyclical swings in the economy at large by using the construction industry and the housing sector as a partial Keynesian regulator, and
> to ensure domestic peace and tranquility by managing the distribution of welfare through the provision of housing.[19]

In the United States, economic growth has been accompanied and to some degree accomplished by rapid suburbanization—a process that has been facilitated by national housing policies, many of these conducted through the Federal Housing Administration. Cyclical swings in the economy have been broadly contained since the 1930s and the construction industry appears to have functioned effectively as a major countercyclical tool.[20]

The social militancy of the 1930s has largely been defused by a government policy that has created a large wedge of middle-income people who are now "debt encumbered homeowners" and consequently unlikely to rock the boat.[21] The evident militancy of the 1960s exhibited by blacks and the urban poor provoked a political response in the housing sector—a response that has not provided a "decent house in a suitable environment" for many of the poor but that has successfully created a debt-encumbered class of black homeowners. [22] It appears that national policies are designed to maintain the existing structure of society intact in its basic configuration, while facilitating economic growth and capitalist accumulation, eliminating cyclical influence, and defusing social discontent.

Federal, state, and local government form a three-tiered political hierarchy and an independent bureaucracy is attached to each level. [23] The federal bureaucracy is itself hierarchically organized, however, so that it is in a position to relate national housing policies to local housing markets. The FHA administers a wide range of government programs and operates autonomously from bureaucracies created at the state and local levels.

In the United States, the main mechanism for coordinating national, local, and individual activities lies in the hierarchical structure of financial institutions operating under government regulation. It is important to note that certain kinds of institutions—the state and federally chartered savings and loan institutions—operate only in the housing sector. [24] Some of these institutions are community based, depositor-controlled, and operate on a nonprofit basis. They are affected by money market conditions and government regulations. These institutions differ from mortgage banks, savings banks, and commercial banks, which are strictly profit oriented. All of these institutions operate together to relate national policies to local and individual decisions and in the process create localized structures within which class-monopoly rents can be realized. While Harvey demonstrates the point by examining Baltimore, this conflict between city and suburb that contributes to the realization of class-monopoly rents on the suburban fringe can be generalized for many cities.

A city has a geographic structure to its housing market that contributes to the potential for realizing class-monopoly rents (another contributor is the conflict between city and suburb). This geographic structure is produced by the interacting policies of financial and government institutions. The housing market of a city is highly structured with respect to the type of institutional involvement as well as to the insurance of home purchases by the FHA. The institutional involvement of the six main submarkets of a city is as follows:

The inner city submarkets, in which low-income black tenants live, are financed by cash and private loan transactions. Professional landlords are disinvesting in these areas but are still maintaining reasonable profits. The tenants here are politically powerless and are thus trapped in this submarket. Professional landlords realize a class-monopoly rent, which they refer to as "rate of return."

The white ethnic areas are serviced largely by community-based savings and loan institutions, which are not strongly profit oriented. Residents here are low-income and good housing can be obtained at fairly low prices since little class-monopoly rent is realized.

The black residential areas are inhabited by low- and moderate-income homeowners. Many homes in these areas were sold by way of a land installment contract. A speculator purchases a house, puts in minimum renovations, and interposes his credit between purchaser and financial institution, enabling the sale to transpire. Evidence has been advanced that these purchasers were being exploited: a class-monopoly rent was realized by the speculator who took advantage of financial and government policies and who was successful in large part because of problems of racial discrimination.

The transience areas are serviced by mortgage banker finance and FHA insurance. Various programs were created in the late 1960s to try to establish a debt-encumbered, stable class of home-owners among the black poor. These programs led to the creation of this FHA-insured, black, low-income housing submarket. One main facet of these programs was the "no down payment" policy. In these submarkets, speculators purchase houses at deflated values, put in minimal repairs to meet FHA quality standards, and sell, at windfall profits, to low-income blacks. Since FHA quality control standards are poor, class-monopoly rents are realized by these speculators.

The middle-income submarkets were created by FHA programs in the 1930s. Currently homeownership is financed by federal savings and loan institutions. Financial institutions are uncertain about risks in these areas. There is political friction in boundary zones of these areas and a struggle to preserve them from erosion at the edges—an erosion that would force residents to seek housing in the suburbs.

The more affluent groups are serviced by savings banks and commercial banks. These groups exercise considerable political power and can fend off speculative intrusions. Class-monopoly rents are realized because of status considerations.[25]

This class structure of submarkets forms a decision environment where individual households make housing choices. These choices are likely to conform to the structure and to reinforce it. The structure is a product of history.

In the long run, the geographic structure of the city is continuously being transformed by conflicts and struggles generated by the ebb and flow of market forces, the operations of speculators, landlords, and developers, the changing policies of government and financial institutions, changing tastes, and the like. But in the short run, the geographic structure is fixed and it is this rigidity that permits class-monopoly rents to be realized within submarkets and between submarkets as a variety of processes seek to erode the boundaries of the submarkets themselves (every submarket has its speculator-developer fringe).[26] In some parts of the city, these conflicts may be dormant at times; boundaries may be stabilized (often with the help of natural or artificial barriers) and accommodation between opposing forces may be reached within submarkets.

The implications of class-monopoly rent for residential structures are of interest. Residential differentiation has long been explained in terms of social ecological processes, consumer preferences, utility maximizing behavior, and so on. There have been attempts to integrate sociologic and economic perspectives on residential differentiation and these together with the growth of statistical techniques to explore patterns of residential structure have generated much literature. The diversity and sophistication of this literature is primarily a result of differences in technique and in details of specification, and not of theoretical structure.

Most theories of residential differentiation make use of concepts of class and income and the use of such concepts indicates that these theories are regarded either as derivative from or as a component of some more general theory of the structure of society. Harvey uses the concept "class" as a vehicle to explore the link between residential differentiation and a more general theory of societal structure. He begins by setting forth a version of the theory of class and then seeks to integrate this theory with materials on residential differentiation.

A concept of class has meaning in relationship to the situation to which it is applied. Class has different meanings under different modes of production. This relational view of class provides us with a standpoint from which to understand the basic forces shaping class configurations under the capitalist mode of production, the same forces that govern the inner movement of capitalism. These forces are, for the most part, in contradiction to each other. In the capitalist mode of production, labor, which produces the means of production, produces the means for its subordination to capital. This power relation is expressed directly through a market mode of integration. The market system requires a wide variety of institutional, legal, coercive, and ideological supports if it is to function. Labor power has to assume a character that enables it to be freely bought and sold and these rights of contract are guaranteed. Ownership and control over the production process have to be guaranteed to protect the interests of those in control to earn a certain rate of return.

Harvey suggests that three kinds of forces making for residential differentiation in advanced capitalist societies can be identified:

(1) A primary force arising out of the power relation between capital and labor.

(2) Certain derivative forces arising out of the contradictory and evolutionary character of capitalism which affect:

(a) The division of labor—As the technical and organizational basis of society is changed, so are the concomitant shifts in social relationships. The possibility for social and, thus, residential differentiation on this basis arises in part out of the specific skills which individuals have to possess in order to perform particular functions—hence, the distinction between manual and intellectual skills reflected in the distinction between blue collar and white collar workers.

(b) Consumption patterns—Profits can be realized on an expanding scale and accumulation sustained only if consumption patterns can be induced to provide a growing internal market to absorb the increasing quantities of products.

(c) Authority relations—The primary relationship structuring capitalist society is the power relation expressed in the market place between business and labor. This power relation requires a variety of institutional supports if it is to be sustained to accomplish increasing investment of capital. The government must be reordered so that they replicate relations expressed in this market.

(d) Political awareness—The separation between the economic and political administrative spheres is significant; by holding out the prospect for legal and political equality and creating specific political structures through which individuals may seek but never really

have control over conditions of their existence, the government apparatus diverts attention from the subordination of workers to
business in the market place. It results,
typically, in trade union awareness on the
part of workers and is consistent with the
emergence of a distinctive kind of middle-
class awareness that focuses on questions of
civil and political liberties to the exclusion of
questions of economic control.

(e) Mobility chances within the population—Most
movement takes place between one strata
within the division of labor to another (e.g.
from the manual to the white collar category).
Insofar as mobility chances are restricted,
they permit the definition of certain large and
relatively permanent aggregative groupings in
society.

(d) Residual forces reflecting the social relations established in a preceding or a geographically separate but subordinate mode of production.[27]

If class has a meaning internal to the capitalist mode of production, then it follows that residual forces cannot produce classes
in society. Confusion on this point may arise because the forces
that structure class under capitalism frequently etch class boundaries along lines established by reference to residual social structures. Thus, in the United States it is generally true that an underclass consists mainly of blacks and Indians (historic residual groupings) and Puerto Ricans, Mexican-Americans, and some recent
black immigrants (residual groupings defined by neocolonialism).
However, Appalachian and other poor whites and women are also to
be found in this underclass. There is, therefore, no necessary
correspondence between residual groupings and class configurations.

The changing scale of urbanization consequent upon capital
accumulation may be conducive to increasing residential differentiation in the city but it is difficult to see how it can necessitate it.[28]
Likewise, the inequitable distribution of income explains the ability
to make choices but it does not serve to explain the reasons choices
are made. A more convincing explanation of the necessity of residential differentiation in the city can be constructed by examining
the way in which the derivative forces of class structuration interact with each other in the context of the changing scale of urbanization. These forces function to keep capitalism intact in the face of
its own contradictory tendencies. If residential differentiation is

explained in terms of derivative forces, then it follows that residential differentiation stems from and probably contributes to the
survival of the capital labor relation rather than to the transcen-
dence of capitalism. Harvey's basic hypotheses are as follows:

(1) Residential differentiation is to be interpreted in
     terms of the reproduction of the social relations
     within capitalist society.
(2) Residential areas (neighborhoods, communities)
     provide distinctive milieus for social interaction
     from which individuals, to a considerable degree,
     derive their values, expectations, consumption
     habits, market capacities, and states of aware-
     ness.
(3) The fragmentation of large concentrations of
     populations into distinctive communities serves
     to fragment "awareness" and thereby frustrates
     the possibility of collectivity among the population.
(4) Residential differentiation must reflect and in-
     corporate many of the contradictions in society
     and it is therefore likely itself to be a source of
     instability and contradiction. [29]

Residential differentiation in the capitalist city means differential access to scarce resources required to acquire market capacity. This differential opportunity is particularly important in the
area of education—understood in broad terms as those experiences
derived from family, community, and classroom. [30] Differential
access to educational opportunity facilitates the intergenerational
transference of market capacity. [31] A white-collar labor force is
reproduced in a white-collar neighborhood, a blue-collar labor
force is reproduced in a blue-collar neighborhood. The community
is the place that reproduces labor power suitable for the place of
production. [32] Residential groupings that reproduce labor power to
meet the needs of a division of labor in society may also form distinctive distributive groupings. This gives residential differentiation a much stronger class character.
The community provides a milieu out of which distinctive
value systems, aspirations, and expectations may be drawn. Insofar as residential differentiation produces distinctive communities,
a disaggregation of this process can be anticipated. Blue-collar
neighborhoods, for example, produce individuals with values conducive to being in the blue-collar class and these values, deeply
embedded as they are in the cognitive, linguistic, and moral codes
of the community, become an integral part of the conceptual equipment that individuals use to deal with the world. [33]

The stability of such neighborhoods and the value systems
that characterize the people in them have been remarkable considering the dynamic of change in most capitalist cities. The reproduction of value systems facilitates the reproduction of consumption
classes and groupings with respect to the division of labor, while it
also functions to restrict mobility chances. The homogenization of
life experience, which this restriction produces, reinforces the
tendency for relatively permanent class groupings to emerge within
a relatively permanent structure of residential differentiation. Consequently, the value systems vary according to position in the overall social structure. In some cases these value systems are translated into a form of class awareness through political action that,
more often than not, reinforces residential differentiation by manipulating government action to preserve the integrity of the neighborhood. If the neighborhood is the main focus of political action, then
community awareness replaces class awareness as the springboard
for political action.

The large core of unskilled workers necessary to preserve
the capitalist order may crystallize into a distinctive underclass
capable of surviving under dilapidated abysmal conditions in the
worst part of the city. They acquire a set of values (sometimes
inappropriately labeled a "culture of poverty")[34] adaptive to these
conditions. Blue-collar groupings possess certain attitudes to work
and the workplace that tend to be reflected in an approach to the
community that is neighborly and mutually protective—hence we
may find working-class neighborhoods integrated socially according to principles of reciprocity.[35] The self-image of the white-
collar worker is colored by the work experience and a strong attach-
ment to the ideology of possessive individualism that manifests itself
in the white-collar neighborhood. The managerial, technical, and
professional elite also tend to form a distinctive grouping. Herein
lie the roots of a social differentiation that likely will be reflected
in residential differentiation.

Once these groupings are formed they are easily perpetuated.
Reciprocity exhibited in working-class neighborhoods is to a large
degree a perpetuation of an ancient and well-tried mode of economic
integration. Immigrant waves, at particular periods in history,
brought to the United States a particular strong ethnic flavor to certain occupational groupings as well as to residential differentiation
that persists to the present day.[36] The domination of blacks and
some other ethnic groups has produced the slum as a "Third World
Colony" in the American city, and the underclass in American
society is identified with a repression based in racism.[37]

The middle-class life style is registered in the city by the
creation of middle-class neighborhoods and, particularly in the
American city, with the process of suburbanization. How does one

explain the way in which the emergence of such grouping relates to
the process of residential differentiation? Harvey claims that the
macrofeatures are produced by the activities of speculator-developers, speculator-landlords, and real estate brokers backed, in
many instances, by financial and government institutions.[38] These
institutions are hierarchically ordered by authority relations consistent with the support of the capitalist order. These institutions
regulate the dynamic of the urbanization process and wield their influence so that certain broad patterns of residential differentiation
are produced. The creation of distinctive housing submarkets
(largely through the mortgage market) improves the efficiency with
which institutions can manage the urbanization process. The result
of these actions is the creation of a structure that individuals can
potentially choose from, but that individuals cannot influence the
production of.

The market mechanism curtails the range of an individual's
choices. The shaping of preferences of more affluent groups poses
a more serious problem, as considerations of status and prestige
are important. A white-collar worker forced to suburbanize, because of deteriorating conditions in the inner city, actually has no
choice. Consumption values attached to suburban living are not
open to choice once the location decision is made. Yet is is also
the case that the preference for suburbanization is associated with
certain values that attach to being in a white-collar labor force.

The political power of the suburbs defends a life style that reflects the differential advantages suburban areas possess with respect to the individual acquisition of market capacity. In the process, a deep irrationality emerges in the geography of the capitalist
production system (residential and job opportunities become spatially separated from each other in grossly inefficient ways). The protective posture of the suburban middle class, largely expressed in
the United States through exclusive zoning, can inhibit growth.[39]

A pattern of residential differentiation and its associated class
configuration, both created to sustain order and mutually supportive
of each other, can work to exacerbate the internal crisis within the
capitalist order.[40] This conclusion applies to all aspects of class
and residential differentiation. The creation of a permanent underclass (or lower class) turns counterproductive if this class is so
deprived of job opportunities by confinement to the inner city, is so
deprived of opportunity to acquire market capacity of any kind, that
it abandons the work ethic altogether and begins to act in ways that
run strongly counter to the preservation of order (for example, riots
in the 1960s) and, in the process, acquires a form of class awareness deeply antagonistic to the perpetuation of its existence.

RESIDENTIAL DIFFERENTIATION
AND SLUM RENTS

Given structurally determined housing submarkets and the
barriers between them, it makes no sense to treat rent determination with a single competitive model. An analysis of structural
forces suggests that rents may be determined by different mechanisms in different submarkets. An examination of these submarkets
reveals that the degree of class-monopoly power differs across
housing submarkets. Slum submarkets are structured so that class-
monopoly rents are realized and low-quality housing is obtained at
exploitative prices, whereas white ethnic nonslum submarkets are
structured so that little class-monopoly rent is realized and reason-
ably good housing is obtained at a fairly low price.

In conclusion, we can hypothesize that, in general, the forces
generating submarkets are endogenous, reflecting the accumulation
process and class structure. Once established, the characteristics
of any given submarket will reflect the interaction among many
processes. Finally, rents are determined through different mechanisms in slum areas than nonslum areas. More specifically, slum
rents (lower quality housing and neighborhood) are higher than nonslum rents (better quality housing and neighborhood) regardless of
residents' incomes.

NOTES

1. Robert Park, Ernest Burgess, and Roderick McKenzie,
The City (Chicago: University of Chicago Press, 1925).
2. J. Barnbrock, "Prologomenon to a Debate on Location
Theory: The Case of von Thunen," Antipode, April 1974. See also
William Alonso, Location and Land Use (Cambridge, Mass.:
Harvard University Press, 1964).
3. David Harvey, Social Justice and the City (Baltimore:
Johns Hopkins University Press, 1973), pp. 163-66.
4. See R. M. Kirwan and D. B. Martin, "Some Notes on
Housing Market Models for Urban Planning," Environment and
Planning 3 (1971): 243-52.
5. Frederick Engels, The Condition of the Working Class in
England in 1844 (London: G. Allen and Unwin, 1950), pp. 46-47.
6. Data for New York City on buildings in REM (Real Estate
Management) substantiate this.
7. George Sternlieb, The Tenement Landlord (New Brunswick,
N.J.: Rutgers University Press, 1966). Sternlieb finds evidence of
owner occupiers (people who own one building and live on the

premises) and concludes that these landlords are not making huge profits. He does postulate, however, that large-scale landlords in inner city ghettos are probably reaping huge profits. Jerome Rothenberg in An Economic Evaluation of Urban Renewal (New York: National Bureau of Economic Research, 1967) shows how the ownership of slum properties can be profitable without showing profit. The federal income and capital gains tax systems play an important role here. A landlord can report accelerated depreciation on his property, thereby obtaining a substantial deduction from taxable income. This depreciation is not offset by maintenance outlays. When the property has been completely depreciated for tax purposes, it is still habitable, despite a lack of physical maintenance of the property, with little impairment of its competitive market position relative to the rest of the neighborhood. The property then can be profitably sold, because the new purchaser can subsequently take depreciation on the property anew, while failing to maintain it, and can in turn sell it profitably. Thus, where market conditions permit undermaintenance of property, the income tax provides an incentive to keep the property in existence longer and at a much lower level of quality than its age would warrant in the absence of the tax.

8. Frederick Engels, The Housing Question (New York: International Publishers, 1935).

9. Ibid., p. 23.

10. Ibid., p. 74.

11. David Harvey, "Class Monopoly Rent, Finance Capital and the Urban Revolution," Regional Studies 8 (1974): 240.

12. See J. S. Keiper, F. Kurnow, C. Clark, and H. Segal, Theory and Measurement of Rent (Philadelphia: University of Pennsylvania Press, 1961).

13. Harvey, "Class Monopoly Rent," op. cit.

14. Harvey, Social Justice and the City, op. cit., pp. 179-82.

15. Harvey, "Class Monopoly Rent," op. cit., p. 241.

16. Karl Marx, Capital (New York: International Publishers, 1967), vol. 3, Chapter 45. See Martha Stires, "The Sybarite Excrescence—Marx's Theory of Rent," unpublished paper, New School for Social Research, 1974.

17. Harvey, "Class Monopoly Rent," op. cit., p. 245.

18. Ibid., pp. 243-44.

19. Ibid.

20. Ibid.

21. Ibid.

22. Brian Boyer, Cities Destroyed for Cash (Chicago: Follett, 1973).

23. Harvey, "Class Monopoly Rent," op. cit., p. 244.

24. Ibid., pp. 244-45.

25. Ibid., pp. 245-49.

26. Ibid., p. 249.

27. David Harvey, "Class Structure and the Theory of Residential Differentiation," in Bristol Essays in Geography, ed. M. Chisolm (London: Heineman, 1974).

28. Ibid., p. 7.

29. Ibid., p. 9.

30. Patricia Sexton, Education and Income: Inequality in Our Public Schools (New York: Viking, 1961); also W. Lee Hansen and Burton Weisbrod, Benefits, Costs and Finance of Public Higher Education (Chicago: Markham, 1969).

31. Herbert Gintis, "New Working Class and Revolutionary Youth," Socialist Revolution, May-June 1970.

32. See John Legget, Class, Race and Labor (New York: Oxford University Press, 1968).

33. Ibid.

34. The controversy over the culture-of-poverty thesis is instructive. Conservatives argue that the poverty of the poor is due to their psychological inadequacies. See Edward Banfield, The Unheavenly City (Boston: Little, Brown, 1968). Liberals deny that such a thing exists and suggest that it can be remedied by upgrading the conditions of life for the poor. See Charles Valentine, Culture and Poverty (Chicago: University of Chicago Press, 1968).

35. Karl Polanyi, The Great Transformation (Boston: Beacon Press, 1944).

36. Oscar Handlin, The Newcomers (Cambridge, Mass.: Harvard University Press, 1959); also Nathan Glazer and Daniel P. Moynihan, Beyond the Melting Pot (Cambridge, Mass.: MIT Press, 1963).

37. William Tabb, The Political Economy of the Black Ghetto (New York: W. W. Norton, 1970).

Systematic discrimination sets off the vast majority of blacks from the rest of the working class. In its relation with the dominant white society, the black ghetto stands as a unit apart, an internal colony exploited in a systematic fashion. The economy of an underdeveloped country is heavily dependent on external markets where its few basic exports face an inelastic demand. Much of the small modern sector of the economy is owned by outsiders, therefore, local entrepreneurship is limited.

38. David Harvey, "Absolute Rent and the Structuring of Space by Financial and Governmental Institutions," Antipode (March 1974).

39. John Seeley, R. A. Sim, and E. W. Loosley, Crestwood Heights: A Study of the Culture of Suburban Life (New York: Basic Books, 1958).

40. Harvey, "Class Monopoly Rent," op. cit., p. 249.

3
RESIDENTIAL DIFFERENTIATION AND SLUM FORMATION: THE CASE OF NEW YORK CITY

This chapter takes the framework developed in Chapter 2 and applies it to the historic development of neighborhoods in New York City. In reviewing neighborhood structure development, the choice of neighborhoods for study derives from the framework and pays proper respect to the concrete historic development of New York City. The chapter focuses on the specific structure and character- istics of submarkets and the specific institutions that have played an important role in reproducing those submarkets.

SPATIAL FORM AND SOCIAL STRUCTURE

This section attempts to answer these general questions: Why did New York City's social structure and spatial form develop as they did? In particular, why did slums proliferate in some areas and attractive neighborhoods in others? What pressures caused transportation networks to assume certain forms and not others? The most popular answers to these questions attribute causative power to market forces or to economic and/or technologic necessities. This section offers an overview of New York City's development, which incorporates such explanations within a broader economic, social, political, and legal framework, and presents a clearer picture.

In attempting to answer these questions, it will be argued that both the nature and quality of urban living and the city's spatial form have been shaped by social and economic forces mediated by forms of housing tenure. These forces arose out of New York City's class structure and the struggles between and within groups over time. The struggles and the interactions between groups has

31

broadly determined the aspirations of the members of each group, their differential abilities to participate in the land and housing markets, and either directly or indirectly defined the structure of these markets.[1] With these parameters set, the autonomous actions of individuals or corporate bodies in the land and housing markets, mediated by the tenure relations, has led to the observed social and spatial structure of the city.

The following were the forces: the search on the part of the middle class for an existence within their means that captured the essence of their bosses' life styles; the separation of the upper and middle class from the lower class (along with this, the separation of blacks from whites); the efforts to increase New York City's capital accumulation potential; the impoverishment of the lower class such that they constituted an abundant, cheap, and adaptable labor force; and the struggle on the part of the middle strata of workers to separate themselves from the rest of the workers and to establish a place for themselves in society. These forces were the major constituents of the whole. They have been abstracted only in order to facilitate a clearer understanding of why New York City's social and physical fabric evolved as it did.

One pressure that shaped New York City's growth arose out of the aspirations of the growing middle stratum of clerks, public employees, and professionals for an existence that captured the essence of the successful businessman's life style but was appropriately depreciated to something they could afford. This translated into a search for attractive, sanitary residential environments that were accessible to their workplaces in the center. The development of outlying areas and of transportation systems (which were predicated upon innovations in both the social and economic relationships surrounding the housing process and in urban transportation technologies) were crucial in facilitating the massive outward migration of the middle class, which gathered momentum from the 1930s. The result has been the rapid growth of Nassau County and parts of Suffolk County.

Many of the prospective suburbanites could not afford to engage their own builders. Speculative builders and developers filled this slot.[2] While large building firms were prevalent in the construction of commercial and public buildings, small firms predominated in the residential construction industry.[3]

Renting from landlords remained the most frequent means whereby the middle class was housed. Owner occupation sometimes meant owning a house and renting an apartment. Banks and the federal government, lending money directly to occupiers and to speculative builders and landlords, were an important form of home finance and were destined to dominate the homebuilding industry after the 1930s.[4]

Another pressure that shaped New York City's social and spatial character was the effort by members of the upper class, and to a lesser extent of the middle class, to separate themselves from the lower class into socially homogeneous neighborhoods. The greater economic and political power of wealthy employers and merchants meant that they were more successful than clerks, professionals, and public employees in this endeavor. As the productive distributive and exchange functions of New York City's economy grew (during the latter part of the nineteenth century), so did the space they occupied in these central areas. External economies enticed new banks, offices, factories, and warehouses to cluster in areas where these activities had established a foothold. In their wake came thousands of unskilled and semiskilled workers who were forced to live close to sources of employment. The combined effect of these pressures on the central area land market was an increase in land values and congestion and a reduction in the space available for residential land use. The importance of central locations for their businesses meant that businessmen migrated from the city and its surroundings.

Upper-class homeowners maintained much of the physical infrastructure or saw to it that their neighborhoods were properly maintained. They prevented other homes in the neighborhood from falling into disrepair or being converted to undesirable uses, by means of social and/or legal pressure, for example, zoning regulations.[5] As a result of social and economic relationships, these residential neighborhoods of New York were well built and remained in good repair as long as their upper-class homeowners continued to live there.

The middle class was numerically larger than the upper class, and the bulk of its members received only moderate though adequate earnings. As they descended the earnings scale, the quality of their housing diminished. Many of these people were essentially forced out of the central area, though they were not unwilling to leave as newly developed suburban areas came onto the market (and as mortgages were easy to obtain), and as transportation systems developed (the Long Island Railroad, New York Central Railroad), making the journey to and from work feasible within their budgets.[6]

What did these middle-class suburbs look like? They were speculative ventures referred to as "developments." Design standards in these developments were low and repetitive with small modifications. Fashionability was the most important measure of aesthetic quality. Having secured the rights on a few acres of land, the speculative builder had a strong economic incentive to pack as many houses on to it as was socially and technically feasible. This enabled him to increase his return on investment. But the builder was constrained to a certain extent by his image of the future occupants' social and physical requirements. They would walk up only a certain number of stairs; they valued a certain amount of open space adjacent to their houses for light, air, and relaxation; they required a street frontage; and so on. [7]

The socioeconomic rationale behind the drive to separate classes in the residential environment is as follows: The institutionalization of markets in labor and essential commodities, upon which the economic system is based, drives a wedge between employers and workers. [8] It is logical for the sociological expression of the division in the workplace to extend into the residential sphere; for employers want to live apart from the employees. [9] In a field interview conducted in New York City, a New York City Housing and Development Administration director explained: "I believe it is the view of the city, and I agree with this totally, that houses for the low-income blacks and houses for the middle class of people to which, if you will allow me to say so, I belong, should be kept very widely apart." [10]

In addition to this, there are similar economic reasons for this class separation in the living environment. The proximity of the respectable neighborhoods of the middle class and wealthy to the lower-class residential areas, especially slums, seems to be undesirable for two reasons. Property values in respectable neighborhoods are assumed to be adversely affected and often depressed below their assumed potential if the connection could be effectively severed. [11] Local slums are a potential health hazard as epidemics usually originate in unsanitary areas and sometimes spread into adjacent areas. In addition, it is assumed that services in these areas are of a lower quality, especially education, police protection, and sanitation.* Besides, slums are simply an eyesore, and a constant reminder of the deprivation upon which dominant class existence is based. Those who have the power to remove this assault on their senses and consciences are unlikely to pass up any opportunity to do so.

Class division was achieved in three ways: suburban migration; barriers such as railways (elevated trains have a depressing effect on areas), creation of "wrong side of the tracks," and transportation networks that facilitated suburban migration; and construction of public housing and urban renewal. Suburban migration has

---

*Many long-term residents of New York City neighborhoods who "lived through" the neighborhood's changes have witnessed this drastic reduction in municipal services.

already been discussed. The effects of barriers and the development of transportation networks and of public housing and urban renewal are discussed in this section. In sum, the lower-class areas have been separated from more affluent areas by the erection of barriers, which have limited access from one area to another and which spatially define the limits of each neighborhood for its occupants.

Railway lines have been powerful social and physical barriers. Railway viaducts carry trains noisily past lower-class neighborhoods, constricting neighborhoods socially and intersecting them physically. Such isolation has tended to accelerate the decline of many areas so that they have rapidly become slums, and segregation on the wrong side of the tracks has often had disastrous effects on land values in "bad" areas, further accelerating their decline. The LL train, which passes through Brownsville and East New York, is a prime example of this.

Another way in which class separation has been accomplished in the residential sphere is by homogenization of predominantly affluent or respectable neighborhoods. Not all lower-income populations are confined to the slum areas. Sizable lower-income populations are still to be found in more desirable neighborhoods. The majority of these areas are ethnic enclaves; in New York City, there are several communities of Italians, Germans, Irish, and so on. Because of the close-knit nature of the residents of these areas (the population being homogeneous in an ethnic sense as opposed to an economic sense), blacks and Puerto Ricans will continually be restricted from such areas as Highland Park, Ridgewood, and Glendale. In addition, the full cooperation of local banks and financial institutions in the refusal to grant mortgages will protect this situation.

The ability to segregate the various segments of society is one of the virtues attributed to the federal government and local housing authorities. Social and architectural uniformity is one of the major goals in the construction of public housing. In fashionable areas, where the power and preferences of landowners and tenants coincide, the task is easier and the goal is often accomplished. A certain class of houses is constructed for a certain class of people. The architecture of an entire area becomes the physical embodiment of the class of its inhabitants and of their relative power in the land and housing market.

In slum areas, the architecture is of a different sort. Landowners' and tenants' power and privileges clash. Many slum areas in New York City (for example, Brownsville, Arverne) are inundated with high-rise public housing projects, constructed for a certain class of people—low-income black and Puerto Rican families.

In most cases, projects are constructed in slum areas, on lots that housed many old-law tenement residents. The institution of public housing has reinforced and further ghettoized these slum areas. These neighborhoods cannot absorb the density of population that these buildings require. As a result, municipal services that were at one time poor are now disastrous.[12]

In those areas where the power of the landowners has not been enough to accomplish socially homogeneous neighborhoods, the federal and state governments step in. Legislation has been enforced to facilitate the removal of the human riffraff who are seen as undesirable elements within otherwise attractive residential areas. The legislation to which I am referring is that of urban renewal.

The legislation allows inspectors to enter and inspect unsanitary or overcrowded property, predominantly older, low-rent housing in designated areas, and to instruct the owner to make good those elements that are deemed harmful to the health of the inhabitants or the surrounding community. If no action is forthcoming, then property could be condemned and demolished. Many landlords, having prior knowledge of plans relating to urban renewal, allow their properties to deteriorate with hopes of selling them to the city. Since no effective rehousing requirements exist, tenants are often faced without an apartment for several months. This is especially true for large families who have problems securing apartments.[13] Evicted tenants, limited to a certain area, merely move to adjacent streets, increasing overcrowding and rents in the remaining houses, which soon come to pose as health hazards. Without effective rehousing obligations and actions, the legislation does little to remove health hazards and generally makes life worse for the lower class.

In sum, then, housing legislation has been most useful in the attractive and generally sanitary environments of the middle and upper classes.[14] Among other things, it has facilitated the removal from their neighborhoods of undesirable concentrations of lower-class slums. The legislation did little to improve the quality of lower-class areas, which was the ostensible reason behind it. It made matters worse for these displaced families.[15]

This same process was highlighted by Marx in 1867 in comparing the treatment of landowners evicted from their land by railways and street improvements and workers evicted from unsanitary housing:

> Admire the capitalist justice! The owner of land, of houses, the businessman when expropriated by "improvements" such as railways, the building of new streets, not only receives full indemnity. He must,

according to the law, human and divine, be comforted
for his "abstinence" over and above this by a thumping
profit. The labourer, with his wife and children and
chattels, is thrown into the street, and, if he crowds
in too large numbers towards quarters of the town
where the vestries insist on decency, he is prosecuted
in the name of sanitation.[16]

Thus, it seems that the sanitary problems of the lower-class
areas have been a means of justifying and legitimizing increased
government intervention to accomplish other goals (class and racial
segregation in the case of New York City), which have served the
interests of the upper and middle classes. As a result, the spatial
segregation of races in New York City has become more sharply
defined.* The outcome of this separation has been directly reflecting "the form of the city"—the architectural uniformity of various
areas being a direct expression of the broad uniformity of needs
and socioeconomic status of their inhabitants.†

Another pressure that shaped the social and spatial fabric of
New York City has been a composite of the on-going efforts to increase its capital accumulation potential, to increase its economic
efficiency as a center of production, exchange, and distribution.
This drive has been concretely realized in two broad dimensions.
First, by the growing clustering of economic activities in the central area, especially the exchange and service sectors. Second, by
improving existing modes of transportation and developing new ways
of moving people and goods within the city and between New York
City and other national and international regions. This can be
divided into three parts: dock development, railway development,
and the development of modes of transportation (roads and subways).
All of these developments have had the same effect on the lower
class: those residents have been forced (through demolition) to
compete for reduced amounts of accommodation at higher cost in
adjacent areas.

Railway determination is essentially subservient to the power
relations inherent in the land and housing markets of twentieth-
century New York City. Railways could function only if large areas
of the city were exclusively set aside for their fixed routes and
separate rights of way. Though railways brought destruction,

---

*The increasing migration of minorities to New York City has
also helped to sharply define racial segregation.

†This is especially true in public housing neighborhoods.

pollution, and congestion, they enabled higher prices to be charged for urban and suburban land. Landowners benefited even more as the inflated awards were translated into market prices. Railway development generated windfall gains for landowners.[17]

Railway location is related to power in the land and housing market. Lower-class neighborhoods were the weak areas and large areas of housing in these areas were owned by a few substantial proprietors. The results have been that demolitions have also forced the lower class to compete for reduced amounts of housing accommodations at higher costs in adjacent areas.

Much of New York's suburban development was accomplished through the work of Robert Moses.[18] The construction of roads opened up new areas for development. Moses's prewar parkways had caused vast population increases in Brooklyn and Queens and in suburban Nassau and Suffolk counties. Subways also opened areas to development. High-density apartment houses were constructed close to subway stations. Some areas in the city consisted of single-family homes, but these houses were built on small plots within walking distance to the subway. Suburbanites traveled to and from work by automobile. Realizing this, building developers built on large plots of land, since traveling for suburbanites was relatively easy.

Once growth in the New York metropolitan region had been upward—people were piled on top of people in apartment houses. Moses's policies made it impossible for jobs to follow people to the suburbs. His parkways were barred to commercial traffic. Land adjacent to the parkways was zoned residential, keeping it closed to commercial development.

In the decade following the opening of the Southern State Parkway, 200,000 new residents (50,000 families) moved into Nassau County, but only 12,000 new jobs were created. The better-off residents of northeast Queens, not having a subway nearby, were forced to take a bus or car to the nearest subway. For the impoverished southeast Bronx residents, not having a subway nearby and not owning a car meant taking a bus to the subway and paying a double fare each way—a hardship many of these residents couldn't afford. That meant that many of these residents walked a mile or more in the morning and evening. In addition, that meant that on weekends, these families could not take their children on trips or to a museum or movie. The prohibitive cost of transportation trapped these people in their homes.

Moses' policies were doing more than simply not helping the people. They were hurting them. They were even limiting their freedom to choose a place to live. His

denial of funds for mass transit extension meant that
new homes and apartments would be occupied by car
owning families. Whether by design or not, the ulti-
mate effect of Moses' transportation policies would
be to help keep the city's poor trapped in their slums.
They were policies not only of transportation but of
ghettoization, policies with immense social implications.[19]

Another pressure that shaped New York City's growth arose
out of the impoverishment of the lower class so that they formed a
cheap, abundant, and docile labor force. The lower-class struggle
for adequate housing has been an outcome of the ways in which production relations have changed in the process.

The nature and necessities of the lower-class position in the
productive process has shaped their housing decisions in two important ways: it has determined their lack of economic, social,
and political power as "actors" in the land and housing markets;
and it has confined feasible residential locations for this class to a
limited spatial area adjacent to their workplaces.

The necessities of their jobs mean that most workers have
very little effective choice of residential locality. Many laborers
are crucially dependent on hearsay and personal contacts for information on possible employment. As a result, commuting would
involve journeys for, rather than to, work. They have been effectively forced to live within relatively short distances of potential employment sources, the bulk of which have been located in
Manhattan.

Other factors helped in confining the poor to the center and
played an important role in perpetuating the functioning of this class
of the labor market and in sustaining the overall process of impoverishment. Credit has been easier to obtain from local shops
(sometimes through installment sales, which are often more
damaging than helpful).

The changes in New York City's social and spatial structure,
arising out of the realization of these pressures, affected the central area lower-class housing market in two major ways: They led
to drastic reductions in both the absolute space available for lower-
class housing and in the availability of financial resources needed
to sustain an adequate network of urban social and physical infra-
structure in lower-class areas.

The imperatives of the process of capital accumulation and
the residential needs of the lower class came into direct conflict in
the central city land market. The increasing profitability of commercial and productive facilities was strongly dependent on central

locations, on the construction of docks and railways, and on the improvement of major thoroughfares. These productive and service land uses consumed large proportions of central area land, which was, on the other hand, the only feasible location for lower-class housing.

Land that supported lower-class housing, being economically and politically the weak point in the land market, most frequently fell victim to the encroachment of productive and service activities. Because practical spatial locations for lower-class housing were limited to the central areas, these takeovers were tantamount to a drastic reduction in the amount of space available for lower-class residences. Consequently, overcrowding and the potential for exploitation increased enormously in the remaining inner-city lower-class residential areas.

The rents that black tenants pay, in the degrading inner-city environment, are exorbitant in relation to their wages, in relation to rents in other sectors of the housing market, and when measured against the quality and quantity of the commodity housing they receive. As Lickchese, a rent collector, confides to Trench, in George Bernard Shaw's Widowers' Houses,

> Tenement houses, let from week to week by the room
> or half-room—aye, or quarter room. It pays when you
> know how to work it, sir. Nothing like it. It's been
> calculated on the cubic foot of space, sir, that you can
> get higher rents letting by the room than you can for a
> mansion in Park Lane.[20]

These overcrowded dwellings are machines for manufacturing rent. Many houses in South Jamaica and East New York and to a lesser extent, Crown Heights, have been subdivided into apartments. Bungalows in Arverne, Edgemere, and Hammels (the Rockaways) have been converted into single-room occupancies.

The flight of the upper class and the middle class from Brooklyn and Queens, and the growing homogenization of social classes within discrete residential areas, was obviously accompanied by the corresponding flight of the financial resources necessary to establish and sustain adequate levels of urban social and physical infrastructure in lower-class neighborhoods. Lower-class neighborhoods, which have needed the greater infrastructure investments, have received the least. Thus, the spatial environment of the city gradually replicates the social and economic disequilibrium of production relations.

The real basis of high rents in the slums is the powerlessness of the lower class. Rents are set in the monthly struggle between tenants and landlords, whose motive is to extract as much rent as possible. The workers' social, economic, and political powerlessness, and the fact that their locational choices are restricted to the central area slum, means that they come off worst in these interactions, almost irrespective of the quality or quantity of housing they rent. The pressure to increase returns by overcrowding houses has been ruthlessly intensified during the last decade or so. Tenants have been exploited by landlords whose only object has been to make as much money as possible. In the words of Henry Trelawny Boodle, an agent for the Westminster and Northampton Estates, in 1887:

> I have heard it stated over and over again, and I believe
> it to be true, that if a man hardens his heart and treats
> his fellow creatures like brute beasts and crowds them
> like pigs, this system of rooming houses is the most
> remunerative thing possible. . . . All [landlords] care
> about is the matter of "interest" in merely to screw as
> much as they possibly can out of their tenants. [21]

The same situation prevails throughout New York City. Landlords in South Jamaica and the Rockaways have enjoyed this position since the 1940s.

Absentee landlords are insulated from any contact with their slum properties. If tenants agree to pay the rents for substandard accommodations, landlords have little incentive to improve scale standards. Small landlords who live on the premises usually do not have the capital to keep their property in decent repair, often because they themselves have been exploited by more powerful prior real estate operators[22] and financial institutions. In sum, the conversion of smaller houses into multiunit structures has led to extreme overcrowding, lack of sanitary precautions, an almost total absence of management and maintenance, and exorbitant rents.

THE DISTINCTION AMONG HOUSING SUBMARKETS IN NEW YORK CITY

The macrofeatures of residential separation in the environment are produced by the activities of speculator-developers, speculator-landlords, and real estate brokers backed, in many instances, by financial and government institutions. These institutions are hierarchically ordered by authority relations consistent with the support of the capitalist order. They regulate the urbanization process and wield their influence so that certain broad patterns of residential differentiation are produced. As mentioned in Chapter 2 (see pp. 19 and 20), the creation of distinctive housing submarkets (largely through the mortgage markets) can be attributed to policies of financial and government institutions. Housing submarkets in a city are distinguished by the type of institutional involvement in the housing sector and by the insurance of home purchases by the Federal Housing Administration. The geographic structure of a city's housing market contributes to the potential for realizing class-monopoly rents. Each of the submarket approaches adheres to the laws of classical political economy as embodied in a paradigm similar to the demoralization paradigm prominent in London in the 1800s. [23]

Public Housing

The construction of high-rise public housing was the earliest public response to the problem of housing the poor. [24] Enacted in 1937 primarily as a job creation program, it intended to serve the "submerged middle-class," the white temporary poor of the depression years, but in the postwar period it was increasingly called on to serve the permanent poor. [25] Housing reformers viewed the slum problem as one of badly planned, designed, built, or managed housing that perpetuated urban degeneration, rather than as a problem of overcrowding. [26] They argued that this was caused by the fact that commercial builders and landlords felt that well-built and managed housing for the poor would not produce an adequate return on invested capital, and therefore there was no incentive to provide decent accommodations. The reformers assumed that good, well-managed housing improved the occupants by raising their morale and giving them an incentive to better themselves. Thus, their solution was to set examples for private enterprise, to show that adequate and sanitary high-density projects were practical and compatible with a fair return on capital, and that "moral were almost equal to physical benefits." [27]

With little exception, only the better-off skilled workers could afford to rent apartments in projects. [28] Besides, the prohibitive rents, the stringent regulations demanding regular advance payment of rent, prohibiting subletting and lack of large apartments put these apartments beyond the scope of many poor families. In addition, many of those who can afford to live in projects prefer to remain in overcrowded private housing than to suffer the paternalistic supervision and hostile architecture of most projects. Consequently, these houses serve only a small portion of the urban poor who are regularly employed and receive moderate

Incomes.[29] The poorest workers are merely displaced into surrounding areas, increasing overcrowdedness.

By making it seem as though the problems are temporary
malfunctions on their way to solution, while reinforcing the structural forces that originated them, the reformers and the city
planners inadvertently have served the purpose of legitimating the
continued existence of housing problems. Furthermore, projects
are an effective means of extending control over the poor. Workers
are controlled in their workplaces and also in their homes.

Urban Renewal

Slum clearance has been another response to housing problems since the passage of the Urban Renewal Act in 1949. Under
this approach, the crux of housing problems was conceived to lie
in the existence of vast areas of substandard dwellings and undesirable surrounding areas. Urban renewal projects have had to
meet some broad conditions, including "an overall plan for the
development of a locality."[30] The poor are seen as unable or unwilling to pay the increased rents that new or more spacious accommodations would necessitate. In addition, urban renewal is a
method by which the tax base of a community may be improved by
encouraging the middle-class suburbanite to move back to the city.
In the words of Martin Anderson, an urban renewal critic,

> The federal urban renewal program allows those in con-
> trol of the program to change one kind of neighborhood
> into another kind by destroying the old buildings and re-
> placing them with new ones. Naturally, the new uses
> they choose for the cleared land—perhaps high rent
> apartments instead of low rent apartments, for exam-
> ple—are those they feel are desirable from their point
> of view of what the public good is.[31]

Since slum dwellings continue to yield handsome profits to
large-scale landlords, there is no incentive for improvement or
new construction.[32] Thus, the solution has been to arrogate to
local housing authorities compulsory purchase powers and to charge
them with the tasks of acquiring slum property, compensating the
owners, demolishing the buildings, and turning the land over to
private developers. In contrast with the local housing authority,
these developers would construct urban renewal houses on the
sites.[33]

One theoretical assumption, a new addition to the accepted
wisdom on dealing with housing problems, justified the slum

clearance approach in the minds of reformers and city planners, even though this approach has made matters worse. It is known as the filtering theory. According to this theory, better-off workers would move into the more expensive new housing erected on the cleared land, and the displaced poor would occupy the houses that they vacated, which were assumed to be in better condition than the demolished housing.[34] In this way, the physical condition of the housing stock would gradually improve. But the theory is untenable because its assumptions are wrong. It assumes that better-paid workers would indeed move into the newly constructed housing, or at least migrate to the suburbs, that the central city low-income population would remain almost constant, and that a unified housing market exists, with housing quality being a function of the physical condition of the housing stock and independent of the social and economic relations between landlord and tenant.

There are powerful forces that have constrained the urban poor in the center and have made suburbanization unrealistic for them. The pressure of population increase has been made worse by the diminishing supply of central land. The persistence of vacancies in the suburbs, while used in support of the filtering theory, is purely academic from the point of view of the central city poor. These vacancies exist in a housing submarket that is beyond their reach and, therefore, irrelevant to their needs. Indeed, surpluses in the suburbs and crowding in the center are testimony to the centrality of social relations in the determination of housing quality and distribution.

While conflicting conclusions have emerged on the effects of urban renewal, my own research supports the view that urban renewal has proven to be disastrous for the urban poor. Under the Urban Renewal Act, large areas in which the poor had been concentrated were the consistent targets for demolition. In most cases, this was tantamount to eviction. Most workers could not afford the high rents of the new accommodations and even if they could, the time lag between demolition and rebuilding was often so long as to make the new housing irrelevant to their needs.[35] They were forced into even more overcrowded dwellings in the surrounding areas, and the increased pressure on the diminished supply of housing forced them to pay higher rents or settle for lower standards.

The situation has been exacerbated by the fact that the act has entailed financial loss for the authorities charged with implementing it. The power relations of the land market have been such that generous compensation clauses have been written into the act, and local housing authorities have found themselves overpaying for land. Compensation has been based on rental receipts. This is an incentive to landlords to herd as many people into their dwellings as possible, charge exorbitant rents, and allow their property to deteriorate in hope of receiving high compensation for an extremely small investment. Racketeering and fake sales at higher prices are also encouraged.[36] As a result of considerable losses sustained by local housing authorities in what amounts to a process of subsidizing property owners, there have been long delays between demolition and reconstruction.[37] Thus, the only people who benefit from the program are the owners of slum property, the demolition and development companies, and the middle and upper classes.[38]

As a result, overcrowding has been made appreciably worse and rents have risen significantly.[39] The act serves to legitimate housing problems by making it seem as though they are on the way to solution. The optimism surrounding the shifting of responsibility from corrupt businessmen to the government, the improved appearance of the new dwellings, and the belief in the validity of the filtering theory contribute to the feeling that something is being done and, therefore, the problems will be solved.

A subsidy program for homeowners was the next response to housing problems after the passage of the Housing and Urban Development Act of 1968. Under this program of interest rate subsidies, moderate-income families were able to purchase new, existing, or rehabilitated homes. A raft of exposés by the General Accounting Office, the Civil Rights Commission, and the House Banking and Currency Committee have uncovered scandals in these programs in so many cities that the Department of Housing and Urban Development (HUD) suspended the program. Housing prices were sharply inflated, with speculators purchasing older, dilapidated homes in transition areas at panic-sale prices, then reselling them at huge profits. Many of the dilapidated houses were cosmetically repaired to meet FHA standards before being sold to moderate-income families.[40] The program resulted in chaos as foreclosures became common and entire neighborhoods were destroyed.

FINANCIAL AND GOVERNMENT INSTITUTIONS AND THE PRIVATE HOUSING SECTOR

Class-monopoly rents arise because as a class, the owners of property have the power always to extract a positive return above some arbitrary level. The process of slum formation can be explained by examining the conflicting class interests of landlords and low-income tenants:

Suppose there exists a class of people who, by virtue of their income, social status, credit-worthiness and

> eligibility for public assistance, are incapable of finding
> accommodation as homeowners or as residents in public
> housing. . . . This class of people has no alternative
> but to seek accommodation in the low-income rental
> market; they are trapped within a particular housing
> submarket. . . . This class has certain options as to
> where it puts its money but much of its capital exists
> in the form of housing. On the basis of the potential
> yield of money on the capital market, professional
> landlords may set their expected rate of return on the
> estimated market value of their fixed capital assets at,
> say, 15% per annum. Suppose there is an abundance of
> low-income units in a particular city for some reason
> and that rates of return are in fact as low as 5%. A
> rational landlord strategy is to reduce maintenance,
> milk properties of value and actively disinvest, using
> the money so extracted on the capital market where it
> earns, say, 15%. With declining maintenance, the
> housing deteriorates in quality and eventually the worst
> units will be taken out of use—scarcity is successfully
> produced. Rents will gradually rise until the 15% rate
> of return is obtained (and there is nothing to stop rents
> from going higher if circumstances allow). The class
> interest of the landlord is to obtain a minimum of 15%
> or else to find some way to get out of the market. [41]

In this case, class interests of landlord and tenant are in opposition.
If housing quality deteriorates and rents rise, tenants may seek
housing elsewhere, but, since they are trapped in this submarket,
their locational choices are restricted. Tenants are politically
weak, there is usually a shortage of suitable housing (because of
population shifts and urban renewal), and landlords have considerable power since they can simply sell or transform to other uses
(for example, upper-income housing). Consequently, the landlord
class will be able to raise rents, forcing low-income tenants, in
many instances, to subdivide space, with the inevitable result:
overcrowding and slum formation.

Class-interest conflict of this sort between tenants and landlords can be documented in any capitalist city. The rate of return
set through the working out of this conflict is best interpreted as a
class monopoly rent even though the landlord usually considers it a
rate of return on invested capital. The realization of this rent depends upon the ability of one class-interest group to exercise its
power over another class-interest group and thereby to assure for
itself a certain minimum rate of return.

The evidence from New York City indicates that the housing submarket structure created by urbanization is a series of distinct islands on which class monopolies produce absolute scarcities. Absolute spaces, created by human practices, are essential to the realization of class-monopoly rent. These absolute spaces are constructed by dividing space up into parcels and segments, each of which can be regarded as a thing in itself, independent of other things.

The private property relation is the most basic institution by means of which absolute spaces are formally created. Political jurisdictions define collective absolute spaces that are carved up by the bureaucratic regulation of land use. These forms of absolute space create the possibility to realize class monopoly rents. It is primarily through the informally structured absolute spaces of submarkets that such rents are realized. The New York City evidence suggests that financial and government institutions play an active role in shaping residential differentiation and that the active agent in the process is an investor seeking to realize a class-monopoly rent. The small neighborhood savings and loan institution in New York is, in effect, a community institution that fits neatly into a social ecological view of urban community structure. But the major portion of housing finance comes from institutions seeking profits or the expansion of business. Faced with a choice between supporting a risk-absorbing landlord operation and a vulnerable homeowner in the inner city, business rationality dictates support of the former at the expense of the latter. The options of the profit-maximizing or expansion-conscious financial institutions are limited. As a result, these institutions become a fundamental force in shaping the residential structure of the city.

Considerations of race and ethnicity, social status and prestige life-style aspirations, and community and neighborhood solidarity increase the potential for realizing class-monopoly rent because they help to maintain the housing submarket structure, to create the absolute space of the community.

Financial institutions and government manage the urbanization process to achieve economic growth, economic stability, and to defuse social discontent. If these aims are to be realized, then new modes of consumption and new social wants and needs will have to be produced. The urbanization process achieves this quite successfully. By structuring and restructuring the choices open to people, by creating distinctive decision environments, the urbanization process forces new kinds of choice.

If the dynamic of urbanization is powered by financial and government institutions, mediated by speculator-developers and speculator-landlords in pursuit of class-monopoly rent, and necessitated by the requirement to reproduce the capitalist order, it can be suggested that housing classes may be produced at the same time. Individuals can strive or choose to join one or other grouping or shift (if possible) from one consumption class to another. In like manner they can strive or choose (depending on circumstances) to move from one housing submarket to another. The structure of these submarkets, however, cannot be chosen, since these are dictated by forces far removed from the realms of consumer sovereignty.

DERIVED HYPOTHESES FOR NEW YORK CITY

The test neighborhoods—Brownsville, Crown Heights, East New York, Southeast Queens, and the Rockaways—were focused on over the period 1950-70. These neighborhoods had experienced change in their neighborhood characteristics, tending to become slums. As their neighborhood characteristics changed, the structure of their housing submarkets changed. The control neighborhoods—Ravenswood, Ridgewood, and Highland Park-Cypress Hills-City Line—were focused on over the same time period (to a limited extent), and these are areas whose neighborhood characteristics and submarket structures remained unchanged over the same period.

Part II of this book will focus on the institutions that produce and reproduce slums by examining the historic development of the test neighborhoods. The following hypotheses were developed and tested through extensive field research in the test areas:

The policies of financial and government institutions have affected urban neighborhoods through public housing and FHA homeownership programs. Neighborhoods with predominantly black populations have been adversely affected by these policies, while neighborhoods with white populations have not.

The actions of speculator real estate interests in black neighborhoods have caused decay (and sometimes destruction) of the private housing stock. The city (primarily the Department of Social Services), by renting substandard apartments for welfare tenants in slum areas (at astronomical rents), has contributed to the success of these speculators, whose aims are to withdraw essential services from their buildings while seeking maximum compensation.

The city's distribution of services has differentially affected neighborhood quality so that neighborhoods with black populations have declined at the expense of neighborhoods with white populations.

In order to test for the existence of distinct housing submarkets and rent determination mechanisms, an econometric analysis was implemented (see Chapter 5) for the test and control areas. In using factor analysis to examine interdependence among various neighborhood quality variables, factors were derived as dimensions to these neighborhoods, which were compared across neighborhoods. Once the distinction among submarkets was made, a test for different rent mechanisms in different submarket types was derived and implemented. One more hypothesis was tested:

Slum rents (rents in inner city, high transience, and black residential submarkets) are higher the lower the neighborhood quality variables, while nonslum rents (rents in white ethnic submarkets) are higher the higher the neighborhood quality variables.

Specifically, given the data I have, I would expect Brownsville (1960, 1970), Crown Heights (1960, 1970), East New York (1970), Southeast Queens (1960, 1970), and the Rockaways (1960, 1970) to conform to a slum rent determination model (high rents, an undesirable neighborhood). Furthermore, I would expect Ridgewood (1960, 1970), Ravenswood (1960, 1970), and East New York (1960) to conform to a nonslum rent determination model (high rents, a desirable neighborhood).

NOTES

1. See David Weinberg, "The Dialectics of Urban Living," Ph.D. dissertation, Massachusetts Institute of Technology, 1974, for an analysis of nineteenth-century London.

2. See Marion Clawson, Suburban Land Conversion in the United States (Baltimore: Johns Hopkins University Press, 1971).

3. For a discussion on the structure of the construction industry in the United States, see Dorothy Nelkin, The Politics of Housing Innovation (Ithaca, N.Y.: Cornell University Press, 1971).

4. See Appendix B, "History of Federal Housing Programs." Also see President's Committee on Urban Housing, A Decent Home (Washington, D.C.: U.S. Government Printing Office, 1968).

5. See Seymour Toll, Zoned American (New York: Grossman, 1969) and R. Linowes and D. Allensworth, Politics of Land Use (New York: Praeger, 1973).

6. See Robert Caro, The Powerbroker (New York: Knopf, 1974).

7. Ibid.

8. Weinberg, op. cit.; also see David Harvey, "Class Structure and the Theory of Residential Differentiation," in Essays in Geography, ed. M. Chisolm (London: Heineman, 1974).

9. J. Legget, Class, Race and Labor: Workers Consciousness in Detroit (New York: Oxford University Press, 1968).

10. In response to a question on the effects of public housing on the neighborhood, a New York City Housing and Development Administration official expressed his feelings concerning public housing site selection.

11. There are conflicting conclusions on this that have evolved from a series of studies. See Appendix "The Literature Survey" for a survey of these studies in Diane Gold, "Class Structure and the Economics of the Housing Problem," Ph.D. dissertation, Graduate Faculty, New School for Social Research, 1977.

12. The Census Tract, in which public housing is constructed, generally witnesses a drastic increase in population. See Appendix, "Initial Occupancy" in ibid.

13. Chester Hartman, "The Housing of Relocated Families," Journal of the American Institute of Planners 30, no. 4 (November 1964): 266.

14. See Martin Anderson, The Federal Bulldozer (Cambridge, Mass.: MIT Press, 1966), for an analysis of urban renewal. See Lawrence Friedman, "Public Housing and the Poor," in Housing Urban America, ed. J. Pynoos, R. Schafer, and C. Hartman (Chicago: Aldine, 1973), for an analysis of public housing.

15. Anderson, op. cit. Also see Jerome Rothenberg, Economic Evaluation of Urban Renewal (Washington, D.C.: Brookings Institution, 1967). For a conflicting conclusion concerning urban renewal, see Charles Abrams, The City is the Frontier (New York: Harper & Row, 1965).

16. Karl Marx, Capital (New York: International Publishers, 1967), p. 660, as quoted in D. Harvey, Social Justice and the City (Baltimore: Johns Hopkins University Press, 1973).

17. For an analysis of this in the Boston area, see Mathew Edel and Eliot Sclar, "Distribution of Real Estate Values in Boston 1870-1970," Boston Studies in Urban Political Economy, 1972. Caro, op. cit., came to a similar conclusion for New York City and its surrounding suburbs.

18. Caro, op. cit.

19. Ibid.

20. Quoted in H. Dyos and M. Wolf, Victorian City (London: Routledge and Kegan Paul, 1973), pp. 380-81.

21. Quoted in E. Olsen, Urban Analysis of London (London: Oxford University Press, 1964), p. 105, as referred to in Weinberg, op. cit.

22. This is documented by George Sternlieb, in The Tenement Landlord (New Brunswick, N.J.: Rutgers University Press, 1966).

23. See Gareth Stedman Jones, Outcast London (London: Oxford University Press, 1971), pp. 262-71.

24. President's Committee on Urban Housing, op. cit., pp. 55-56. Also, Michael Stone, "Federal Housing Policy, A Political Economic Analysis," in Housing Urban America, op. cit., pp. 423-33.

25. L. Friedman, "Public Housing and the Poor," in Housing Urban America, op. cit., pp. 448-59.

26. According to L. Friedman, public housing was also constructed to ensure jobs for the large core of unemployed.

27. Weinberg, op. cit., p. 200.

28. President's Committee on Urban Housing, op. cit.

29. This has changed slightly within the last few years as residents displaced because of urban renewal are guaranteed occupancy in public housing. George Sternlieb and B. Indik, Ecology of Welfare (New Brunswick, N.J.: Transaction Books, 1973), pp. 70-71:

> The role of New York City's public housing in relation to welfare households has frequently been misunderstood. Many people assume that the bulk of public housing apartments are occupied by welfare recipients and vice versa, that the bulk of welfare recipients are in public housing. In New York City, neither of these statements is at all true. First is the fact that particularly in New York City, public housing has been the sanctuary for the moderately paid workers. Even when the federal government has assumed the capital costs of construction, the rents and income guidelines have frequently excluded welfare recipients (and the poorest workers). In 1968, the requirements to public housing in New York were substantially reduced.

30. Jewel Bellush and Murray Hausknecht, Urban Renewal: People, Politics and Planning (New York: Anchor Publishing Co., 1968), p. 12.

31. Anderson, op. cit., p. 3. Anderson also claims that "urban renewal may have caused a decrease in cities' tax revenues. Indications are that the chances of urban renewal increasing tax revenues are small, and if they do increase, it is likely that the increase will be slight." p. 221.

32. Sternlieb, op. cit. Although Sternlieb does not find evidence of many large-scale landlords, he postulates that large-scale owners of residential property are probably realizing substantial gains.

33. Bellush and Hausknecht, op. cit., pp. 15-16. Originally redevelopment projects had to be predominantly residential, but in 1954, 10 percent (later increased to 30 percent) of the total federal funds available for redevelopment could be used for projects that were not predominantly residential.

34. Wallace Smith, "Filtering and Housing Standards," in Readings in Urban Economics, ed. M. Edel and J. Rothenberg (Cambridge, Mass.: MIT Press, 1972).

35. Census data collected for this thesis substantiate this statement, as rents in census tracts where urban renewal projects are constructed rise well above average rents for the area, and the rents in census tracts surrounding these urban renewal projects rise well above rents for comparable housing elsewhere. Anderson, op. cit., documents this fact, p. 163.

36. Brian Boyer, Cities Destroyed for Cash (Chicago: Follett, 1973).

37. Anderson, op. cit., p. 222.

38. Ibid., pp. 112-17.

39. This is documented by Jerome Rothenberg, The Economics of Urban Renewal (New York: National Bureau of Economic Research, 1967).

40. See Boyer, op. cit.

41. David Harvey, "Class Monopoly Rent, Finance Capital and the Urban Revolution, Regional Studies 8 (1974): 241-42.

4
THE FIELD SURVEY

The purpose of this chapter is to summarize the results of
the field survey. The chapter will cover the field survey method
and the questionnaire used, as well as the choice of field survey
neighborhoods and the conclusions derived from the field survey.
It focuses on a detailed discussion of how the conclusions were derived from the field survey. Although this evidence was drawn from
a field survey in New York City, there is ample documentation of
similar phenomena existing in other cities. Materials from London
will be drawn upon for comparative purposes.

THE FIELD SURVEY METHOD

The field survey has a clear descriptive purpose, that is, to
provide a researcher with information. Many inquiries aim to explain rather than to describe. Their function may be theoretical—
to test some hypothesis suggested by theory—or severely practical—
to assess the influence of various factors upon some phenomenon—
but whichever the case, the purpose is to explain the relationships
among many variables. This may lead to extreme complexities in
interpretation.

The researcher should look upon surveys as one way of ex-
ploring the field, of collecting data around as well as directly on a
subject so that the problem is brought into focus and the points
worth pursuing are suggested.

In the survey method, information is obtained directly from
individual respondents either through personal interviews or through
mail questionnaires or telephone interviews. Questionnaires are
used either to obtain specific responses to direct questions or to

secure more general responses to open-end questions. A direct
type of question is designed to force the respondent to choose among
a limited number of answers as, for example, in the question, "Has
your neighborhood changed in the last 10 years?" This question
contrasts sharply with the open-end question, "How has your neighborhood changed in the last 10 years?" The open-end question
permits respondents to formulate their own answers.

There have been neighborhood surveys conducted to investigate neighborhood and housing quality from the observer's viewpoint,
or to investigate the effects of the change in socioeconomic status
of residents on neighborhood and housing quality. In many surveys
of housing and neighborhood quality, the research method employed
is participant observation. With this method the observer joins in
the daily life of the neighborhood he is studying. He watches what
happens to the residents of the neighborhood and how they behave
and he also engages in conversations with them to find out their
reactions to, and interpretations of, the events that have occurred.
He studies the life of the community as a whole, the relationship
between its members and its activities and institutions.

The observer's task is to place himself in the best position
for getting a complete and unbiased picture of community life. A
risk with participant observation is that the role adopted by the observer will restrict his understanding of the situation. In playing a
clearly defined role in the community, the observer's understanding
of the situation is thereby restricted. He will have access only to
sources of information associated with that role; by being friendly
to some members of the community, he will be cutting himself off
from others. The ideal of being able to enter into the life of a community at several different levels so as to get a complete picture is
rarely attained by the participant observer. In addition, unstruc-
tured interviewing can lead to difficulty in drawing conclusions.

Participant observation in studying neighborhoods was employed by R. Hunter and J. Lyford.[1] Careful examination of these
studies and various others furnished me with a well-rounded picture
of a community seen as a whole. Neighborhood descriptions in these
studies led to the formulation of questions used in this field survey.

At the other extreme, a common type of housing and neighborhood study might be classified as a quantitative enquiry. The usefulness of this type of survey is often debated, as one does sometimes suspect social scientists of being excessively eager to use
them: to leap into the field as soon as they have a problem, collect
data, tabulate answers, write a report, and regard the research as
finished.

Sometimes good judgment requires the deliberate sacrifice of
quantitative precision for the greater depth attainable by more

intensive methods of attack. An example will make this clear.
There has been much discussion of the problem of racial change in
neighborhoods and the deterioration of neighborhoods. To get the
interpretation of community residents about this trend, the National
Opinion Research Center conducted a comparative survey of ra-
cially-integrated American neighborhoods, collecting a wealth of
information on this trend. [2] The official report put forward a summary of findings that represented tabulations of the number of respondent's answers falling into each of several categories. While
many of these studies focus on the right questions, their usefulness
is impaired because the respondent is not free to formulate his own
answer. This situation is especially true for longitudinal studies,
where the aspect, form, detail, and length of a respondent's answer
can be of utmost significance.

A classic example of this type of quantitative enquiry is the
National Opinion Research Center's study. Questionnaires from
this study and other similar ones served as guides for my own questions. In many instances, the closed-end questions from this study
were reworded to allow for historical interpretation.

For purposes of the present study, the questions constructed
fall into the following six categories:*

Neighborhood: These questions were designed to find out the
respondent's interpretations of the desirability of his neighborhood
and how this has changed over the last 20 years. Included in this
category were questions regarding the neighborhood's good and bad
points, the closeness of neighborhood residents, the effects of public housing and changing property values on the neighborhood. In
designing the questionnaire, the first group of questions centered on
the broader aspects of housing and neighborhood quality. Even
though the respondent's interest may have centered on specific issues, it was a good idea to start with broad questions about the
subject and then to narrow down to the specific issues, using what
is known as a funnel sequence of questions.

Community Facilities: The next group of questions was designed to determine the respondent's interpretations of the quality
of public and private community facilities and how this quality has
changed over the last 20 years. Included in the category of public
facilities were questions regarding health care facilities, street
cleaning and sanitation facilities, day care and educational facilities,

---

*See the full Questionnaire at the end of this chapter.

and public transportation facilities. Private community facilities included shopping, recreational, and religious facilities.

Cultural Pressure: These questions were designed to find out the respondent's interpretation of outside pressures (those exerted by people who come in contact with the community but who are not part of the community) and their effects on the community. Included in this category were questions regarding storekeepers, policemen, courts, school teachers, and welfare workers.

Public Safety Problems: These questions were designed to find out the respondent's interpretations of the quality of private housing (primarily rental housing) and how this has changed over the last 20 years. Respondents were asked questions regarding the general quality of the neighborhood's housing and more specific questions regarding the structure of rents, the rental relationship, and the general maintenance of buildings in the neighborhood (for example, incidence of rats, roaches, heat, hot water, adequacy of laundry facilities, and elevators).

Community Interaction and Support, and Political Networks: This last category of questions was designed to find out the respondent's interpretations of the "closeness" of community residents and how this closeness (or lack of it) affects neighborhood quality. Included in this final category were questions regarding tenants' associations, block clubs, and interaction between the community and various political figures.

THE INTERVIEWS

Most of the data in this report were secured by home interviews and interviews at the place of work with long-term community residents. The quality of the information obtained was of major importance in determining the number of interviews necessary for each area. In-depth interviews in the neighborhoods were not difficult to arrange because the Community News Service and the Housing and Development Administration site offices were cooperative in assisting me in my search for respondents. From these initial contacts, I was able to make additional contacts.

The populations of the test neighborhoods were quite similar except for two factors: age and income levels. Each of these characteristics was believed to make an independent contribution to stability within racially changing neighborhoods. Older people generally have low residential mobility. Higher-income families tend to be homeowners and, as a result, contribute to neighborhood stability.

The objectives of the field work component of this thesis were to obtain information on the housing and residential problems of long-term neighborhood residents, and to obtain information on aspects of life ordinarily hidden from the outside observer.

The primary sources of data were in-depth personal interviews with a sample of neighborhood residents, both men and women, who were, in most cases, area leaders. The age of the interviewee ranged from mid-twenties to late sixties. Respondents were primarily black. Approximately 100 interviews were conducted, 20 in each neighborhood.

The interview process took place between May and December 1975. Interviewing time averaged three hours, and in some instances I was asked to return to complete an interview. Some interviews were conducted with one respondent, many with two and three. The advantage of the latter was that open-end questions were more thoroughly debated. Respondents were preponderantly cooperative and willing to give information, as indicated by a very low refusal rate (one refusal in all).

Most of the data were produced in the form of field notes. These served the purpose of documenting, from the community itself, the causes and effects of changes in the neighborhood and housing quality. In many cases, specific quotes from the interviews are used as documentation. In addition, two sample interviews from each neighborhood are included after each neighborhood analysis in order to provide the reader with continuity.

SELECTION OF STUDY AREAS

Housing submarket behavior could have been studied by examination of neighborhoods in different cities or various areas in one city. On behalf of the multiple-city approach, one can argue that situations drawn from a single city do not give a fair sample of the variation possible. While limiting a study to one community makes it difficult to argue that the results of the investigation have universal application, having the case studies located in the same "control system" is of decided advantage for comparative analysis.

Problems of comparability created by regional factors (city size and age), by variation in economic and social dominance among urban areas, and by the goals and strategies of different local housing authorities are avoided. The single-city approach provides a solid base for comparing the differences among residential areas and the manner in which those differences influence the form and extent of housing submarket behavior. Thus, the one city strategy seems to offer the more useful approach to studying the diversity of neighborhoods and the relationship of that diversity to housing submarkets.

New York City provides an ideal case study for the housing problem. It is an old city containing a large core of old residential districts, many of which have been affected by the changing racial composition of the city. It is this fact that determined the choice of study areas.

The study areas were small neighborhoods in Brooklyn and Queens (about a one-hour train ride from Manhattan) and contained much of the borough's public housing and dilapidated private housing. The needs of the study called for areas small enough to permit intensive study and defined so as to permit comparison with data from other sources. In addition, these had to have undergone racial change during the study period (1950-70).

Five neighborhoods—Brownsville, East New York, Crown Heights, Southeast Queens, and the Rockaways—were selected as best meeting these requirements. Some of the areas are poverty areas, with a substantial amount of substandard housing. Other neighborhoods contain a mixture of middle-class homeowners and poverty-level renters, and one test area (the Rockaways) has virtually no private rental housing. It houses 10 percent of the Queens population and contains 25 percent of its public housing.

Most of the housing in these areas is old; over 95 percent of all private housing was constructed prior to 1929. There are some old-law and new-law tenements, high-rise apartment buildings, and some private one-, two-, and three-family homes.

The median household income in these areas ranged from approximately $4,000 to $18,000, according to 1970 census figures. Some areas had large welfare populations, others had virtually none. Extreme differences also prevailed with respect to public housing distribution.

At one level, these studies report neighborhood analyses: they record the statistics, newspaper and magazine accounts, and the views of community residents expressed of these areas over a 20-year period. Yet, my aim is not to write the definitive history of selected New York City neighborhoods. Rather, I am concerned primarily with those aspects of the neighborhood story that relate the course, characters, and content of neighborhood change to the characteristics of the neighborhood residents.

It is important to emphasize that there are variations among the test neighborhoods; however, an underlying unity was provided by the similarity in racial composition. What is significant at this point is to consider briefly the variations among community populations to determine how the diversity of the neighborhood shaped the activities of local housing authorities and the city: the extent of their participation and the final product emerging from these processes.

While all five areas experienced racial transition, the characteristics of those population movements were critically diverse. A study of census tract shifts by socioeconomic characteristics indicate that Brownsville was as depressed relative to the city average in 1950 as it was in 1960. Low incomes, bad housing, high crime and juvenile delinquency rates, poor health, racial ghettos, and old age were characteristic of that neighborhood.

At the end of the 1950s and throughout the 1960s, the significant population movement in Brownsville was the perceptible inmigration of welfare and other low-income black families (many displaced by urban renewal in the Bronx and Manhattan) taking advantage of the abundance of federal public housing.

Other than a critical loss of white people, Crown Heights during the same decade had not witnessed any startling transformation in the socioeconomic characteristics of its population. While many blacks had moved into the houses left empty by suburban-bound whites, the basic character of the neighborhood's residents remained unchanged.

East New York, however, during the late 1950s and throughout the 1960s, witnessed a dramatic shift in the socioeconomic characteristics of its population as population movements produced a reversal from a white middle-income home-owning community to a black and Puerto Rican lower-income majority and an increasing clash of life styles. Much of the population shift into East New York was from Brownsville. As Brownsville had become a haven for public housing and urban renewal, many families had been displaced from the old- and new-law tenements they had previously occupied. These families were compelled to live in crowded quarters in East New York's small one-family homes. This process was welcomed by slum landlords and, to a lesser extent, by resident owners who couldn't maintain their homes.

East New York was one area in New York City that was severely affected by the FHA scandal and various forms of blockbusting. In many cases, homeowners were forced to crowd families into small one-family homes in order to generate income (to prevent foreclosure). Many landlords had to abandon buildings and the increasing number of FHA foreclosures added fuel to the fire. In the East New York area, approximately 2,500 buildings lie abandoned and boarded up. The surrounding areas have urban renewal projects; East New York has none.

The Southeast Queens study area can be divided into two distinct communities: South Jamaica, west of Merrick Boulevard, has been a low-income black community since the late 1940s. The area contains large poverty pockets, dilapidated housing, and all other indicators of a powerless poverty population. The second community,

St. Albans and Addesleigh Park, east of Merrick Boulevard, has been an upper middle-income black community since the 1940s with many indications of community stability. In recent years, however, the increasing population and overcrowdedness of the South Jamaica area has caused a spillover of what residents call "undesirable elements" into St. Albans. Some homeowners have been leaving the area and many who remain have uncertain feelings regarding the future.

The South Jamaica area, during the late 1940s and early 1950s, witnessed population change. At this time, some black families were permitted to purchase homes north of Atlantic Avenue. Unfortunately, many of these homeowners could not afford to maintain their properties, some were forced to abandon them, others converted their single- and double-family houses into rooming houses, and SROs (single room occupancies). The construction of South Jamaica Houses in 1941 and Baisley Park Houses in 1962 further induced a population shift from white to black.

While the western half of the area experienced racial transition, racial change was also occurring in the eastern half of the area, at a much slower and calmer rate. Since the 1940s, many of New York City's upper-class blacks have purchased elegant houses in the St. Albans and Addesleigh Park sections. The economic strength of the community has been declining because South Jamaica's borders have been moving eastward.

The Rockaways study area, prior to World War II, was a desirable summer resort. The decline of the summer market and an abundance of displaced welfare families helped to transform this community from one of summer use to year-round use, a move that has not been followed by increased services. Many summer bungalows have been converted to all-year use and house welfare families. In addition, the peninsula is "flooded" with public housing, much of which has replaced the summer bungalows that have "fallen beyond repair."

Control areas (in which racial change did not occur and whose "white ethnic" submarket structure still exists) were selected for comparative (statistical) purposes. The areas of Highland Park-Cypress Hills-City Line, Ravenswood, and Ridgewood were selected since each resembled at least one of the test areas in housing and density of population.

The remainder of this chapter contains a presentation of materials obtained from the field survey and supplemented by statistical data. More detailed analyses on specific neighborhoods appear in Part II of this book in the neighborhood histories and in the sample interviews. Reference is made here to specific interviews, many of which appear in Part II. Unless otherwise indicated, all quoted materials are from the field research conducted for this study. Reference is also made, where applicable, to neighborhood statistics.[3]

PUBLIC HOUSING

There are two questions to be asked of the effects of public housing and FHA homeownership programs on urban neighborhoods: Do the policies of financial and government institutions have varied effects on urban neighborhoods through public housing and FHA homeownership programs? Have such variations adversely affected black neighborhoods, while they have had limited impact on white neighborhoods?

Housing legislation has been most useful to the attractive and generally sanitary environments of the middle and upper classes. Among other things, it has facilitated the removal from their neighborhoods of undesirable concentrations of lower-class slums. The legislation has made matters worse for many displaced families. Demolitions have forced large numbers of displaced families to compete for a reduced amount of housing accommodations at higher costs in adjacent areas; a process that eventually leads to overcrowding and subdividing of apartments. The sanitary problems of the lower-class areas have been a means of justifying and legitimizing increased government intervention to accomplish other goals (that is, racial segregation) that serve the interests of the middle and upper classes. As a result, the spatial segregation of races in New York City has become more sharply defined. The outcome of this separation has been directly reflecting the form of the city—the architectural uniformity of various areas (for example, public housing areas) being a direct expression of the broad uniformity of needs and socioeconomic status of their inhabitants.

FHA homeownership programs have had drastic effects on urban neighborhoods with black populations. The low-quality FHA minimum standards have allowed speculators to realize windfall profits by selling houses to blacks at astronomical prices. These programs have resulted in widespread abandonment and have, in the process, created a large class of debt-encumbered black homeowners.

The field survey from New York City neighborhoods indicates that policies of financial and government institutions differ in urban neighborhoods. Public housing has been constructed in different proportions across neighborhoods; FHA-insured low- and moderate-income housing has been located in certain designated areas.

That such variations have racially based effects is also strongly indicated by field survey evidence. Public housing has been constructed in huge proportions in predominantly black neighborhoods and has had a negative effect on the neighborhoods. FHA homeownership programs have concentrated on racially changing (or changed) neighborhoods and have, in many instances, caused them to decline.

Project areas (which are predominantly black) have absorbed huge population increases. This population shift has put a strain on municipal services, which have not increased to accommodate the increased population. A lack of resident project staff is evident in black areas. Stringent income limits imposed by the New York City Housing Authority forced those residents most able to aid the community to leave the area. With virtually no homeownership and private rental housing in black areas in deplorable condition, these families move to other neighborhoods. New York City Housing Authority data indicate that when projects are constructed in black neighborhoods, many site residents are displaced. The concentration of small apartments in projects tends to screen those in need from obtaining adequate housing, since many black families require larger apartments. An erosion of the community's economic base caused by the proliferation of public housing has resulted in depressed shopping areas. Racial discrimination in tenant selection for public housing (by income) is also evident. Black project tenants have average incomes often $2,000 higher than those of white tenants.

Most of the lower-income white tenants, often senior citizens, live in lower-rise projects in predominately white neighborhoods.

This section presents evidence regarding the inequitable distribution of public housing and FHA housing, and their racially based neighborhood effects. This evidence was obtained from the field study of New York City neighborhoods and from municipal agency data on various public housing characteristics.

Project Management

Residents of black neighborhoods are appalled at the apparent lack of resident project staff. A community leader of Brownsville said: "15 to 30 years ago, talk was started about resident management, resident maintenance—we never got it! Resident maintenance is one of the biggest farces; it is so-called in existence but with such stringent conditions that the idea is negated." Project tenants feel that the lack of a resident project manager has a destabilizing effect on the project. Project managers, who live outside the project area, do not understand or care to understand the life styles of project residents. In addition, they are on the premises from 9:00 A.M. to 5:00 P.M. and are obviously unavailable during evening hours, when they are needed most. One Brownsville resident remarked:

> We have 12 projects here, employing many people. But virtually nobody from this community is employed by them. This is bad for both the community and the project residents. Our population remains unemployed and project residents are lacking necessary services that should be available during the evening hours. This situation is unfair—it doesn't happen this way in so-called stable neighborhoods.

Municipal Services

Most of the superblock project sites (which are in predominantly black neighboroods) that now house thousands of families previously contained smaller houses and housed a few hundred families. While the projects have caused the population of the area to increase considerably, the city's distribution of municipal services has not followed suit. A long-term resident of Crown Heights commented about municipal services in the Albany Houses area:

> Of course, services in the Albany Houses area have been drastically cut. The four blocks that projects are on used to have 60 two-family houses, now they house thousands of families and services have not been increased. Garbage collection, for example, is done twice a week, as it was done before. This makes for some filthy streets.

A Brownsville resident added:

> In 1948, when this neighborhood was predominantly Jewish and politically important, things were different. I remember, one winter day, we had a terrible snow storm in Brooklyn. The next day, the streets in Brownsville were clean. Neighboring Bedford Stuyvesant, where most of my friends lived, hadn't been touched. My friends couldn't even move their cars. If this snow storm happened now, the streets of Brownsville would be full of snow until the weather becomes warm enough so that it melts.

Instability of Residence

The stringent income limits imposed by the New York City
Housing Authority secure a transient project population. As residents' incomes surpass this limit, they are forced to move out of
public housing. A Brownsville resident remarked:

> Public housing has a way of destroying the family
> unit . . . income guidelines are not conducive to
> building. Many people did not want to leave Browns-
> ville because they knew what it was like to be a part
> of the community. Many people fought bitter fights
> to be here. Because of income guidelines, people
> were forced to move. Children are in a position to
> be forced to lie about who is working in the household.

Since the private housing in the area is grossly substandard, these
residents often leave the neighborhoods. Residents feel that this
makes the possibility of a communal life and cohesive community
organization remote. A Brownsville leader commented:

> Many people have fought bitter fights to stay here.
> People are forced out of the projects as soon as they
> get on their feet. People who could help the commu-
> nity are forced to leave. And when they move out of
> the project, they move out of the neighborhood. Who
> would want to live in these crumbling houses at these
> inflated costs ?

Displacement of Site Residents

Many of the public housing projects replaced old- and new-
law tenements. These tenements housed large welfare families,
as they usually had a substantial number of large apartments.
When projects were constructed in black areas, many site residents
were displaced and forced to crowd into private housing in the immediate area, since their locational choices were restricted. This
caused overcrowding (since the supply of housing was reduced).
The New York City Housing Authority initial occupancy data indicate
that an extremely small percentage of prior site residents, in
black areas, are rehoused on the site. That such practices are
common was also indicated by a Brownsville housing specialist:

> The projects are supposed to be built for the poor. But
> they are purposely constructed so that the poor can be

almost systematically eliminated from living in them.
Many poor families are large families and most project apartments are small. This controls the influx of
poor families to the projects.

Erosion of Shopping District

Many residents feel that the proliferation of projects tends to
erode the economic base of the community and, as a result, causes
local businesses to move elsewhere. An Arverne resident commented: "The Rockaway Peninsula is flooded with public housing
and old-age nursing homes. This has destroyed our economic base
and has caused all businesses to leave the area. We have no shop-
ing facilities to speak of in this neighborhood." An examination of
statistics from the New York Market Analysis (for 1960 and 1970)
showing retail activity in neighborhoods supports this statement.

Stabilizing or Limited Effect on the Neighborhood

When projects are constructed within reasonable proportions
(housing perhaps 15 to 20 percent of a neighborhood's population),
the neighborhood is not adversely affected: In some neighborhoods,
for example, Kingsborough Houses, located in northeast Crown
Heights, residents see the project as a source of community stability: "The project grounds are kept up. The building is maintained to a certain extent. After all, the Housing Authority could
get but so lax as a slumlord." A similar situation prevails in the
South Jamaica area. The two federal housing projects, Baisley
Park Houses and South Jamaica Houses, are well run and considered to be a neighborhood asset:

> Baisley Houses and South Jamaica Houses are virtually
> the only decent rental houses in the South Jamaica area.
> The tenants are keeping up the property. Recently, the
> outside of one project was painted by tenants. The
> only other sound housing in the area is Rochdale Village,
> a middle-income cooperative in the southernmost sec-
> tion of the area.

Projects in East New York have been located in the periphery of
the area and have pushed the so-called undesirable element in a
northward direction, from the area south of Linden Boulevard (now
referred to as Flatlands Plaza) and in a westward direction from

the area east of Fountain Avenue. This has caused extreme overcrowding in the East New York area, accompanied by increased
rents. An East New York resident explained:

> I have lived in this area for 15 years. When they put up
> this new building, I went right down to the office to apply
> for an apartment. They gave me a green card and a red
> card to fill out and they said they would call me if some-
> thing came up. They never called me. They don't like
> to rent to Puerto Ricans, even though they are residents
> of the community. They just crowd more of us into less
> housing and bring others to live in the new housing.

Brownsville and the Rockaways have become "project neighborhoods" with a small percentage of private housing serving a
transient population. Both neighborhoods have been severely affected by the proliferation of public housing. While both of these
areas show signs of some stability (community organization), efforts are not coordinated and structure and organization are difficult to achieve.

Crime in the Projects

One would expect that as crime in the neighborhood has increased, crime in the projects would increase proportionately.
According to New York City Housing Police data, crime in the
projects has decreased drastically since 1963 (the first year that
project data were collected). The project crime problem, according to residents, remains most severe in the project neighborhoods
of Brownsville and the Rockaways. A Brownsville housing specialist remarked:

> We have more projects here than anywhere else in the
> city. About 60,000 residents of this neighborhood live
> in public housing. The crime problems in the projects
> are terrible. There are only 12 Housing Authority
> Police assigned in this area and they never seem to be
> around when crimes are committed.

This discrepancy can be attributed to any combination of three factors: there is less crime in the buildings and more crime on the
streets surrounding the projects; there is a problem with the re-
cording of statistics—either intentionally or unintentionally; the
Housing Authority Police are inefficient: either there are an

insufficient number of Housing Authority Police in project areas or
the sufficient number of policemen are not controlling the crime
problem in the projects. The project tenants are inclined to think
the third factor is the most important. Residents feel that the
housing police should be distributed according to project population.
A Rockaway resident remarked:

> We are flooded with projects here. Yet the project
> police are not sent here. You see a few, from time to
> time. But most of them are in the so-called stable
> neighborhoods to keep peace between the few project
> residents and the middle class residents around them.

Tenants in the Projects

The projects in the project areas (Brownsville and the Rockaways) have a higher percentage of welfare tenants, a higher percentage of female-headed families, and a lower percentage of
senior citizens than those in other neighborhoods. Projects in
predominantly white neighborhoods have tenants with lower incomes.
They are generally senior citizens. The private housing in project
areas generally serves a transient, welfare population. Private
housing in white areas with projects is generally in good condition.
There is also a considerable difference between income levels
of black and white tenants (median income for the black residents
is often $2,000 to $3,000 higher than that of white residents). This
distinction is a reflective of either discrimination in tenant selection—dual income standards; or black families with higher income
desire to live in a project because the opportunities in the private
housing market (that would be available to white families of similar
income) are deplorable.
In 1974, Langston Hughes Apartments (Brownsville) had 54.2
percent welfare tenants, 48.2 percent one-parent families, and 25
percent senior citizens. Ravenswood Houses (Astoria-Ravenswood),
located in a white ethnic neighborhood, had 6.0 percent welfare
tenants, 14 percent one-parent families, and 40 percent senior
citizens. Private housing in Brownsville is decayed while housing
in Ravenswood is well maintained.

PRIVATE HOUSING

There are three questions to be asked on the effects of
speculator real estate interests in racially changing (or changed)

neighborhoods: Are the actions of speculator real estate interests in black neighborhoods different from those in white neighborhoods? Have such variations in speculator interests caused the housing stock to decay in black areas while housing in white areas remained sound? Has the city, in its distribution of welfare clients, contributed to speculator operations in black neighborhoods?

In racially changing neighborhoods, speculators often pick up houses cheaply, put in minimum cosmetic repairs, and sell them to black families. Banks and mortgage banking interests most often will refuse to grant mortgages to minorities. The speculator then interposes his credit between that of the banker and the buyer, obtaining the credit necessary for the transaction. He then inflates the price (often astronomically) and turns the house over to the black family. In many cases, speculators entice these prospective homeowners by providing false information regarding costs of maintaining housing and by allowing these families to purchase homes they cannot afford by offering them a minimum down-payment plan or no down-payment at all. The process of red-lining (deliberate withdrawal of financial support for the housing market) by financial institutions perpetuates this process.

Real estate speculation is also common in areas where federal or state housing is in the planning stage. Legislation allows inspectors to enter and inspect unsanitary or overcrowded property, predominantly older housing in certain designated areas, and to instruct the owner to make good those elements that are deemed harmful. If no action is forthcoming, then property could be condemned and demolished. Many landlords, having prior knowledge of plans relating to urban renewal, allow their properties to deteriorate with hopes of selling to the city. This has a disastrous effect on the quality of housing in the neighborhood.

The pressure to increase returns on investment by overcrowding has been ruthlessly intensified during the last 20 years (public housing construction and demolitions have facilitated this process). Tenants have been exploited by landlords whose only object has been to make as much money as possible. If tenants agree to pay the rents for substandard accommodations, landlords have little incentive to improve the standards. Since the city pays astronomical rents for welfare tenants occupying substandard housing, they support these landlords.

The evidence from New York City neighborhoods indicates that actions of speculator real estate interests have adversely affected black neighborhoods while having a limited impact on white neighborhoods (regardless of the income levels of residents). Mortgage practices vary across different types of neighborhoods and so do price structures. The city, by exiling welfare clients to substandard housing and paying high rents for apartments, has contributed to the success of speculator operations. Landlords, with no incentive to repair, neglect their properties, knowing their substandard apartments will be rented.

The Effects of Speculator Real Estate Interests and
Financial and Government Institutions on
Urban Neighborhoods

Many Americans who look at abandoned FHA houses and at dilapidated neighborhoods believe that the people brought these conditions on themselves. In reality, urban neighborhoods have been ruined by deliberate and mismanaged government housing programs, money-hungry investors, criminal speculators, and crooked bankers. A Southeast Queens resident said:

> The banks and real estate brokers are the ones who pull
> down these neighborhoods. They allow anyone with $200
> to buy a house. They tell these people that it will cost
> a certain amount to keep it up. But they fool these
> people and the result is that many people have to abandon
> their homes. Real estate interests do not care if these
> houses are abandoned. They are FHA insured. Mean-
> while, entire neighborhoods are destroyed and the so-
> called homeowners are, once again, renters. They are
> generally forced into surrounding areas. The over-
> crowding that persists causes more decline.

Crime, violence, disease, and addiction are nurtured by a ruined physical environment, and there is no poverty so degrading as the one where shelter rots in the day and burns in the night. An East New York resident explained:

> Once the old-time residents move, it is the intent of the
> real estate company (who is generally the landlord) to
> move in and move out as many families as possible so as
> to legally obtain rent increments. Many landlords who
> owned the smaller buildings have left their buildings and
> then FHA steps in and takes over and boards them up.
> Wherever there are FHA houses, there are rats. When
> FHA takes over, they don't spray for rat poisoning, they
> do not keep the houses clean.

Some Relationships between Landlords and Tenants

Landlords often seek maximum compensation (rents) since they realize that their tenants have no real alternative. A Crown Heights real estate agent points out: "The landlords here charge whatever the market will bear. The market in black neighborhoods throughout the city is a dirty market. Prices are much higher than they should be. But with locational choices restricted, landlords can exploit the people all they want." Landlords often cut services in order to secure transiency and increase rents (especially in rent-controlled or rent-stabilized buildings). A Crown Heights resident explained:

> There are many rent-controlled apartments in the apartment houses here. Tenants have been living there for many years and are paying the lowest rents. If landlords cut services, which they claim they are doing because of increased costs, they can get some of these tenants disgusted enough to move. Then they can take in black tenants and charge high rents. This is unfair, as black tenants are paying ridiculous rents and are, in fact, subsidizing the rent-controlled apartments.

Landlords of rent-stabilized and rent-controlled buildings frequently rent apartments to a few "troubled families" in the hope of scaring off the most stable (long-term) residents so that rents for these apartments can be increased and rented to welfare families. A Crown Heights resident remarked:

> On Eastern Parkway, we had some long-term residents in the rent-controlled apartment buildings. The landlords have taken in a few welfare tenants with small children to scare off some of the older people. Landlords have also deliberately cut services in the buildings and have rented their apartments to the highest bidders (welfare tenants).

Rents Paid by Welfare Tenants: The City's Role in This Process

Welfare tenants pay astronomical rents in relation to the quality of the dwellings they occupy. A Crown Heights real estate broker said:

Welfare tenants are the most exploited people here.
They live in the worst housing in the area, much of which
should be condemned, and they pay the highest rents.
Since rents are paid directly to landlords by the welfare
department, the tenant has no power whatsoever. Where
tenants start rent strikes in demand of services, welfare tenants have to accept what they are given. This
gives landlords the power to do what they want, which
isn't much except collect rents.

Since the city (welfare department) pays these rents for welfare tenants and exiles them to substandard housing, they, in effect,
support corrupt and discriminatory housing operations. An East
New York housing specialist remarked:

The welfare tenants in this neighborhood really keep the
landlords in good business. The welfare department
just sends their clients here to rent these horrible
apartments with all the rats, roaches, and mice. They
pay ridiculously high rents for these apartments. Why
should a landlord fix his house if he could rent it to a
welfare family and get a higher rent?

Census data indicate that many welfare tenants occupy the
private housing surrounding projects in the project areas. This
housing is in deplorable condition. In many instances, these buildings were previously abandoned by their landlords and taken over by
the city. There are, for example, 850 buildings in real estate
management in Brownsville. The city, therefore, is subsidizing
its own operations at the expense of the tenants. Census data also
indicate that the bulk of the residents of these dwellings are welfare
recipients (who are refused apartments in public housing, often because of the insufficient number of large apartments in projects).
Housing specialists claim that some are families waiting for a
project apartment and families who are waiting to leave the community and, often, the city. A Brownsville housing specialist said:

The private housing here serves a transient population.
Most of it is occupied by large welfare families who
didn't qualify for public housing, usually because there
were too many children in the family for a project
apartment. Some families are living there until they
buy a home elsewhere and some are waiting for a
project apartment.

Changing Neighborhoods and Absentee Landlords

As the neighborhood's socioeconomic structure changes, many established landlords hold on to their properties and purchase homes for their families in the suburbs (or more desirable neighborhoods). That such practices are common in Southeast Queens is indicated by a South Jamaica resident:

> The people who used to live here still own these houses. They have moved to St. Albans and Long Island but they still own houses in the lousiest sections of South Jamaica. The tenants here have to subsidize the mortgages of the "so-to-speak" black middle class who have made it and moved on. What is not said is that they made it by exploiting their own people.

Landlords' interests in these cases are purely monetary. An angry resident of South Jamaica commented:

> The landlords in South Jamaica don't live here—and they don't care if the housing is kept up. As long as it is occupied, and it will be as long as welfare tenants are sent here, they are content. Landlords are only interested in collecting rent.

A Brownsville community leader explained: "In the past, we had resident owners. When they moved, they rented their houses and allowed them to be abandoned. This caused others to move. Even though the old-timers moved, they still exercised control over the area." Conversions of single- and double-family houses into rooming units has increased landlords' revenues. Using property as a tax shelter, many established landlords invest in slum housing for depreciation purposes. In this way, a tax write-off is allowed for the allocation of the cost of housing over its useful life, which is generally a short period. The property is then purchased by another established landlord, and so on.

MUNICIPAL SERVICES

There are two key questions to be asked of the distribution of municipal services: Does the city's distribution of municipal services have varied effects on urban neighborhoods? Do such variations cause black neighborhoods to decline at the expense of nonblack?

Those who control the city strive to provide a greater range of
services to its more desirable neighborhoods than its run-down
sections.

The flight of the middle and upper classes from the city and
the growing homogenization of social classes within relatively discrete residential areas was accompanied by the corresponding
flight of the financial resources necessary to establish and sustain
adequate levels of urban social and physical infrastructure in lower-
class neighborhoods. Thus, the spatial environment of the city
replicates the social and economic disequilibrium of production
relations.

The evidence from New York City neighborhoods indicates
that levels of municipal services across neighborhoods differ
markedly. Neighborhoods with adequate levels of services are
well-maintained, while neighborhoods whose services are at lower
levels are severely hurt. That such variations have racially based
effects is strongly indicated by evidence from New York City neighborhoods. Municipal services have been deliberately withdrawn
from neighborhoods during (and after) racial transition, regardless
of residents' incomes. This withdrawal of services is most evident
in the areas of education, sanitation, and health care and police
protection.

Inferior Educational Structure

The quality of schooling available to children from black areas
is impaired: schools have difficulty in attracting and retaining
staff, schools do not possess facilities of buildings and equipment
comparable with other schools in white areas. A Rockaway resident
added:

> When the projects were built, a large student popula-
> tion came here. We have these old schools and facili-
> ties have increased a slight bit. But the classes are
> overcrowded, with 60 in a class. The teachers we
> have here do not care about teaching, only about col-
> lecting their salaries. Our children graduate but they
> cannot read or write.

Teachers' attitudes toward their jobs are less than serious.
Parents feel that teachers are in school to secure some experience
in hope of being transferred elsewhere. Teachers often perform
more adequately as babysitters, resulting in poor quality education
for students. A Brownsville community leader said:

> The schools here are terrible. The parents should take
> a class action suit against the Board of Education for
> miseducating their children. Teachers physically
> abuse children and are never brought up on charges.
> They are merely transferred to other locations.

An East New York resident added:

> The schools are old, crowded, and functioning on split
> sessions. There are annexes on wheels but these are
> terrible. I have a son who attends the public school
> here. He is not learning but he is being promoted
> every year. His teachers say he is good but I know
> he cannot read, and he is in the 5th grade.

Many parents from these neighborhoods send their children to parochial schools because facilities in the neighborhood schools are
horrendous. Long-term residents emphasize that a causality exists
between changes in the quality of educational facilities and services
and the changes in the neighborhood's population composition.

Decline of the Shopping Area

Shopping facilities have declined and in many cases disappeared as the neighborhood changed. Residents claim that the remaining stores (except chain stores) are owned by people from
outside the community who come into the community during the day
to exploit the people. A Brownsville resident commented:

> Come through Brownsville on a Jewish holiday. All the
> stores are closed. The storekeepers sometimes have
> Puerto Ricans fronting as owners. The people who
> used to live here own the stores. They have left the
> community but they earn their livings by ripping us off.
> They have the worst merchandise you can imagine . . .
> especially food! The prices are the highest in town.

Merchandise in these stores is inferior and prices are exorbitant.
Many residents who are tied to the community (because of transpor-
tation) are forced to shop in neighborhood stores. A long-term
Brownsville resident recalled:

> Twenty years ago we had good stores here. They sold
> fresh merchandise at reasonable prices. I remember

the Pitkin and Belmont area markets. They had the
best food money could buy, especially fish, fruit, and
vegetables. They used to sell all the fish on Friday
that they had from the week so that it did not spoil.
Now, I think they import the stale fish to sell here.
Shopping here stinks!

The Crime Problem and Police-Community Relations

Disorder and crime are a lasting and permanent threat to residents of black areas. Crimes against property and people are common and police cooperation is minimal. Police are not responsive
to the community they are required to serve. A Brownsville leader
said: "The police here cooperate only with the teachers and the
Pitkin Avenue Merchants Association. They are not at all concerned
with the residents of this area."
Security has not been achieved to any reasonable measure and
crime has not been controlled. A Brownsville resident commented:
"There is a breakdown in relations between the community and the
police. There is no cooperation to keep the community safe and
clean. The police-community breakdown is a major reason for the
high crime rates, which are higher than we should have to put up
with." Traditionally the policeman was a part of the community he
policed; if not actually a native of the area, he would most probably
have grown up in the same kind of area. Over the years, the police
established a working relation with working-class (white ethnic)
communities whereby expectations of both groups were shared.
Residents of black areas feel that a lack of communication between
police and community residents exists because of a difference in
mentality. One community leader of Brownsville commented:
"Once the people move to the suburbs, they develop a suburban
mentality. They come to these neighborhoods and think they are
running a camp. If we see a crime here, we don't call the police.
The police harass you and make you feel like the criminal."
A case illustrating the end result of this process can be made
by examining crime rates across neighborhoods. In 1970, South
Jamaica had 2,700 robberies, 3,900 burglaries, and 3,800 auto
thefts. Ridgewood-Glendale (a white ethnic neighborhood) had 223
robberies, 1,000 burglaries, and 700 auto thefts.
With the movement of the established working class to suburban
areas, the policeman moved away from the areas in which most of
his work was. These old areas have suffered from neglect and decay and from a decline of "community" as the resident population
changed. Matching this neglect has been a loss of police contact and
effectiveness and a rise in the incidence of crime.

Fires: Causes and Consequences

The incidence of fires in these areas is higher than in most surrounding neighborhoods. There were approximately 2,000 structural fires in Brownsville in 1973 and 125 in Ridgewood, 235 in Ravenswood (two white ethnic areas). Structural fires are highest in areas whose housing turnover is high. Residents attribute high rates of structural fires to landlord neglect. Landlords, by failing to provide necessary maintenance and services, allow their buildings to deteriorate. Many residents claim that they have buildings burned down (by hiring teenagers to set them afire) to collect fire insurance or to derent control or destabilize rents in these apartments. Local housing specialists are certain that tenants in these horrendous dwellings sometimes set them afire with hopes of escaping their surroundings. This often translates into getting apartments in public housing. A Brownsville housing specialist explained:

> I have tenants from these destroyed buildings coming
> here to try and find an apartment. They say they had
> nothing to do with those fires in their buildings, but
> I know that they are all not telling the truth. These
> tenants see no way out of these hellholes they are
> forced to occupy and so they burn them down. While
> this happens sometimes, the landlords are responsible
> for most of these fires both intentionally and through
> neglect of the buildings.

Inferior Health Care Facilities and Poor Health

Health care facilities in black areas are generally poor (except in Crown Heights, which is surrounded by doctors and clinics), and consequently the state of community health is seriously deficient. That health care is seriously deficient in black areas is indicated by an examination of health statistics in New York City neighborhoods. Statistical evidence indicates that the highest incidence of venereal disease, infectious hepatitis, and lead poisoning was in the black neighborhoods. Brownsville, for example, had 1,100 reported cases of gonorrhea in 1970, compared with Ridgewood's 22 cases.

"Exploitative Medicaid mills" are often interspersed throughout the community. These health clinics offer inferior services and charge exploitative prices. Since the profit rate on medication is fixed, doctors in these clinics often prescribe far more medicine than is necessary to arrest an illness. A Brownsville community leader explained:

> These Medicaid mills here are so bad. They make you
> wait so long and then they charge you so much—even
> though they are supposed to be for the poor. Then they
> give you so much medicine, most of which you don't
> need. They give you small doses too, so that you keep
> coming back and getting more. They can make only a
> certain amount for each prescription, so they give you
> small prescriptions.

Since there are limited number of private physicians, residents of these areas are forced to use hospital emergency rooms as their private physicians.

Sanitation Problems: Their Effects on the Neighborhood

Residents complain vehemently about neglect on the part of the Sanitation Department in keeping streets clean. Garbage pick-ups are infrequent and inefficient. A Crown Heights resident commented:

> The sanitation workers have some racket. They make
> you bring garbage to the curb and if it is one foot from
> the curb, they refuse to remove it. When they dump
> the cans into their trucks, they leave much garbage in
> the street. They pick up garbage so infrequently that
> much of the garbage left on the curb ends up in the
> gutter and alleys.

Street cleaning (sweeping) is virtually nonexistent. A Brownsville resident remarked: "We have six days' alternate side parking here. But you never see the Sanitation Department cleaning the streets. Once in a while, they throw a little water down—that just soaks the dirt." Residents feel that the regulation forced on them to place garbage bags near the curb causes a problem. Since garbage collection is infrequent, bags are often torn by the time they are to be collected, making the streets filthy. An angry Brownsville resident commented:

> Garbage pick-ups were more frequent before the proj-
> ects were constructed. Now that the population in the
> area has increased, they cut services. The Sanitation

Department's mandatory rule of placing garbage near
the curb has caused our neighborhood to get filthy.
They pick up garbage twice a week, and garbage piles
up on the streets.

Lack of Recreational Facilities

For the most part, recreational facilities are absent from
these areas. The smattering of parks and playgrounds that physically inhabit these areas has been neglected over the years and is
presently unsupervised. A Brownsville resident explained: "There
is only one park for all Brownsville, East New York, and Crown
Heights children. It gets so crowded with all these youngsters. But
I won't allow my children to attend the dirty, full of glass, Betsey
Head Park in the area."
Movie theaters that at one time serviced these areas have
closed down with the changing character of the areas. A Brownsville resident recalls: "We had many movie theaters. We had the
Loew's Pitkin, the Jewish Theater, and so on. This neighborhood
was some place for recreation. Now, we have the burned out shells
from these theaters and the storefront churches that have replaced
them." This has also been the case with bowling alleys and roller
skating rinks. An Arverne resident explained: "My children have
to go to Elmont for any recreation. We have nothing here. We had
movie theaters but they have been closed down. We have no skating
facilities, parks, or recreational centers."

A BRIEF LOOK AT LONDON

In London, the Greater London Council has considerable control over the rental housing market. Council housing (the English
equivalent of public housing) can be built or acquired. It can consist
of apartments or houses. People are housed according to a point
system. According to their conditions, the quality of the accommodation will differ. Families who are homeless or in dire need of
housing are given first preference at rehousing. In most cases, the
quality of the accommodation they receive is less than adequate.
Those families who have been on the waiting list for a considerable
period of time will patiently wait but usually receive far better accommodations. In many instances they receive a house.
The Council Estates (large complexes of Council housing) are,
in many cases, located outside the central area. The two Council
Housing Estates I visited were Aldgate and Brixton. These neighborhoods are located at the periphery of the city (Brixton was the last

underground station on the Victoria Line; Aldgate was the last underground station on the Metropolitan Line). The Council housing estates are a considerable distance from the underground stations. Housing construction in both of these neighborhoods is similar, consisting of a combination of low-rise (three-story) and high-rise (ten-story) buildings situated widely apart. The areas surrounding the Council houses are predominantly industrial. A limited number of private dwellings here are severely overcrowded with illegal aliens (Indians, Pakistanis). The remaining private housing is abandoned, burned out, and boarded up with wood planks.

Shopping areas in Aldgate and Brixton are inadequate. There are no supermarkets in the immediate area. Because of prohibitive fares on the Underground, which vary with distance traveled, people are restricted to the shopping facilities in the immediate area. Health and educational facilities are on the premises or within close proximity. Police and sanitation services appear to be more adequate in these neighborhoods than in comparable neighborhoods in New York City.

It has been contended by Harloe, Issacharoff, and Minns[4] that the Council knocks down more houses than it replaces. Particularly hard hit is the private rental (unfurnished) sector, as many houses have been taken over by the Council and others have been converted to more profitable furnished lettings. While the Council rehouses displaced families, their control over these tenants enables them to successfully manipulate them. This implies rehousing in certain designated areas; a process that further exacerbates the housing problem.

The small percentage of private landlords in the London central area is discouraged from improving its properties because of a prohibitive tax structure. Interest rates are very high and, when available, are only such for a short time period. The small private landlord is forced, in many cases, to charge a higher rent, since he is virtually starved of capital to meet his expenses.

Many lower-class areas of London have recently been invaded by the middle classes. Shabby modest mews and cottages have been taken over when their leases have expired and have become elegant, expensive residences. Victorian houses, which were downgraded in an earlier period and used as lodging houses, have been upgraded once again. Many houses are being subdivided into costly houselets. Once this process begins in a neighborhood, it goes on rapidly until the entire area is displaced and the social character of the neighborhood changes. The main agents at work in these areas are property speculators.

These speculators often seek government financial inducement and take advantage of these low-cost areas. The process includes the destruction of lower-class neighborhoods and a subsequent reduction in the supply of housing for these displaced residents. It results, however, in an extremely high return on investment for property developers in these run-down areas. The ability of mortgage finance and the willingness of the private land-lord to sell encourages these speculators. It has been estimated that the relocation of one middle-class family is equal to the dis-location of two lower-class families. This results in a reduced supply of available housing—a situation that causes increased over-crowding in adjacent areas and increased rents, as the poor compete for this housing.

THE QUESTIONNAIRE

Neighborhood

1. By and large, do you think this neighborhood is a good place to live in? Was this neighborhood more or less desirable 10 or 20 years ago?
2. Can you comment on what you see as the neighborhood's good points and bad points and how these might have changed over the years?
3. Do you think of the neighborhood as your real home (where you really belong) or do you think of it as a place where you happen to be living?
4. Would you like to move out of this neighborhood or would you like to stay here? If you would like to move, do you have any particular area in mind? Why is it that you are not in that area at present?
5. Do you have relatives or close friends in the area? Did you come in following relatives or friends, did you help bring in relatives or friends, or did you know relatives or friends but have no help in moving to this area?
6. Would you say that people in this neighborhood have any-thing in common? If so, what things do they have in common?
7. Please discuss your feelings about this neighborhood in light of past residences in other neighborhoods.
8. How do you feel about the changing property values and rents in this neighborhood?
9. Do you think this neighborhood has a lot of tensions: racial, ethnic, or others? If so, is this recent or has it been going on for a long time?
10. Do you feel that the public housing projects in this neigh-borhood affect the quality of the neighborhood at large? If so, how can you attempt to explain this?

11. Was this neighborhood a good one before the projects were constructed? How has it changed?

Community Facilities (Public and Private)

12. Where do you (and other family members who live here) usually do the following things . . . is it in the area or outside of the area?

        a. grocery shopping
        b. clothing shopping
        c. shopping for household appliances and furniture
        d. going to a park or playground
        e. visiting a doctor or clinic
        f. banking
        g. movies, and other recreational facilities

13. Is the lack of good medical care a serious problem in this area? Has this always been the case?

14. In case of sudden illness or accident, where do you turn? What do you expect to happen?

15. Is the lack of recreation for adults a great problem in this area?

16. Is there a lack of recreation for teenagers in this area?

17. Is there a lack of recreation for children in this area?

18. What recreational facilities do your children use?

19. Do you find the streets and sidewalks in the neighborhood in bad condition? Anything else, for example, broken telephone booths, abandoned cars? Has this always been the case?

20. Are parking regulations enforced in this area, for example, alternate side of the street parking, so that streets can be cleaned?

21. Do you feel that garbage is picked up properly in this area? Was it always so?

22. Do you feel the day-care facilities in this area are inadequate? Have they always been so?

23. Is public transportation in this area a problem or is it adequate? Are train stations safe? Are they clean?

24. Is it safe for children to cross streets when going to school? Are there crossing guards available on street corners so that small children can be assisted in crossing the street?

25. Do you feel that the schools were equipped to handle the influx of new students coming from the projects? In other words, did educational facilities increase with the increase in school-age population?

26. Are the public schools in this area opened during evening hours so that children can use facilities (gym)? Do public schools in this area provide facilities for children during summer months?

27. Is there a public library in the immediate area? Does it have adequate facilities for school-age children?

28. Do the neighborhood groceries have poor quality merchandise? Which items are of particularly poor quality? Have you complained to the Department of Health? What became of this?

29. Have any movie theatres been closed down since you have moved here?

30. Are there many churches in this neighborhood? Are there many storefront churches? Has this always been the case? What degree of importance do you place on the church as an institution within a community such as this?

31. Do you feel that levels of public facilities and services have decreased over time? Which, and in what respect?

32. How would you describe the general quality of public facilities and services in the immediate vicinity of the respondent's home?

Excellent—street lights, utilities, street signs are in perfect condition and lack of rubbish in the streets and alleys is outstanding.

Good —public services appear to be maintained, garbage is not scattered around, although some equipment may need replacement.

Fair —some street lights are inadequate, street signs are in poor condition, there is some litter in the alleys and streets.

Poor —broken and defective public equipment is quite evident and typical of the area, litter is scattered in the street, and the overall appearance of the street is unclean.

Cultural Pressure

33. Do you feel that storekeepers overcharge in this area? Do you feel that storekeepers treat people from this area badly? How? Are storekeepers usually residents of this area or are they from other parts of the city or suburbs?

34. Do you feel that this neighborhood has inadequate police protection? If so, has this been the case for a long time? Do the police harass you? Others? How?

35. How do you feel about the courts in this neighborhood? Are they accessible? Are they just?

36. Do you feel that the schools in this area are good? If not, what specifically is wrong with them? Do you feel teachers harass children from this area? How?

37. Do many welfare workers visit this area? Do they harass the people?

Public Safety Problems

38. These days, for you and your family, is crime a serious problem? If so, is there any particular crime you are in fear of? Has crime been about the same since you moved here or can you note significant changes?

39. Are there many fires in this area? Have there always been many (or few) fires here? If there are many fires, why do you think this is so?

40. Do you feel that this area is a "hangout" for drug users and addicts? If so, has this always been true?

41. Is there any gang problem in this area? If so, how long has this been going on?

42. Is this neighborhood noisy? If so, how do you account for this?

43. Is a lack of places for children to play a problem in this area? Are children generally safe? Is this a good area to bring up (preschool, elementary school, high school, post-high school) children?

44. Do you feel that the existence of cluttered high-rise buildings perpetuates crime or has no effect on crime?

45. Do most of the stores in this area have burglary gates? If so, how long has this been the case?

Housing Characteristics

46. How long have you lived in this neighborhood? Have you lived in the same apartment or house during this period of time?

47. Is bad housing in this neighborhood a serious problem? What things are particularly bad? Was there much bad housing when you moved here? If yes, why did you move to this particular neighborhood?

48. Do you rent this apartment? If so, how much rent do you pay (per month)?

49. How is renting relationship handled with regard to lease, agreements, services, repairs, payments, and so on?

50. How is home ownership handled with regard to holder of and terms of mortgage, major renovations or investments in house (who supplied money, labor, supplies)?

51. Do you feel that your rent is too high for the quality and size of your apartment? What should be a fair rent?

52. Do you feel that rents are high in this area because landlords take advantage of welfare tenants?

53. How many rooms do you have? How are they used?

54. Does the bathroom in your apartment have a window?

55. Does this building have an elevator? If so, does it operate efficiently? Is it safe? Are hallways safe?

56. Is this apartment house rent-controlled?

57. Have you suffered from the following problems recently?

lack of heat and hot water
roaches or rats
holes in the walls and ceilings
broken windows and pipes

Have you complained? What is the attitude toward complaints?

58. (For those people living in multiple dwelling structures of less than 10 units) Does your landlord live in this building? If not, does he live in this neighborhood?

59. (For people in apartment buildings) Is there a laundry room in your building? If so, is there ever a problem doing your laundry in the building?

Community Interaction and Support and
Political Networks

60. Are there many tenants' associations in this area? Are they effective in improving housing conditions?

61. Are there many local neighborhood improvement groups in this area? If so, are they effective in combatting some of the problems in this area?

62. Do you belong to any clubs or organizations in the neighborhood? If yes, which ones?

63. How do you think clubs help the community?

64. Have individuals in your household asked help from the following:

    a. Local councilman
    b. Assemblyman
    c. U.S. congressional representative or senator
    d. District leader
    e. Other political figures

If yes, describe circumstances and nature of interaction.

65. Do household members think of any political figure or contact as a potential source of support?

NOTES

1. See R. Hunter, The Slum (New York: The Free Press, 1964); and J. Lyford, The Airtight Cage: A Study of New York's West Side (New York: Harper & Row, 1966).

2. See National Opinion Research Center, Racial Integration in American Neighborhoods (Chicago: University of Chicago Press, 1970).

3. See Diane Gold, "Class Structure and the Economics of the Housing Problem," Ph.D. dissertation, New School for Social Research, 1977, especially Chapters 7-11 for detailed statistics on various neighborhood indicators.

4. M. Harloe, R. Issacharoff, and R. Minns, The Organization of Housing (London: Sage Publications, 1974).

5
AN ECONOMETRIC ANALYSIS OF RENT DETERMINATION ACROSS NEW YORK CITY SUBMARKETS, 1950–70

Many economic studies have analyzed the effect of individual variables on rents; but it is unsatisfactory to work on the basis of individual attributes when a good many of the variables are highly correlated. Moreover, the effect and relevance of particular influences vary according to the race and social class of households— the geographic structure of the housing submarket and the quality of the neighborhood. It is therefore necessary to understand the underlying structure of determinants of rents in order to appreciate the potential influence of any variables and to make reliable estimates of their effects.

The determination of rent levels involves more than the quality of amenities contained in and around the building. Housing is more accurately described to include both the internal and external attributes of a dwelling, the characteristics of its occupants, and the quality of the neighborhood.

The analysis in Chapter 2 suggests that within certain types of submarkets, class-monopoly rents are realized. Class-monopoly rents exist when the rate of return (rent) is set by the outcome of conflict between landlord and tenant. Class-monopoly rents arise because there exists a class of owners of housing who are willing to release the units under their command only if they receive a positive return above some arbitrary level. Landlords behave in accordance with a well-defined class interest. They gain their class power in part from the fact that individually they can survive quite well without releasing all the resources under their command. The realization of class-monopoly rent depends upon the ability of one class-interest group to exercise its power over another class-interest group and thereby to assure for itself a certain minimum rate of return. When landlords maintain this position, they supply poor quality housing to a class of renters at inflated prices.

In the central city, the submarkets whose populations are pre-dominantly black are subject to class-monopoly rent realization. This concept (for purposes of this study) is synonymous with racial rent differentials.

This chapter examines the structure and determinants of rents across eight New York City neighborhoods via principal components and regression analysis by examining the relationship between popu-lation, housing quality, neighborhood quality, and rents in different neighborhoods (corresponding with different submarkets) between 1950 and 1970. Neighborhoods (test areas), where class-monopoly rents are realized are compared with control areas (where class-monopoly rents are not realized). In this way, a test for the exis-tence of distinct submarkets and the different rent determination mechanisms in these submarkets can be performed.

In order to analyze the structure of rents in different neighbor-hoods, measures of factors affecting neighborhood quality and rents are needed. In addition, an appropriate unit of observation must be chosen and tests must be developed to determine rent mechanisms. In order to test for interdependence within neighborhoods, the ap-propriate unit of observation has to be smaller than a neighborhood. The census tract was chosen as the unit of observation. The prob-lems with small area analysis are then reviewed. The second sec-tion of this chapter discusses the development of neighborhood indi-cators adopted for this study, showing the quantitative variables that most clearly measure neighborhood quality. The method and uses of principal components factor analysis for this study are then reviewed. The third section of the chapter summarizes the factor analysis re-sults, reviewing the factors and characterizing them. This shows that there are some common qualitative dimensions to these neigh-borhoods that can be measured and compared. In the fourth section, a test for distinct submarkets is developed. Using factor scores, a test for the clustering of factor scores on every factor by submarket type was designed. In the fifth section, a test is developed for rent determination. Specifically, it is expected that slum rents are higher, the lower the neighborhood quality, and that nonslum rents are higher, the higher the neighborhood quality. A discussion of the results fol-lows and implications for further research are discussed.

THE USE OF NEIGHBORHOOD SOCIAL INDICATORS
AS A MEASURE OF NEIGHBORHOOD QUALITY

The Census Bureau has acknowledged serious shortcomings in the accuracy, if not the meaningfulness, of the data in the decennial Census of Housing. Unfortunately, the bureau, as a result, has contracted rather than deepened its fact-gathering efforts in this area. The few more attempts by Wilkinson, Sternlieb, and Kain and Quigley to construct new indicators, from segregation indexes to housing gap measurements, are too limited in their concerns to serve well as neighborhood indicators.[1]

One approach to the development of effective neighborhood indicators is suggested here, showing the necessary variables for analysis of neighborhood quality. Though the intention here is not to elaborate on the statistical problems involved in the use of neighborhood social indicators, some discussion of the broader technical issues involved—especially in the use of small area data—is relevant.

The main essentials of neighborhood indicators are that they should be applicable over the country as a whole, they should be comparable over the country as a whole (there should be no definitional problems), they should be easily and cheaply available, they should be simple, and they should be based on as small an area as possible. Neighborhood quality may be, and often is, manifested in small pockets, often only a matter of a few streets or blocks. For this reason, data based on cities or even boroughs are inadequate. Since in this study I wanted to test for interdependence among neighborhood characteristics within a neighborhood, the appropriate unit of observation had to be smaller than the neighborhood. The only data source that fulfilled these requirements was the census tract data in the decennial census. In this way, comparisons were made between and within neighborhoods. All data assembled in larger units (that is, health areas, police precincts, fire companies) were transformed to the census tract level on the basis of population.

Census tract data are not without faults. At present, decennial 100 percent census are available, but with some data analyzed on a 10 percent basis. In addition, fresh data are unavailable for the years in between census years and the situation arises where data five years old have to be used. While this is far from ideal, it is unlikely that major shifts in the relative status of neighborhoods examined in this study have occurred since the 1970 census. A third shortcoming arises with the 10 percent census tract data, which are liable to bias and sampling errors. This is a more intractable problem, but not one serious enough to destroy the validity or usefulness of the data.

At a more basic level, the choice of social indicators to identify neighborhood quality involves value judgments. By including statistics on crime, juvenile delinquency, fires, health, and so on, an assumption is made that neighborhood quality has something to do with levels of crime, juvenile delinquency, and so on.

Neighborhood indicators are operationalized concepts—the manifestation in quantifiable form of some notion that in itself may not be quantifiable. In order to derive "indicators of neighborhood quality," the first task is to clearly define the concept "neighborhood quality." Having produced a definition, the way is clear to derive suitable indicators of operationalized measures of that concept. This process of derivation is constrained by the availability of data. All assumptions regarding neighborhood quality represented neighborhood characteristics described by New York City neighborhood residents. Many of these characteristics have been documented in previous studies. One example is as follows:

> The slum is a locus of adult crime and juvenile delinquency. Substandard areas have been ascertained to contain a greater percentage of delinquents per one thousand population than true in non-slum sections. Wherever physical deterioration characterizes an area, delinquency rates are invariably high.[2]

An extensive body of literature regarding housing and health has been developed, tracing the contributions of decayed, unsanitary, overcrowded, or poorly ventilated, heated, and lighted housing to a number of illnesses, including tuberculosis, and to tensions that contribute to emotional depression and the breakdown of family life. One important health hazard of inadequate housing is the widespread menace of lead poisoning to children.

> As much a scourge of slum life as the more easily recognized peril of fire, lead poisoning, caused primarily when youngsters swallow bits of pieces of paint and plaster that drop from decayed walls and ceilings, is today a silent epidemic among the nation's poorly housed. Despite the general belief that the substitution for lead-based paint marked the end of the problem, lead poisoning has remained a widespread affliction. The scientists' committee in New York City, based on testing programs in slum neighborhoods, estimated that 18,000 small children were going around with lead poisoning in their systems.[3]

> Housing is the brick and mortar aspect of environment, and as such, is not without its effects upon the individual. Medical science has traced its connection to health. The designation of tubercular afflictions as house diseases typifies the relationship. The same is also true for the communicable diseases of childhood, syphilis, and gonorrhea.[4]

TABLE 5.1

Neighborhood Quality Variables, 1950, 1960, 1970

1950		1960		1970	
TDU	Total dwelling units	TDE	Total dwelling units	TDU	Total dwelling units
OCU	Owner-occupied units	OCU	Owner-occupied units	OCU	Owner-occupied units
LGU[1]		LGU[1]		LGU[1]	
MY	Median income	MY	Median income	MY	Median income
RMS	Median rooms	RMS	Median rooms	RMS	Median rooms
TP	Total population	TP	Total population	TP	Total population
BP	Black population	BP	Black population	BP	Black population
CRT	Contract rent	AGE[2]		AGE[2]	
PBP	Percent black population	TR	Total residents	TR	Total residents
POO	Percent owner-occupied units	LTR	Long-term residents	LTR	Long-term residents
PLU	Percent[1]	MUR	Murder	BPL	Below poverty level
		RAP	Rape	TF	Total families
		ROB	Robbery	FHF	Female-headed family
		FAS	Felonious assault	COU	City-owned units
		BUR	Burglary	NAR	Narcotics
		GL	Grand larceny	MUR	Murder
		AT	Auto theft	RAP	Rape
		TMD	Total misdemeanors	ROB	Robbery
		TCR	Total crime	FAS	Felonious assault
		STR	Structural fires	BUR	Burglary
		RES	Resident fires	GL	Grand larceny

90

VB	Vacant buildings		AT	Auto theft
OUT	Outside fires		TMD	Total misdemeanors
TB	Tuberculosis		TCR	Total crime
SYP	Syphilis		STR	Structural fires
GON	Gonorrhea		NSTR	Nonstructural fires
YVD	Youth venereal disease		TRA	Transp. fires
JDR	Juvenile delinquency		EMG	Emergencies
PBP	Percent black population		FA	False alarms
PCO	Percent owner-occupied units		TB	Tuberculosis
PLU	Percent[1]		SYP	Syphilis
PAG	Percent[2]		GON	Gonorrhea
PLT	Percent long-term residents		YVD	Youth venereal disease
CRT	Contract rent		JDR	Juvenile delinquency rate
			IH	Infectious hepatitis
			LPOL	Lead poisoning
			PBP	Percent black population
			POO	Percent owner-occupied units
			PLU	Percent[1]
			PAG	Percent[2]
			PLT	Percent long-term residents
			PFH	Percent female-headed families
			PCO	Percent city-owned units
			CRT	Contract rent

[1]Structures with five or more units.
[2]Number of units constructed before 1929.

Source: U.S. Bureau of Census, Census Tract Statistics for New York City (Washington, D.C.: U. S. Government Printing Office, 1971. Compiled by author.

> Mortality rates, particularly during infancy, child-
> hood and even adult years, appear to be higher for
> those in poverty areas than for the rest of the popu-
> lation. [5]

Neighborhood variables used in this study are derived, in part, from those mentioned above (see Table 5.1). The nature of this study has warranted the addition of some variables. Neighborhood stability is assumed to be a function of neighborhood quality. Stability can be measured in a neighborhood by rates of owner occupancy and rates of housing turnover. It is postulated that high rates of owner occupancy and low turnover rates are indicators of a desirable neighborhood. Variables on the number and types of abandoned buildings, incidence of fires and false alarms are also considered to be prime indicators of neighborhood quality. In addition, the number of buildings in REM (Real Estate Management), abandoned by private landlords, and taken over by the city was an important neighborhood indicator.

A STATEMENT ON FACTOR ANALYSIS

Factor analysis is a generic term representative of several multivariate statistical techniques designed to analyze the inter-correlations of a large variable data set. [6] Primarily developed by psychologists, most applications lie in that field with the pioneering study being initiated in the area of mental abilities. In the field of urban studies, Berry applied factor analysis toward classifying cities according to specific demographic, political, and socioeconomic characteristics;[7] in a study on neighborhood housing, Wilkinson derived an index of environmental quality using factor analysis and observed it to be significantly correlated with housing prices;[8] while Robson found factor analysis useful in reducing a large set of explanatory variables in order to study the social structure of a city. [9] These studies demonstrate that factor analysis is a useful analytical tool in a variety of situations, especially where traditional statistical techniques have failed to produce meaningful results.

In this study, the objective of factor analysis is to summarize the data on neighborhood quality parsimoniously. This is done by reducing the dimensionality of the data set by educing a smaller set of latent or unobservable variates (factors). Patterns of regularity are initially identified, analyzed to determine the variables involved, and ultimately assembled in the form of factor scores to test for distinct housing submarkets and different rent determination mechanisms.

Basic to the concept of factor analysis is the idea that if several variables exist and are intercorrelated, the relationships that accrue may be due to the presence of one or more underlying factors. Those variables that are most highly correlated with a particular underlying factor (that is, those the factor loads heavily upon) should in such case be most highly related to each other. The high correlation between a factor and its associated variables produces independent clusters (since in this study, the principal components solution is chosen)[10] of high intercorrelation. The assumption is made that the high intercorrelation within each cluster and the low relationship between clusters is due to the presence of a single factor representing the particular cluster. Factors are associated with clusters until all the clusters have been isolated. When this is complete, the variables within each cluster are examined to determine the presence of a common element. The common element among the indexes is presumed to be the factor associated with the cluster and is named accordingly.

Successive factors are extracted in order of decreasing contribution to the total variance. The first component pattern delineates the largest portion of relationships in the data (highest eigenvalue), the second delineates the next largest pattern that is uncorrelated with the first (next highest eigenvalue), the third delineates the third largest pattern that is uncorrelated with the first and second, and so on. The eigenvalue is equal to the sum of squares of loadings for each factor and the sum of eigenvalues is identical to the sum of communalities (R^2 in multiple regression analysis). Eigenvalues indicate when all significant factors have been extracted; as they decline in size, the percentage of the total variance explained by each factor declines.

A problem associated with principal components arises when the same variable loads heavily on several factors, making it difficult to identify and interpret factors. A number of analytical rotation schemes have been advanced to transform principal components in such a way as to preserve its basic feature of parsimony, while simplifying its structure, making it easier to interpret. The varimax approach, which is used here, has the desirable feature of yielding high loadings for a few variables on each factor, leaving the remaining loadings near zero. A formal varimax criterion is thus proposed, according to which the orthogonal (independent) rotation of factors is stopped when it appears that the maximum variation possible has been explained. Orthogonality is retained if any rotation schema is employed. Each factor is rotated until it defines a distinct cluster of interrelated variables.

NEIGHBORHOOD ASPECTS OF HOUSING PRICES

Neighborhood quality was measured and compared by initially grouping 34 (1960) and 44 (1970) variables, via principal components factor analysis, which were either originally tabulated on a census tract base or transformed to one. This facilitated the reduction of the overlapping patterns of variation present in many of the variables and thus makes study possible of more concise statements about the neighborhoods.

Factor scores, that is, the value of each census tract on a factor, were derived for 161 census tracts within five test areas and three control areas. Using these factor scores, a test was implemented for the existence of distinct submarkets. Furthermore, the existence of different rent determination mechanisms in different neighborhoods can be examined.

The 34 (1960) and 44 (1970) variables summarizing the dimensions contained in Tables 5.2 and 5.3 were reduced to 5 and 6 factors via the factor analysis. To provide independent dimensions to the analysis, the orthogonal (varimax) rotation scheme was chosen with factors being selected for rotation if their eigenvalue exceeded unity. The resulting factor structure explaining 85.1 (1960) and 86.6 (1970) percent of the variance is also set forth in Tables 5.2 and 5.3.

Factors Underlying New York City's
Neighborhoods, 1960 and 1970

The following summaries of the factor estimations have concentrated on summarizing the factor analysis results, reviewing the factors, and characterizing them. This shows simply that there are some common qualitative dimensions to these various neighborhoods that can be measured and compared. As a rule, variables that were most highly correlated with a particular underlying factor (that is, those the factor loads heavily upon) and had a loading of at least ± .5 were associated with that factor. The choice of ± .5 was made because of the nature of the data. This rule has been applied in other urban housing studies (for example, Sternlieb, and Kain and Quigley).[11]

TABLE 5.2

Factor Analysis, 1960
Crown Heights, Brownsville, East New York, Highland Park, South Jamaica,
St. Albans, Addesleigh Park, Queensbridge (Ravenswood), Ridgewood

	Varimax Rotation Matrix				
	Factor 1	Factor 2	Factor 3	Factor 4	Factor 5
TDU	0.33721	0.81363	0.36982	0.21004	0.07244
OOU	0.06936	-0.06015	0.11127	0.85300	-0.10063
LGU	0.33140	0.78416	0.40151	-0.05566	0.00457
MY	-0.28082	-0.20978	-0.90727	0.42165	-0.44492
RMS	-0.04927	-0.40654	-0.05053	0.28245	-0.13314
TP	0.40244	0.73564	0.44812	0.21255	0.09612
BP	0.92009	-0.10823	0.13573	0.02730	0.06598
AGE	0.35153	0.90470	0.35709	0.14223	0.23674
TR	0.38529	0.75912	0.49394	0.22123	0.09493
LTR	0.26836	0.80709	0.25262	0.39672	0.06223
MUR	0.87935	0.31189	0.14291	-0.16602	-0.09628
RAP	0.94435	0.06827	0.22388	0.03931	-0.00893
ROB	0.96963	0.43509	0.12854	-0.05854	-0.05141
FAS	0.93426	0.15898	0.16798	-0.07471	-0.05450
BUR	0.68621	0.61636	0.36109	-0.10827	-0.04369
GL	0.88781	0.34783	0.12599	0.19099	0.00887
AT	0.79791	0.33836	0.22311	0.25423	0.07607
TMD	0.92111	0.26924	0.20577	0.00606	-0.01285
TCR	0.90662	0.23188	0.20864	-0.00527	-0.02327
STR	0.23180	0.42092	0.80087	-0.03334	-0.06623
RES	0.11735	0.39853	0.81597	-0.09036	-0.02992
VB	0.36131	0.15690	0.88483	0.01375	-0.09594
OUT	0.17914	0.09185	0.78052	0.24182	0.09333
TB	0.69149	0.14662	0.54178	-0.08840	0.49533
SYP	0.69265	0.24235	0.43494	-0.11449	0.35587
GON	0.70712	-0.07362	0.14146	0.04423	0.41345
YVD	0.69117	0.07041	0.36744	-0.02825	0.47977
JDR	0.23315	0.29274	0.78549	-0.02606	0.24707
PBP	0.60159	-0.35771	0.09166	0.06481	-0.09354
POO	0.03594	-0.85114	-0.00351	0.37290	-0.27574
PLU	0.15400	0.79577	0.17221	-0.27675	0.01525
PAG	-0.17613	0.25993	-0.06842	-0.11279	0.64060
PLT	-0.35917	-0.05013	-0.40339	0.33303	-0.19103

Note:	Factor	Eigenvalue	Percent of Variation
	1	17.2726	52.3
	2	5.1246	15.5
	3	2.4862	7.5
	4	2.1156	6.4
	5	1.0962	3.3

Source: Compiled by the author.

TABLE 5.3

Factor Analysis, 1970
Crown Heights, Brownsville, East New York, Highland Park, South Jamaica,
St. Albans, Addesleigh Park, Queensbridge (Ravenswood), Ridgewood

| | Varimax Rotation Matrix | | | | | |
	Factor 1	Factor 2	Factor 3	Factor 4	Factor 5	Factor 6
TDU	0.66610	0.27918	0.08686	0.47594	-0.03929	0.45451
OOU	0.25144	-0.03585	-0.01947	-0.53091	-0.29434	0.59869
LGU	0.55676	0.29541	0.04415	0.70035	-0.01677	0.17441
MY	-0.17735	-0.09094	-0.04786	-0.36529	-0.56861	0.20160
RMS	-0.20841	-0.05981	-0.12300	-0.81683	-0.19154	-0.09809
TP	0.72581	0.32406	0.23094	0.35240	0.09417	0.39142
BP	0.78126	0.35935	0.28854	0.12310	0.32309	-0.05404
AGE	0.57716	0.24038	0.08977	0.43202	-0.01279	0.41662
TR	0.73241	0.29308	0.18178	0.35672	0.06161	0.41922
LTR	0.72334	0.19308	0.05589	0.25021	-0.33600	0.40277
BPL	0.08996	0.09164	0.62442	0.16577	0.53837	-0.18530
TF	0.67308	0.29820	0.12014	0.42208	0.00281	0.48960
FHF	0.67299	0.46361	0.35545	0.31875	0.21161	0.06444
COU	0.12517	0.28450	0.85187	0.18446	0.08002	-0.14174
NAR	0.42304	0.87623	0.03729	0.09978	0.01003	-0.06886
MUR	0.09352	0.98430	0.06196	0.08126	0.03200	0.00334
RAP	0.01276	0.99195	0.00116	0.04669	0.01985	0.02277
ROB	0.90786	0.29279	0.13695	0.12286	0.08500	-0.12680
FAS	0.14590	0.97642	0.08307	0.09889	0.01577	-0.01710
BUR	0.74942	0.55956	0.03702	0.28233	0.08360	-0.02971
GL	0.94501	0.09846	0.14179	0.01248	-0.02457	-0.17539
AT	0.80236	-0.09803	-0.12214	-0.20673	0.01754	0.15389
TMD	0.94602	-0.06937	0.13488	0.20467	0.03186	-0.00944
TCR	0.97270	-0.02666	0.09043	0.15173	0.02264	-0.04900
STR	0.25330	0.74120	0.52565	0.16844	0.04125	0.00558
NSTR	0.13561	0.94389	0.24793	0.00057	0.01144	0.04991
TRA	0.21932	0.16149	0.86129	0.03918	0.09283	0.06894
EMG	0.07656	0.87887	0.12247	0.09568	0.00579	0.03282
FA	0.07618	0.94569	0.22581	-0.03872	0.08970	0.06809
TB	0.37783	0.66665	0.34742	0.19310	0.23348	0.03828
SYP	0.58691	0.52677	0.34514	0.18055	0.30901	0.02503
GON	0.84522	0.32491	0.22631	0.14191	0.17671	-0.13359
YVD	0.55859	0.42894	0.44049	0.17848	0.21817	-0.00704
JDR	0.80962	0.50978	0.64416	0.15569	0.27514	0.19446
IHEP	0.34723	0.31382	0.66484	0.00610	0.28306	0.33645
LPOI	0.17618	0.50340	0.55631	0.04606	0.48162	0.18395
PBP	0.60949	0.10433	0.22651	-0.28826	0.39462	-0.44361
POO	-0.11784	-0.04778	-0.20069	-0.84607	-0.26980	0.03644
PLU	0.28523	0.09303	0.17585	0.86631	0.01029	0.03167
PAG	-0.06091	-0.02604	0.06238	0.12917	0.03292	0.02823
PLT	-0.05671	-0.05256	-0.24244	-0.28060	-0.80647	-0.05485
PFH	0.12285	0.04269	0.20499	-0.07019	-0.05469	-0.36339
PCO	-0.04800	0.02927	0.84162	0.16490	0.02858	-0.27967

Note:	Factor	Eigenvalue	Percent of Variation
	1	20.56565	47.8
	2	5.91777	13.8
	3	4.44780	10.3
	4	3.36628	7.8
	5	1.87160	4.4
	6	1.08457	2.5

Source: Compiled by the author.

Housing and Neighborhood Factors (1960)

Component 1: Race, Crime, Health (FSA)

The list of variables most highly correlated with component FSA clearly shows that it is closely associated with a range of crime, health, and population composition variables. It is most highly associated, positively, with various crime measures and black population. The second highest association is with the health variables: gonorrhea, syphilis, youth venereal disease, and tuberculosis. This component explains 52.3 percent of the variation in the data. All variables loaded positively on this component.

Component 2: Neighborhood Structure (FSB)

Component 2 is likewise easily identifiable. The individual associations show that it is a measure of neighborhood structure. It is most highly associated, positively, with total dwelling units, number of housing units constructed prior to 1929, number of long-term neighborhood residents, total residents, number of structures with five or more units. It loads negatively on percentage of owner-occupied units, number of rooms, and percentage black population. This component most clearly identifies high density, older housing, and a stable neighborhood. It thus emerges clearly as being positively associated with high-density housing and with the neighborhood's population structure and explains 15.5 percent of the variation in the data.

Component 3: Vandalism (FSC)

Component 3 explains only 7.5 percent of the total variation and this is reflected in the appreciably lower vectors of the variables. Nevertheless, these weightings do make a coherent pattern that can be identified. The positive associations with fires and juvenile delinquency point to a positive association with the factor of vandalism. Essentially, this third component appears to be isolating, positively, those neighborhoods that are characteristic of high fire rates and juvenile crimes (which many argue are synonymous). A New York City Fire Department official estimated that 50 percent of structural fires in the city are set by juveniles. Community leaders claim that the incidence of fires set by juveniles accounts for two out of three structural fires.

Component 4: Low Density (FSD)

The number of owner-occupied housing units and median family income both load positively on this component. This component is most closely associated with the housing density and income class of a neighborhood. To this extent, it is partly a mirror image of Component 2 but, unlike Component 2, it adds an income and density differential to its isolation of social characteristics.

Component 5: Housing Constructed Prior to 1929 (FSE)

Component 5 is the most difficult one to give a specific identity. This is not surprising in that one is dealing with a component that explains as little as 3.3 percent of the total variation so that the total proportion of the variable that is accounted for is correspondingly low. As one moves to successively lower components they become increasingly difficult to interpret. The elements appropriate to each vector show that the variable most highly related to Component 5 is the percentage of housing built before 1929 with a vector weight of .64; the second most highly related is median income, which is negatively associated with old housing and has a vector weight of .44.

Housing and Neighborhood Factors (1970)

Component 1: Race, Property Crimes and Misdemeanors, and Venereal Disease (FSA)

The first factor has high loadings on 15 variables that are descriptive of property crimes and misdemeanors (robbery, burglary, grand larceny, auto theft, total misdemeanors, and total crime), population composition, and family structure (black population and female-headed families), and nonhousing-related diseases (gonorrhea, syphilis, and youth venereal disease). This component explains 47.8 percent of the variation in the data. All variables had positive loadings on this component.

Component 2: Crime against Persons, Fires (FSB)

The second component clearly measures crime against persons and fires. Rape, murder, felonious assault, and narcotics load heavily and positively on this factor. False alarms, emergencies, structural and nonstructural fires also load heavily and positively. This component explains 13.8 percent of the variation in the data.

Component 3: Abandonment, Poverty, Poor-Quality Environment (FSC)

This component clearly measures abandonment (since it loads positively both in number and percentage of city-owned real estate, that is, buildings that have been turned over to the city because of tax default by landlords), quality of the environment (since it loads positively on transportation fires and housing-related diseases such as lead poisoning and infectious hepatitis), and low income (since it loads positively on the variable percentage below poverty level). This component explains 10.3 percent of the variation in the data.

Component 4: High-Density Old Housing (FSD)

This component has high loadings on the variables that are descriptive of the housing stock, namely, the age, size, and type of house and is a measure of dwelling characteristics. Since the variables measuring age of structure and structures with five or more units load positively on this component, and variables measuring the extent of owner-occupied housing and number of rooms per apartment load negatively, this component is indicative of high-density old housing. This component explains 7.8 percent of the variation in the data.

Component 5: Transience (FSE)

This component is clearly a measure of a low-income, transient population. The variable percentage of long-term residents is most highly related to component FSE (-.80647), the second most highly related is median income (-.56861). This component explains 4.4 percent of the variation in the data.

Component 6: Owner-Occupied Housing (FSF)

This component is a measure of the number of owner-occupied units (it loads positively on this component, .59869) and explains only 2.5 percent of the variation in the data.

FACTOR SCORE DISTRIBUTIONS: THE EXISTENCE
OF DISTINCT HOUSING SUBMARKETS

1960 and 1970

Having identified the context of each of the first five (and six) principal components, it is now possible to allot scores appropriate to each component for each of the eight study neighborhoods (161 observations). This is done by using the elements of the latent vectors of each variable, for each of the five (or six) components in turn, as weights that are applied to the original data expressed in standardized form. The five (1960) and six (1970) sets of component scores that were produced for the 161 census tracts have unit variance and zero mean.

Using factor scores, a test was implemented for the existence of distinct housing submarkets. If there was continuous variation in any or all of these factors across all submarkets, then between-neighborhood differences would be small and within-neighborhood differences would be wide. Instead, this analysis would suggest that the interdependence and interaction in slum formation would result in the distinct clustering of factor scores on every factor by submarket type.

The estimation and distribution of factor scores is straightforward. One can divide the range of possible factor scores into discrete ranges and compute the number of census tracts with factor scores in that range for any given factor. In the tables that follow, the distribution of factor scores is presented for 1960 and 1970. The factor analysis isolates important housing and neighborhood indicators. The distribution of scores on these housing and neighborhood factors strongly resembles the relative qualities of these neighborhoods (as described by residents and personal observation). For each of the factors, every census tract falls within the general range which is identified for each submarket.

The final stage for purposes of this empirical analysis proceeds quite easily from the plotted distributions. Given the distributions of the neighborhood and housing quality factors in Tables 5.4 through 5.8, it is necessary to hypothesize different rent determination mechanisms in different neighborhoods. Specifically, the hypothesis in this analysis is that rents in the test areas (slums) will be higher, the lower the quality of the neighborhood and that rents in the control areas (nonslums) will be higher, the higher the quality of the neighborhood.

1960

Component 1 (FSA), on which crime, health, and race load highly and positively, is clearly a measure of an undesirable neighborhood. Examination of the distribution of factor scores for the eight New York City neighborhoods studied reveals differences in neighborhood quality across housing submarkets. The low factor scores (ranging between -.9 and -.6) for white ethnic areas were indicators of a desirable neighborhood. The black residential areas, which consisted primarily of black middle-class homeowners, were less desirable (with factor scores ranging between .1 and .4), the inner city areas, in which residents were predominantly black and poor, were most undesirable, with factor scores ranging between 6 and 1.

TABLE 5.4

Factor Score Distribution, FSA—Race, Crime, Health, 1960
(undesirable neighborhood)

	Submarket	Factor Score Value	Number of Census Tracts
Test areas	White ethnic	(-) .9 -.8	13
		(-) .79 -.7	7
		(-) .69 -.6	5
	Black residential	.1 -.2	12
		.21 -.3	14
		.31 -.4	12
	Inner city	.6 -.7	19
		.71 -.8	17
		.81 -.9	20
		.91-1.0	8
Control areas	White ethnic	(-) .9 -.8	9
		)-) .79 -.7	21
		(-) .69 -.6	17

Source: Compiled by the author.

TABLE 5.5

Factor Score Distribution, FSB—High Density,
Neighborhood Stability, 1960

	Submarket	Factor Score Value	Number of Census Tracts
Test areas	Inner city	(-) 1.0 -.9	17
		(-) .89 -.8	16
		(-) .79 -.7	17
		(-) .69 -.6	14
	Black residential	(-) .4 -.3	13
		(-) .29 -.2	10
		(-) .19 -.1	15
	White ethnic	.5 -.6	5
		.61 -.7	4
		.71 -.8	8
		.81 -.9	8
Control areas	White ethnic	.6 -.7	10
		.71 -.8	10
		.81 -.9	17
		.91-1.0	10

Source: Compiled by the author.

TABLE 5.6

Factor Score Distribution, FSA—Race, Health, Property Crimes, 1970
(undesirable neighborhood)

	Submarket	Factor Score Value	Number of Census Tracts
Test area	Black residential	.1 -.2	9
		.21 -.3	2
	High transience	.6 -.7	23
	and	.71 -.8	13
	Inner city	.81 -.9	31
		.91-1.0	32
Control areas	White ethnic	(-) 1.0 -.9	18
		(-) .89 -.8	9
		(-) .79 -.7	9
		(-) .69 -.6	13

Source: Compiled by the author.

TABLE 5.7

Factor Score Distribution, FSB—Fires,
Crime against Persons, 1970
(undesirable neighborhood)

	Submarket	Factor Score Value	Number of Census Tracts
Test areas	Black residential	0 -.1	3
		.11 -.2	8
	High transience	.4 -.5	22
		.51 -.6	15
		.61 -.7	20
		.71 -.8	19
		.81 -.9	15
		.91-1.0	8
Control areas	White ethnic	(-) 1.0 -.9	10
		(-) .89 -.8	9
		(-) .79 -.7	9
		(-) .69 -.6	7
		(-) .59 -.5	7
		(-) .40 -.4	7

Source: Compiled by the author.

TABLE 5.8

Factor Score Distribution, FSC—Abandonment,
Poor Quality Environment, Poverty, 1970
(undesirable neighborhood)

	Submarket	Factor Score Value	Number of Census Tracts
Test areas	Black residential	0 −.1	4
		.11 −.2	7
	High transience	.6 −.7	24
	and	.71 −.8	35
	Inner city	.81 −.9	24
		.91−1.0	16
Control areas	White ethnic	1.0 −.9	7
		.89 −.8	9
		.79 −.7	11
		.69 −.6	11
		.59 −.5	11

Source: Compiled by the author.

Component 2 (FSB) measures neighborhood stability. Examination of factor score distributions reveals differences in neighborhood stability across housing submarkets. The high factor scores (ranging from .5 to 1) indicate that the white ethnic areas were stable neighborhoods. Black residential areas were somewhat less stable, having factor scores between −.1 and −.4. Inner city areas were the least stable, with factor scores between −.6 and −1.

1970

Component 1 (FSA), on which race, property crimes, and health load positively and highly, is clearly a measure of neighborhood quality. High factor scores on this component would indicate that a neighborhood is undesirable, low scores would indicate a more desirable area. The distribution of factor scores indicates that white ethnic areas were most desirable (with factor scores between −1 and −.6), black residential areas less desirable (with factor scores between .1 and .3), and high transience and inner city areas were least desirable (with factor scores between .6 and 1.).

Component 2 (FSB), having high positive loadings on fires and crime against persons, is also a measure of neighborhood desirability. Examination of the distribution of factor scores for the eight neighborhoods reveals a pattern similar with FSA. The white ethnic areas had factor scores between -1 and -.3, black residential areas had factor scores between 0 and .2, and factor scores in high transience and inner city areas ranged from .4 to 1.

Component 3 (FSC) is also a measure of neighborhood desirability since variables measuring poverty, abandonment, and a poor-quality environment loaded highly and positively. White ethnic areas had the lowest factor scores, ranging from -1 to -.5, black residential areas had factor scores between 0 and .2, high transience and inner city areas had factor scores between .5 and 1.

THE DEVELOPMENT OF A TEST FOR RENT DETERMINATION MECHANISMS

There is an overabundance of studies that have examined certain aspects of price differentials in the housing market. Authors have stressed how conflicting much of the data seem and how they require subtle analysis. There is a recognized need to distinguish among housing submarkets within a city before attempting to analyze the determinants of rents in different types of neighborhoods. In addition, it is necessary to derive a suitable measure of neighborhood quality since the quality of the neighborhood should have a strong influence on rent levels. Finally, it is advantageous to examine neighborhoods over time, comparing the changes in neighborhood quality with the changes in rent levels.

For the most part, the existing literature suffers from lack of the foregoing characteristics. Classic housing studies (for example, by Muth)[12] treat the entire metropolitan housing market as being affected by the same mechanisms of price and quantity determination, arguing that there are price intercepts as a result of racial price discrimination. These studies are formulated in relative space, in a static equilibrium framework, failing to consider the monopoly characteristics of absolute space and the mechanisms that reproduce differences between neighborhoods. While some studies by Sternlieb and Kain and Quigley have considered the influence of neighborhood quality (to a certain extent) on rent determination, they suffer from the first two limitations, impairing their usefulness.[13]

This section will explore the possibility that the relationships between rent and neighborhood quality are determined by different mechanisms in different neighborhoods. The factor score distributions that have been described and summarized indicate that neighborhood quality differs markedly across housing submarkets. In this section a comparison of rent levels in these neighborhoods with the neighborhood quality variables derived from the factor analysis is made. Given the known submarket structures of the neighborhoods, the distribution of factor scores enables one to measure rents across different submarkets and the phenomena that explain these rents in different time periods as the submarket structure of a neighborhood changes.

This study concentrates on the period 1950-70. Since the census tract was chosen as the unit of analysis, estimations were performed for the census periods of 1950, 1960, and 1970. In 1950 (used in this study as a base period) there were no available data on neighborhood quality. It was therefore necessary to measure the influence of various census variables (population and housing variables) on median rents, ignoring neighborhood quality. A multiple regression analysis (using ordinary least squares) was performed for 1950. For 1960 and 1970, the factor score distributions for the various submarkets served as measures of neighborhood quality and were compared with rent levels in these neighborhoods.

1950

Model Specification

Characteristics of the housing stock used in defining submarkets include the number and percentage of owner-occupied units, the size of the building and the apartment, and the age of units. Age serves as a proxy for a variety of characteristics of the housing stock, such as room size and layout. Size of the building serves as a proxy for housing density. In addition, the number and percentage of blacks in a census tract, total population, and median income served as population characteristics. The following variables were included in the multiple regression model for 1950:

Exogenous

TDU   Total Dwelling Units
OOU   Total Owner-Occupied Units
LGU   Total Large Units (structures with five or
        more units)
MY   Median Income
RMS   Number of Rooms
TP   Total Population
BP   Black Population
PBP   Percentage Black Population

POO Percentage Owner-Occupied Units
PLU Percentage (structures with five or more
     units) large units

Endogenous

CRT Median Contract Rent

All data were compiled from census tract statistics.

Estimation of the Model

All data were taken from the 1950 Census of Housing and the
1950 Census of Population. The model is estimated by ordinary
least squares, using a sample of 161 census tracts. For purposes
of exposition, an estimate of the equation is shown in Table 5.9.
The results of this analysis are similar to those of many conventional studies, such as Muth,[14] since neighborhood quality is not
measured. While obtaining very similar results, these authors
conclude that higher-income renters pay higher rents than do lower-
income renters. The introduction of measures of neighborhood quality would significantly alter the results, primarily by showing that
the relationships between rents and neighborhood quality are different in different types of neighborhoods:

Equation: CRT = 11.52867 + .00591TDU - .00198OOU
- .00466LGU +* .01001MY - 3.39969RMS - .00056TP
+ .00228BP + 6.35828PLU +* 8.52351PBP +* 19.37327POO

The equation exhibits a fair statistical fit, with many of the
coefficients exhibiting the expected sign and some of the ratios approaching 2 or higher. Median income and percentage black population have the highest t ratios, followed by percentage owner-
occupied units. The number of rooms variable had a t ratio of approximately -2, thereby implying that the number of rooms exerts
a negative influence on rents. The equation has an R^2 of .524. The
median income variable (R^2 contribution = .213) and black population variable (R^2 contribution = .114) account for most of the calculated R^2. The F ratio for the equation (with 10 and 150 degrees of
freedom) is significant at the 1 percent level.

The estimated coefficients reveal that median income (the
higher the income, the higher the rent) and black population (the
higher the black population, the higher the rent) have a positive influence on rents.

---

*t $\geq$ 2.

TABLE 5.9

Multiple Regression, 1950
(Crown Heights, Brownsville, East New York, Highland Park,
South Jamaica, St. Albans, Addesleigh Park,
Queensbridge (Ravenswood), Ridgewood

	Variables in the Equation			
Variable	B	Beta	Standard Error B	F
TDU	0.00591	0.48374	0.00804	0.540
OOU	−0.00198	−0.02688	0.01180	0.028
LGU	−0.00466	−0.34463	0.00629	0.550
MY	0.01001	0.68270	0.00114	76.596
RMS	−3.39969	−0.31487	1.24175	7.496
TP	−0.00056	−0.14405	0.00136	0.168
BP	0.00228	0.17107	0.00146	2.446
PLU	6.35828	0.23885	5.85441	1.180
PBP	8.52351	0.25772	3.90278	4.770
POO	19.37327	0.54159	8.02287	5.881
Constant	11.52867			

			Summary Table			
Variable	Multiple R	R Square	RSQ Change	Simple R	B	Beta
TDU	0.14359	0.02062	0.02062	−0.14359	0.00591	0.48374
OOU	0.29323	0.08598	0.06537	0.21847	−0.00198	−0.02688
LGU	0.37706	0.14217	0.05619	−0.15094	−0.00466	−0.34463
MY	0.59676	0.35612	0.21395	0.56560	0.01001	0.68270
RMS	0.59697	0.35637	0.00025	0.24184	−3.39969	−0.31487
TP	0.60284	0.36342	0.00705	−0.14784	−0.00056	−0.14405
BP	0.69098	0.47745	0.11403	0.01951	0.00228	0.17107
PLU	0.69492	0.48291	0.00546	−0.20621	6.35828	0.23885
POO	0.31762	0.56555	0.02263	0.17001	8.52351	0.25772

Note:
		Analysis of		Sum of	Mean	
Multiple R	0.72391					
R Square	0.52405	Variance	D.F.	Squares	Square	F
Adjusted		Regression	10	5225.98	522.59	16.51
R Square	0.49568	Residual	150	4743.36	31.64	
Standard						
Error	5.62516					

Source: Compiled by the author.

The Relationship between Rent and
Neighborhood Quality

As stated earlier, it is a premise of this study that rents are determined through different mechanisms in slums than outside slums. An examination of the factor score distributions revealed the existence of distinct housing submarkets. Given the distributions of the neighborhood and housing quality factors, it is necessary to test for different rent determination mechanisms in different neighborhoods. In order to measure the strength and direction of the relationship between rent and neighborhood quality, simple correlation coefficients were calculated for the test areas and control areas for 1960 and 1970, using median contract rents and factor score FSA (poor quality neighborhood).

If the premise of this study is accurate, the simple correlation coefficient will be strongly positive for the test areas (indicating that rents and a poor-quality neighborhood have a high positive association) and strongly negative for the control areas (indicating that rents and a poor-quality neighborhood have a high negative association). If the direction of association were the same for the test and control areas, any racial price differences must be attributed to different price intercepts, as opposed to different rent determination mechanisms.

The estimated coefficients for 1960 reveal that in the control areas, median contract rents and poor neighborhood quality had a high negative association (-.99) and in the test areas, median contract rents and poor neighborhood quality had a high positive association (.97). The estimated coefficients for 1970 also reveal that in the control areas, median contract rents and poor neighborhood quality had a high negative association (-.87), while the association was highly positive (.89) in the test areas.

1960

In explaining actual observed differences in rents and neighborhood quality between test (slum) and control (nonslum) neighborhoods, the quality of the neighborhood must be considered, along with housing and population characteristics. Examination of factor score distributions for factors FSA (race, crime, health—neighborhood desirability) and FSB (high density, stable neighborhood—neighborhood stability) showed that the neighborhood quality of the test areas was much lower than the neighborhood quality of the control areas. Census data indicate that median rents in the test areas averaged $75, while median rents in control areas averaged $56.

This supports the hypothesis that nonslum rents are higher, the higher the neighborhood quality, while slum rents are higher, the lower the neighborhood quality.

1970

In the 1970 factor analysis, three factors (FSA, FSB, and FSC) were examined by census tracts within neighborhoods to characterize neighborhood quality. Examination of the distribution of their factor scores showed that on factor FSA (race, health, property crime—neighborhood desirability) the test areas had very high scores, whereas the control areas had very low scores. Similarly, on factor FSB (fires, crime against persons—neighborhood desirability) the distribution of factor scores showed that the test areas had high scores where the control areas had low scores. The distribution of factor scores for factor FSC (abandonment, poor-quality environment—neighborhood desirability) followed the same pattern. Census data indicate that median rents in the control areas averaged $80, while median rents in the test areas averaged $110. This confirms the hypothesis that nonslum rents are higher, the higher the neighborhood quality and that slum rents are higher, the lower the neighborhood quality.

A BRIEF INTERPRETATION

It seems sufficient to conclude, at this stage of interpretation, that the interdependence and interaction in slum formation results in the production and reproduction of geographically distinct housing submarkets. The racial composition of a neighborhood is important in mediating the influences of financial and government institutions in local housing submarkets. The housing submarkets where the black population lives are structured (largely through financial and government institutions) so that rent determination mechanisms are different from those of other submarkets. The stratification of these New York City neighborhoods and examination of their factor scores appear to reveal differences in housing and neighborhood quality and rents that are reflective of the ways in which class-monopoly rents (racial rent differentials) are realized.

SUMMARY

In this chapter, a test for submarkets and rent determination mechanisms (class-monopoly rent realization) was designed and implemented. This test demonstrated that rents are a function of the submarket structure of a neighborhood. The black population, because of the structure of the housing submarkets in which it lives, has experienced increased housing costs, beyond the cost increment experienced by residents of so-called stable neighborhoods. In this summary section, a discussion of some of the implications the test carries for further research in housing is presented.

It has been argued in this chapter that neighborhood quality and race of neighborhood residents reflect with some accuracy the distinctions between lower and higher rental expenditures. It seems necessary to review some of the problems with the test for class-monopoly rent realization in order to judge the cogency of these claims.

One of the central problems with factor analysis is that different analysts might disagree about the interpretations of the factors estimated in the analysis. An additional warning about the results of this chapter should be raised. Although the method of variable transformation used is clear cut and neat, it is an estimate and is therefore subject to error.

One final warning about the results of this experiment is that it was, in fact, conducted solely as an experiment. Now that this experiment has been completed, it is possible to analyze data from other neighborhoods and cities and specify the procedures of the test more precisely than it seemed possible to do the first time through the process. Data sets might be more clearly defined, variables for inclusion more precisely chosen, and hypotheses about factor loadings more thoroughly identified. Given this evidence of class-monopoly rents in New York City, a wide variety of substantive questions come to mind. Do similar situations prevail in other cities, countries? What does this imply about the 1974 Housing and Community Development Act with regard to Section 8 (direct cash assistance)? Should the Department of Housing and Urban Development employ multiple standards of fair market rentals?

NOTES

1. R. Wilkinson, "Indicators of Neighborhood Quality," The Economist, August 1973; J. Kain and J. Quigley, Housing Markets and Racial Discrimination (New York: National Bureau of Economic Research, 1975); George Sternlieb, Housing, An AMS Anthology (New York: AMS Press, 1976).

2. Frederick Thrasher, The Gang (Chicago: University of Chicago Press, 1922), pp. 2-3. This is also documented in Irving Halpern, Slums and Crime (New York: New York City Housing Authority, 1934).

3. Joseph Fried, Housing Crisis U.S.A. (New York: Praeger, 1971).

4. Paul Insel and Rudolf Moos, Health and the Social Environment (Lexington, Mass.: Lexington Books, 1974), p. 12.

5. Anne Somers, Health Care in Transition (Chicago: Hospital Research and Education Trust, 1971), p. 125.

6. See Harry Harman, Modern Factor Analysis (Chicago: University of Chicago Press, 1967).

7. See Brian Berry, City Classification Handbook (New York: Wiley Interscience, 1971).

8. See Wilkinson, op. cit.

9. See B. Robson, Urban Analysis (London: Cambridge University Press, 1969).

10. Harman, op. cit.

11. See G. Sternlieb and J. B. Indik, The Ecology of Welfare and the Welfare Crisis in New York City (New Brunswick, N.J.: Transaction Books, 1973); George Sternlieb, The Tenement Landlord (New Brunswick, N.J.: Rutgers University Press, 1966); Kain and Quigley, op. cit.

12. R. Muth, Cities and Housing (Chicago: University of Chicago Press, 1969).

13. Sternlieb, The Tenement Landlord, op. cit.; Kain and Quigley, op. cit.

14. Muth, op. cit.

6
CONCLUSION

This study investigated the process of slum formation and maintenance and its effects on urban housing submarkets. Within this general objective, the following hypotheses were developed and tested:

The policies of financial and government institutions have affected urban neighborhoods through public housing and FHA home-ownership programs. Neighborhoods with predominantly black populations have been adversely affected by these policies, while neighborhoods with white populations have not.

The actions of speculator real estate interests in black neighborhoods have caused decay (and sometimes destruction) of the private housing stock. The city (primarily the Department of Social Services), by renting substandard apartments for welfare tenants in slum areas (at astronomical rents), has contributed to the success of these speculators whose aims are to withdraw essential services from their buildings while seeking maximum compensation.

The city's distribution of services has differentially affected neighborhood quality so that neighborhoods with black populations have declined at the expense of neighborhoods with white populations.

Slum rents (rents in inner city, high transience, and black residential submarkets) are higher, the lower the neighborhood quality variables, while nonslum rents (rents in white ethnic submarkets) are higher, the higher the neighborhood quality variables.

In order to test the first three hypotheses, an in-depth field survey in five New York City neighborhoods was undertaken. The field survey served the purpose of gathering descriptive historical data on changes in housing and neighborhood quality from the neighborhood.

112

The field survey materials support the first hypothesis, indicating that black neighborhoods have been adversely affected by public housing and FHA homeownership programs, while white neighborhoods have not. According to many New York City residents, project areas (which house predominantly black populations) have absorbed huge population increases. The population shift has put a strain on municipal services, which have not changed to accommodate the increased populations. Residents' complaints (in project areas) also focus on the lack of project staff and the stringent income guidelines imposed by the housing authority that guarantee a transient population. The construction of projects causes mass displacement of residents, since many large families who occupied these sites were unable to qualify for public housing. Residents have also witnessed the decay of shopping areas caused by an erosion of the community's economic base.

Many New York City housing specialists support the claim that the low FHA minimum-quality standards have allowed speculators to realize windfall gains through the sale of FHA homes in black areas. Black families, unable to obtain their own mortgage financing, have been forced to pay a "black tax" in order to purchase housing. Furthermore, housing specialists claim that these programs have resulted in destruction, high foreclosure rates, and abandonment, while a large group of debt-encumbered black homeowners has been created.

The field survey materials support the second hypothesis, indicating that the actions of speculator real estate interests in black areas have caused decay of the housing stock and that the city (in its distribution of welfare clients) has contributed to the success of speculator operations. According to many New York City residents, black neighborhoods have been ruined by hungry real estate investors, criminal speculators, and crooked bankers. In addition, residents assert that landlords receive exploitative rents while providing minimum service since they exercise a class power over tenants. Furthermore, landlords' interests in their properties are purely monetary, often resulting in large welfare population movements (they pay the highest rents), subdividing of apartments, and overcrowding, contributing to the initial decay caused by the lack of maintenance.

The field survey materials support the third hypothesis, indicating that the city's distribution of services has allowed black neighborhoods to deteriorate at the expense of nonblack neighborhoods. According to many New York City residents, municipal services have been deliberately withdrawn from neighborhoods during (and after) racial transition, regardless of residents' incomes. The withdrawal of services has been most evident in the areas of education, sanitation, health care, and police protection. Residents of black neighborhoods also complain of the lack of recreational facilities and the adverse effects of high structural fire rates on neighborhood quality.

The econometric analysis supports the fourth hypothesis, indicating that racial rent differentials exist across New York City neighborhoods. The interdependence and interaction in slum formation results in the production and reproduction of geographically distinct housing submarkets. The housing submarkets where the black population lives are structured so that rent determination mechanisms are different from those of other submarkets. The stratification of the eight New York City neighborhoods and examination of their neighborhood qualities and rents support the claim that slum rents are higher, the lower the neighborhood quality, while nonslum rents are higher, the higher the neighborhood quality.

While the New York City field survey materials lend support to the first, second, and third hypotheses, one can question their meaningfulness by arguing that situations drawn from neighborhoods within a single city do not give a fair sample of possible variation. The field survey results can also be questioned because the sample size was restricted. In addition, most of the statements made by residents and housing specialists cannot be proven beyond a doubt. They are rather suggested by the theoretical approach taken and supported by trends in New York City neighborhoods as described by residents and housing specialists.

The examination of the structure of New York City's housing market would be more complete if additional neighborhoods were examined and if data on mortgage practices, financial institutional involvement, and real estate interests were available.

Despite these qualifications, the results of this study are important for two reasons. First, current neighborhood and housing patterns have been shaped by developments that occurred during the period of this study: the sharpening of racial segregation in housing, the changing interests of financial institutions in local housing markets, and so on. Second, this study has shown how public housing has worsened the minority predicament. The fact that demolitions have forced displaced families to pay higher rents or settle for lower standards is proof of this. This study suggests that public housing has served a small number of regularly paid families and has been inconsequential in affecting the situations of those it has ostensibly aimed to serve.

Whether this tendency toward increasing discrimination and exploitation in housing will lead to the destruction of entire cities is unclear. The continuing flight of the middle class from the city will make matters worse. It appears as though the changing interests of financial and government institutions, speculator real estate interests, and the city's distribution of services will continue to aid in the destruction of neighborhoods as they have for the last 25 years.

2
THE NEIGHBORHOOD
ANALYSES

> How illuminating a [study] may become, how specific
> and how vivid are the [descriptions] and what reality
> some of the intangible and unformalized aspects of
> [community life] assume when seen through the mirror
> of an actual man's heart and brain and not through the
> interpretations of an outsider. And surely, there still
> remains the [study] for them to interpret better and
> more profoundly.[1]

Part II of this study sets out to elucidate the process of slum
formation and maintenance by means of a detailed case study of New
York City neighborhoods. I was particularly sensitive to the specific history and to the historically determined role of the community resident in describing its course. I also felt that there was no
way to keep the individual and his actions and feelings from being
the central datum of investigation. For these reasons, the neighborhood analyses were, to a large extent, derived from interviews
and conversations with long-term community residents, community
leaders, and real estate brokers.

The methodology employed in this field study was not novel.
Foundations for this approach were found within the discipline of
anthropology. As early as 1887, Franz Boas discussed this method
in his Study of Geography. Boas emphasized that the "individual
fact" is of paramount importance. He illustrated this in detail by
comparing the method of the historian with that of the physicist:

> The physicist compares a series of similar facts, from
> which he isolates the general phenomenon which is com-
> mon to all of them. Henceforth the single facts become
> less important to him, as he lays stress on the general
> law alone. The historian, on the other hand, denied that
> the deduction of laws from phenomena was the only ap-
> proach to eternal truth. There was also the method of
> understanding, and for those who chose this route, the
> attitude toward the individual fact or event was quite
> different from the physicist's. Its mere existence en-
> titles it to a full share of our attention; and the knowledge
> of its existence and evolution in space and time fully
> satisfies the student, without regard to the laws which
> it corroborates or which may be deduced from it. Inso-
> far as the historian was interested in law, it was in
> order to explain the actual history of the phenomena
> from which it had been deduced. Sociological laws of

functional interdependence have not yet been established
in social anthropology, no general theory has so far
emerged, and a succession of testable hypotheses have
led not to abstract formulae of social life but to empirical generalizations. Rather than now possessing a solid
theoretical basis . . . social anthropology is in a state
of conceptual confusion expressed in proliferating technical taxonomies and definitional exercises, each new
field study offering enough anomolous features to lead to
yet more typological and methodological pronouncements.
We have reached a point of empirical plenitude and propo-
sitional futility . . . that we must take each case as it
comes. Ethnographic facts will be much easier to understand if we approach them free of all . . . a priori assumptions. Our concern is with what social categories
are; not what they ought to be.[2]

Boas's critique of field studies (the type conducted by social anthro-
pologists) can be applied to existing field studies on slum formation
and maintenance. These studies are based largely on empirical
generalizations, at one point in history, resulting in the "conceptual
confusion" that Boas described.

In this part of the study, historical information gleaned from
books and documents was used sparingly since the object here was
to offer data from the community itself. Reports from the U.S.
Census Bureau and the Health Department, Housing Authority, Police Department, Fire Department, and Youth Services Agency of
New York City were drawn upon for background material.

In short, the method developed was based on a study of changes
in the neighborhoods that were observed by community residents.
The study refrains from the attempt to solve the fundamental problem
of slum formation until processes that are now going on are un-
raveled.

Each neighborhood has its own unique history, dependent partly
upon the peculiar inner development of the residents, and partly upon
the outside influences to which it has been subjected. Consequently,
each of the following chapters is somewhat different in emphasis.

NOTES

1. From introduction, Paul Radin, Method and Theory of
Ethnology (New York: Basic Books, 1966).

2. From introduction, George Stocking, ed., The Shaping of
American Anthropology: A Franz Boas Reader (New York: Basic
Books, 1974).

7
BROWNSVILLE

POPULATION

Brownsville takes its name from Charles Brown, who subdivided lots in 1865. By 1883 there were 250 frame buildings in
Brownsville. Two years later, an immigrant Jewish tailor named
Jacob Cohen moved from the Lower East Side because his ailing
wife needed a country environment. Many other Jewish immigrants
from the Lower East Side and Williamsburg followed, sparking the
first sizable growth of the neighborhood at the turn of the century.
Brownsville was described as follows:

> Brownsville became the Long Island, the suburb of the
> Lower East Side. Many who had their businesses in
> Manhattan moved to Brownsville where it was clean
> and healthy. Sunlight entered their rooms and tempted
> them to cleanliness, the watchword of their religion.[1]

Brownsville witnessed the development of one of the largest
communities of East European Jewish immigrants during the last
decade of the nineteenth century and the first two decades of the
twentieth. Of the nearly 2 million Jews who migrated to the United
States during that period from Russia, Poland, Austria, Hungary,
and Rumania, the overwhelming majority settled in New York City.
Most of the newcomers established themselves in the Lower East
Side, and when it became overcrowded, many took up residence in
Brownsville.

As tenements on the Lower East Side were razed for construction of the Williamsburg Bridge, many families from these blocks
moved to Brownsville. At this time Brownsville was described as

a "land of sweat shops and whirling sewing machines, of strange Russian baths, of innumerable dirty and tiny shops, of cows which are milked directly into pitchers and pails of customers at eventide, of anarchists, of Jewish dancing schools and of a peasant market.[2]

The extension of the IRT (Interborough Rapid Transit) along Livonia Avenue to Junius Street in 1920 triggered more building, some of which is still a part of the area's housing stock.

When the Jewish immigrants formed their island within the village of Brownsville, they did not displace the earlier residents from their homes. The immigrants of Brownsville moved into new houses, which were built on large stretches of land. Much of the building was done in haste and without adequate planning. Rows of frame houses, frame factories in back yards, frame privies, and small frame tenements were quickly and cheaply constructed. The result was a duplication of the experience of other congested areas— so much so that Jacob Riis in the late 1890s stigmatized Browns-ville as a

> nasty little slum. Most of the houses are without
> sewers or drains. Families are so huddled together
> in the sweat shop tenements that even the ordinary
> precautions of cleanliness are next to impossible.
> The goat, cat, or dog is as much a member of the
> family as the baby, and makes itself generally at
> home with him in the living room. The streets are
> nothing but mudholes—and where the streets are not
> miry with filth, they are deep in dust. There is only
> one bath, or common wash house, in Brownsville,
> and on Fridays, Saturdays and Sundays, it is in-
> variably crowded to the doors.[3]

The postwar decade of the 1920s saw many changes in American life. Despite a slight depression in 1920, there was an economic upsurge and the period was one of relative economic security. War prosperity reached Brownsville, and as a result, many of the older settlers and their children were able to abandon their old tenements and purchase new homes being constructed in large numbers in the Eastern Parkway (Crown Heights) and adjoining sections. Row upon row of two-family homes were constructed on Union, President, Carroll, Crown, and other streets in this section.

The period of prosperity in the late 1920s came to an abrupt and dreary end in October 1929. For more than a decade (from the Great Crash until World War II) the United States experienced one of the most devastating financial depressions in its history. With the depression, Brownville was assailed on all sides. The men

began to lose their jobs and appeared wheeling baby carriages.
They began to shop for their wives and argue with the peddlers. And
as times grew worse, the long, fascinating noses of our Jews got
closer to the ground and began to sniff through the very walls to see
what was transpiring on the other side.

Up to 1940, Brownsville was an exciting neighborhood, pre-
occupied with building institutions, and alive with the sense of aiming toward a more meaningful life and a happier society. Since the
end of World War II, the neighborhood had been on the decline. As
the second and third generations of youth grew up and graduated
from schools and colleges, they sought to establish themselves in
other environments. Many of them moved to Flatbush, Long Island,
and later to Canarsie.

The growing prosperity and the change in the ethnic composition of the area prompted a wholesale exodus, beginning about 1960,
of the remaining Jews, with the result that the white community has
virtually disappeared. Much of old Brownsville has been razed to
make room for a conglomeration of housing projects. The projects,
as well as the remaining old tenements, are now occupied by blacks
and Puerto Ricans. The proliferation of public housing in Brownsville has resulted in a wholesale influx of welfare families to the
community. While the population of the neighborhood as a whole
has not increased, there is extreme overcrowding in the public
housing area. Thousands of units were constructed to replace the
few hundred units that previously occupied the sites. Much of the
surrounding housing has been demolished. The increasing number
of large welfare families unable to qualify for public housing crowd
into tenements.

There were approximately 170,000 residents in 1940, 142,000
in 1950, 118,600 in 1960, and 100,000 in 1970. There are a disproportionate percentage of Brownsville residents in the dependent
section of the population—those under age 16 and over age 65.
Women are the principal wage earners in many families. Community leaders estimate that 85 percent of the population is receiving
welfare benefits. Unemployment is approximately 40 percent and
many of those who work do not make a living wage. The great majority of Brownsville's citizens are poor persons who eke out a sub-
sistence through a combination of welfare payments and temporary
work. Many of them who are employed are subject to frequent
layoffs.

Resident landlords, merchants, businessmen, and professionals who could help provide an economic base for the community
are almost absent from its population. There are, however, a
group of active community leaders who have a deep sense of commitment to the area and will continue to struggle to improve their
neighborhood:

> I would never like to move out of Brownsville. The
> transportation is great. We need more jobs, there's
> too much welfare, we need better educational facili-
> ties. I have lived in Brownsville for 20 years and it's
> home to me! I will continue to fight to make Browns-
> ville a better place to be.

Although some residents perceive conflicts of interest among
leaders—"Politicians in Brownsville allow their personality differences to affect the community; if leaders and residents band together like those in Bedford Stuyvesant did, the community would
be better"—they realize that some of these groups are aiming to improve conditions in Brownsville.

PUBLIC HOUSING

As early as 1940, the Brownsville community recognized
many of its slum problems. Unemployment, poor-quality housing,
lack of medical facilities, and juvenile delinquency were only some
of Brownsville's problems. At that time, it was felt that public
housing construction would improve the physical, moral, and economic health of the area.

> Brownsville abounds in shacks and hovels which are
> flimsy, ill-designed, and badly equipped to start with
> and have grown tenfold worse with age, neglect and
> poor management. These so-called homes lack ade-
> quate light, air, sunshine, space, water, heat and
> safety, in bad smelling streets, germ-ridden struc-
> tures, abutting upon crowded, ugly barren streets,
> live about 100,000 members of the community.
>   The type of construction in Brownsville—a sort
> of bastard rural in its balmiest days, fixed its status
> as a "cheap section."[4]

After the depression, Brownsville's transformation to a slum
area was completed. Most landlords of small means who owned
Brownsville properties either abandoned their buildings, were
wiped out by foreclosures, or could not afford upkeep on their buildings. As early as 1934, the Committee on Crime and Delinquency
labeled Brownsville a high crime area; in fact it ranked first among
the districts studied as to total number of crimes.
  Beginning in 1948, areas of slum housing gave way to redevelopment in the form of public housing. By 1961 the Brownsville areas

had four low-income projects. A Brownsville housing specialist
remarked:

> Since 1948, the city Housing Authority has spent more
> than 60 million dollars to build four low-income hous-
> ing projects that stretch from East New York Avenue
> to Livonia Avenue and from Rockaway Avenue to Stone
> Avenue, a 28-block area that was the rotten core of
> the Brownsville slums.
>
> Some 18,000 persons now live in 77 towering,
> graceless buildings that are divided into 4,754 plain
> but sanitary apartments. For this privilege they pay
> an average rent of $13.01 a room per month. The
> housing projects have removed a blighted area, but
> they have also swelled Brownsville's low-income
> population. They have brought together people with
> similar problems, and we don't know if the community
> is really better off.

These projects, while representing comparatively sound housing at
the time, were not properly planned or constructed. "Twenty years
ago when Howard, Van Dyke, and Brownsville Houses were constructed, I remember going up the stairs, my legs used to get
caught between the stairs. There were sewer rats then!"
Since 1961 the New York City Housing Authority has spent an
additional $10 million on public housing in Brownsville. In one
small section there are enough low-income apartments built since
1948 to house the entire populations of Bronxville and Scarsdale.
They house more than 6,500 families and represent nearly all the
"sound" apartments in the neighborhood. Once again, these projects
were not properly planned. Projects were uncoordinated with each
other, and with schools, recreation space, health facilities, and
job training.

> Brownsville is the biggest project area in the city. The
> city has been building houses, but no parks, schools,
> municipal services. Projects here are too cluttered,
> too high. Van Dyke Houses as 1,326 units—it takes up
> four blocks. The projects here are too close together.
> Criminals could get out without being seen. Planning
> for these projects takes eight to nine years; a process
> of elimination comes into being when it comes to quality.

The buildings replaced slums and displaced many families; they also
helped institutionalize poverty and the slum.

The largest part of the neighborhood is Public Housing. Most projects here are so-called low-income projects; low cost, I mean! They have attracted lower-income people, among these are some with problems. Forest Hills, an area with a small project population, has some problem families, but the community is a self-sufficient community—able to absorb problems and make sure that they don't affect the community. Instead of having the dog wagging the tail, in Brownsville we have the tail wagging the dog. If we had a stable resource population, with 20 percent problem families, it wouldn't be so bad. But, thanks to the city, we have the reverse—with maybe 10 to 15 percent of the population trying to deal with 85 percent of the population's problems, one can easily assume that Public Housing has affected the quality of life in Brownsville.

In addition, the Housing Authority seems to send all welfare families and problem families to Brownsville. People, seen as undesirable, who apply to Pink Houses are sent to Brownsville. We have more welfare people than anywhere else in the city. Residents are simply not screened.

Project residents have paid especially dear for the breakdown in community organization. Having no organized voice, they suffered for years with unsanitary conditions in the halls and in the surrounding outside areas; with broken window panes, poorly functioning toilets, vandalism, and general deterioration of the projects.[5]

In the 1960s, as economic times were good, thousands of long-term residents moved to Long Island, to the west. "I was born here—a lot of my so-called friends moved out. All my relatives lived here once and moved. They climbed the economic ladder of success and moved out—to Maryland, Long Island, New Jersey." Into Brownsville came new people; into its organizations some new people, but without voice. New people did not staff committees.

Poorly planned public housing was not the only destructive force at work. Brownsville's vacant apartments became a dumping ground for many of the city's poor, including welfare clients, dislocated by urban renewal in other areas. The process fed on itself. As panic spread, tenements emptied out as though hit with plague.[6] Many landlords walked away, abandoning their buildings. Other landlords welcomed welfare tenants, milked their buildings for all their worth, and had their buildings burned to the ground—many recovered substantial sums of money from insurance companies.

Brownsville today testifies that slum clearance and massive building of low-income projects alone are certainly no solution to problems of the slums. While projects for the most part represent structurally sound housing, they can be a detriment to the community, especially if they predominate the area and house the bulk of its population.

PRIVATE HOUSING

Amboy Street, Brownsville 30 years ago: there it was. That dirty stinking block. The ugly gray and red tenements, tombstones of disease, unrest and the smoldering violence which has its girth in misery, were crowded close together and rose straight up on both sides of the street to shut off all but a narrow expanse of sky. It was as if nothing bright would ever shine on Amboy Street. [7]

If one turns the corner of Pitkin Avenue and Amboy Street today, there are vacant, littered lots looking like ground zero in a bombing run. Halfway down the block, the last tenement remains, with its glassless windows, awaiting the wreckers. There are no cars parked here, no overflowing garbage cans, no people lounging on the stoops. [8]

Brownsville's private housing is, at present, composed primarily of decayed and crumbling three-story frame dwellings and four-story tenements. Multifamily dwellings occupy two-thirds of the residential acreage; two-family houses cover about 26 percent and one-family homes about 7 percent.

Plaster crumbles at the touch and the stairs groan onerously. Until about 1958, a largely Jewish working class community, today it is largely black and Puerto Rican and largely forgotten. Row after row of apartment houses—brick and masonry structures, as well as older tenements—have sunk into decay. More than 500 buildings have been completely deserted. Whole blocks are silent; only the sounds of glass crunching underfoot and the gurgle of water from vandalized pipes echo through the burned out hulks. The decline in Brownsville started after World War II. When whites moved out, landlords just cut off services. [9]

Much of the construction of private housing in Brownsville was done in haste and without planning. Rows of houses were quickly and cheaply slapped together. While the most noticeable decline occurred after World War II, housing conditions were deplorable 50 years ago.

There was worse housing here 50 years ago, when I moved here. Housing was on the way out years ago and this recent transient population has made it crumble faster. Where I used to live in a cold water flat, we had no heat or hot water either. We used to get water from the hydrants. Another reason for bad housing is the extent of overcrowding. Because of the tremendous number of fires, people are forced to relocate. The construction of public housing also worsens this process. The supply of housing is low and rents are high and so, people are forced to crowd together and live in old, deteriorating buildings until they are burned to the ground. Then, if they're lucky, they'll get into public housing.

Brownsville's private housing has served a highly transient population, especially since the 1960s. Many large welfare families, displaced from urban renewal and public housing sites, have had no alternative but to rent these decrepit apartments. Landlords, aware of the situation, seek maximum compensation and provide minimum services.

Landlords take advantage of welfare clients. They charge the maximum. The landlords have many sets of prices. Welfare clients are exploited and discriminated against. Public housing tries to screen out the large welfare families and these people are the ones who should live in public housing.

Tenants in private housing live from month to month, leases are almost nonexistent. "Lease agreements, when they exist, do not mean a hill of beans—a lease in Brownsville is just a piece of paper so that the landlord can get his money. The landlord doesn't make repairs—try and take him to court—his brother is the judge."

As noted here earlier, instability of residence is extraordinary. One survey of a section of Brownsville indicates that 56 percent of the population has lived there fewer than ten years.[10] With a high rate of tenant turnover, landlords have been able to increase rents, irrespective of any possible rent controls. Housing specialists indicate that there is "no rent control" to speak of in Brownsville. "Rent control in Brownsville is nil. Landlords charge as much as $275 for a decrepit apartment." Rents are set in month-to-month struggles between landlords and tenants and are not a function of the quality of housing or the neighborhood.

> Rents, I don't understand this! I would think that there are two basic things that should influence rents. What makes a piece of property valuable? The property itself and the street on which it stands . . . the workmanship of the house, facilities, etc. Some houses are sound as far as workmanship is concerned, but they haven't been kept up. When city services decrease, property values decline. Conditions of the population also cause property to decline. People here have problems, from the moment they get up until they go to sleep.
>   Anyway, near the railroad tracks, there was an old, decayed house. We had to put people in this house. Rents were $280 a month—when I touched the walls, they caved in. Rents should have some relationship to service. We understand why they charge high rents on Park Avenue. Here, Riverdale Houses, near the train that passes every ten minutes, streets are filthy, police are inadequate, public services are at a minimum, rooms are very small—but rents are exorbitant.

Community leaders feel that this structure of rents in Brownsville secures the transience of its population.

> Marcus Garvey Houses—they'll never rent it—raise the rents for existing tenants and force them to leave the area.

> It's absurd—Marcus Garvey Housing rents for $300 to $350 for four rooms. Anybody who can afford such a rent will certainly move elsewhere.

> The Welfare Department is the only one who will pay those rents. They send all the large families to Brownsville. The private housing market has become a transient market—a temporary residence until you get an apartment in public housing or until you move elsewhere.

Less than 10 percent of families in the community owned their homes in 1963 and this number has obviously dwindled further in recent years.[11] Nearly 25 percent of the 1,300 structures demolished in 1968 in the city were in this neighborhood.

> When they had demolition money, they went through this place. They didn't examine the structures at all. Across from my house, the whole street was demolished. They did the whole block. I didn't understand this so I called HDA [Housing and Development Administration]—they told me that this was the wrong block.

An additional 650 structures have been abandoned and are now vacant. There remains a small group of resident homeowners who are trying desperately to maintain their properties. Many have been forced to abandon their property as banks have foreclosed on their mortgages.

> Let me tell you something about the homeowners in this neighborhood. We have had a tremendous turnover in homeownership over the past few years. These homeowners put in their last dollar and they want to stay here. They paid ridiculous prices for their houses and had difficulty in obtaining mortgages. These facts, coupled with bad advice, have resulted in an enormous number of foreclosures. My advice to most people is don't buy a house unless you know something about it. So many people have been misled by hungry realtors who gave bad advice.

As a result, the bulk of the private housing stock in Brownsville is either in real estate management (operated by the city) or owned by absentee slumlords. Data from the Real Estate Department indicate that as many as 5,800 units in Brownsville are in "real estate management," taken over by the city because of tax default. Housing specialists in the neighborhood indicate that many of the remaining units are owned by a few absentee slumlords.

> We had one of the biggest slumlords in New York City here. He wanted tenants to take over Powell Street after he milked the property and let it fall to the ground. These landlords live well outside the community—they come in to collect rents. They provide minimum service and extract maximum compensation.

> About three landlords own all the private rental housing in Brownsville. One real estate agent, whom I suspect

is the biggest slumlord in the neighborhood, sells fire
insurance and, at the same time, owns many houses.

They feel that the landlord-tenant relationship partially explains
the high rates of structural fires in the neighborhood:

> Yes, there are many fires here. There are many fires
> here because, if you live in deplorable conditions and
> you have no way of escaping and you have five or six
> kids and the only way you are going to get housing is if
> there is a fire, you'll make sure one exists. I've
> talked to people and, while they never admit to setting
> the fires, I know they set some of them. They come
> in here and complain about lack of heat and hot water—
> a cycle of endless complaints. Some money-hungry
> landlords also burn buildings, but many landlords turn
> their buildings over to the city, especially if they owe
> back real estate taxes.

With virtually no homeownership, a disproportionate number
of problem families, and very few commercial sources to support,
Brownsville's population is at a serious disadvantage. Aside from
resources that are necessary for organizational effectiveness
(money, communications, and legal assistance), Brownsville lacks
a stable social base, and it is difficult to sustain community action.
To a large extent, what is available tends to be impermanent, in
many cases after showing signs of success (Vista, student help,
local antipoverty programs) and high turnover in personnel is
commonplace.

Housing conditions in Brownsville and the demolition of old
buildings are partly to blame for its high transience, but the city
has done nothing to encourage population stability. For example,
the New York City Housing Authority requires that any family earn-
ing above a stipulated income must vacate a public housing apartment. In effect, this prevents upwardly mobile tenants and those
most likely to provide leadership from permanently settling in
their community, since the limited supply of private housing in
Brownsville is grossly substandard.

NEIGHBORHOOD

> Brownsville would be a good place to live in if people
> could be left alone to decide their own fortunes. This
> neighborhood was a well-run and well-organized small

> Jewish community—facilities that were needed existed.
> The old Hebrew Education Society, Day Care Centers,
> shopping facilities were adequate. We had small pri-
> vate homes and small apartment houses and the city
> services were there! When you start with high rises,
> facilities must be increased—but in Brownsville, they
> weren't. How has this neighborhood changed? How
> did Europe change after the war? Brownsville has
> subsequently become a disaster area. All the small
> private homes are gone, all the sound apartment
> houses are gone, marketplaces have left. Once upon
> a time, children went to school and faced people that
> expected them to learn—now, they go to school and
> face everything but that!

Community leaders remember Brownsville when it was a self-
contained community, with teachers, storekeepers, landlords, and
politicians living together and working toward building a community.
Community leaders and residents feel that the separation of residence from ownership and control has been one of the major reasons
for the deterioration of the area. This separation has been enforced by the political and institutional structure of the city.

> Twenty to twenty-five years ago, people who migrated
> to Brownsville had hope. They were young and strong
> and they started working to build a community. Many
> tried to work within existing organizational structures.
> Those structures started to change, people moved out
> and on. The new residents attempted to take over but
> this was not allowed to be. Schools, stores, every-
> thing is just hooked up with politics. Abe Stark and
> his development came out of this area—it was Demo-
> cratic, a Democratic base in Brooklyn in the 1940s.
> In the past, Brownsville had resident homeowners—when
> they moved, they rented their houses and allowed them
> to be abandoned. This caused others to move. The
> landlords rented to Puerto Ricans where blacks were
> not accepted. That was a piece of the evil. This
> created a division instead of unification of a black and
> Puerto Rican community. Even though the old-timers
> had moved, they still exercised control over the neigh-
> borhood. They couldn't control the services so they
> took them along when they left. There has been an
> increasing need for these services and as the need
> becomes more evident, the services disappear.

Twenty-five years ago, pushcarts lined Brownsville's congested streets. Pitkin Avenue and Belmont Avenue were active shopping streets. An open drug store, a well-stocked market, and quality merchandise are memories.

> There used to be drug stores, delicatessens, sporting goods stores, good shopping facilities. We had good bakeries, linoleum stores, and furniture stores on Rockaway Avenue and Pitkin Avenue. I remember the good-quality fish that I used to buy on Belmont Avenue. The merchants used to sell all the fish they had left from the week on Friday evening because they didn't want it to spoil. Now, they freeze this fish and sell it at exorbitant prices to residents of Brownsville. These storekeepers know they will have customers; people are too poor and too tired to shop elsewhere.

Residents view the causes of exploitative practices by neighborhood merchants as being representative of a certain mentality.

> Storekeepers do overcharge. They do not treat customers as they should. This comes, in part, from customers not demanding that quality service. Storekeepers are from other areas of the city and suburbs. When you have a suburb mentality and you come into areas like Brownsville with this mentality, you are going to have a derogatory attitude toward the people. I stopped shopping on Pitkin Avenue a few years ago. I did this because I used to walk in—when the storekeepers saw my face, they would say, "we'll take care of you. There are some black and Puerto Rican people here too. We'll take care of them first and give them some merchandise. We want to give you something special, something you'd like. So, we'll just give them the other stuff and give you something nice.

When merchants were residents of the area, their attitudes toward customers and the area were different.

> The storekeepers here live far outside the community. They come here, exploit the people, dump the garbage in the streets, take the money and run outside the community. Come through Brownsville on Jewish holidays— all the stores are closed. Most of the stores here are owned by Jewish people who have moved out of the area. Sometimes they have Puerto Ricans fronting as owners.

The colorful crowd of pushcarts and open stands along Belmont
Avenue is a problem to the community because of foul odors from
garbage and rats. "The Sanitation Department does a very bad job,
especially near the market. Fish markets and fruit stores leave a
lot of garbage and since it is not picked up, the streets stink. I
passed by once and I thought someone was dead: the stink was that
bad!" The trash problem is also particularly severe in Brownsville. Windblown refuse accumulates and scatters throughout the
area. Garbage pick-ups are infrequent and highly inadequate.

> Garbage pick-up is a joke. I remember how different
> the situation was years back. . . . The newest gim-
> mick is the garbage compressors and compactors, the
> most unsanitary, health hazardous thing that housing has
> forced on its tenants. There are worse problems with
> rats and roaches due to these compressors and com-
> pactors. The Sanitation Department has demanded
> that all garbage be placed near the curb in plastic bags.
> But when it takes five days for them to pick it up, most
> of the garbage ends up on the streets.

As one travels north of Brownsville, the conditions of the streets
begin to change. Less trash is seen on the sidewalks, potholes do
not seem to be so prevalent.

> There are many potholes in the streets of Brownsville,
> streets aren't paved. Services aren't what they should
> be. Coming off Rockaway Avenue, down from Fulton
> Street, the streets are paved pretty well up until about
> East New York Avenue. Then everything stops—you
> know you have reached Brownsville.

The situation is identical when traveling south of Brownsville.
Abruptly one comes to a wide boulevard that is Brownsville's south-
ernmost boundary. Past this thoroughfare, all avenues are blocked
off by a railroad siding and large vacant lots interspersed with industrial buildings. This sight stretches for several miles along
the width of Brooklyn and acts as a border for Brownsville and
Canarsie.

One of Brownsville's most pressing needs is good medical
care. Unsanitary living conditions coupled with inadequate health
facilities cause poor health. Venereal disease, infections, hepatitis,
tuberculosis, and lead poisoning are two to four times the city's
norm. "Good medical care is a problem. Brownsville throughout
has Medicaid mills. We had private doctors here in the past, now

the hospital emergency room has become our private doctor. Even
the Medicaid mills close at 2:30 P.M.!" The 344-bed Brookdale
Hospital, a voluntary institution with a community mental health
center, simply cannot properly service the entire Brownsville population. Most residents are forced to leave the community (many go
to Kings County Hospital) and since many cannot afford the $.50
carfare, they attend the exploitative Medicaid mills within the
neighborhood.

The quality of schooling available in Brownsville has gotten
appreciably worse over the last 50 years. If pupils copy homework,
they often cannot read the pages assigned from the textbook, because the teachers often do not allow the books to be taken home.

> Stop a friend in Brownsville and ask him "How would
> you feel if your child were to lose half a year of
> schooling?" The answer could be "It would make no
> difference. The kind of education that my child gets—
> with no books allowed home, with substitute teachers,
> with no remedial help in a building 100 years old, with
> 60 children in a class." Another might say, "Margaret
> graduated. She got a diploma. She entered Junior High
> School but she cannot read a fifth grade reader. Be-
> yond a fourth grade book she cannot go."[12]

Brownsville students are the victims of a racist educational structure. Facilities in the Brownsville public school systems are almost nonexistent, teachers are basically "securing some experience
so that they can move elsewhere." Students, aware of the limited
expectations of their teachers, perform accordingly.

> Many parents are sending their children to Catholic
> schools, out of the area, because the educational
> facilities here are horrendous. Parents try to see
> that children get adequate education. There's no
> chance of this in the Brownsville public school sys-
> tem. Educational facilities are poor. Buildings are
> old and not well-maintained. Teachers are baby
> sitting and our children are not learning. One man
> I know has a child in the Brownsville public school
> system. This child comes home with all As. His
> father asked him to read a book and he didn't know
> how! His father went up to the school and inquired
> about this. The teacher told him, "Your son is well
> disciplined."

Schools are quite inadequate. I am waiting for the day
to come when parents take a class action suit against
the Board of Education for miseducating their children.
Teachers don't expect anything of children. When teachers physically abuse children they are not brought up on
charges. They are merely transferred to other school
districts. Children are more or less left to use their own
judgment; it seems as though many are there to do custodial services in the schools. Administration of the
schools is corrupt and so are the policy makers who are
paying members or friends in political clubs. Recently,
a school principal was replaced with a man who should be
put to pasture. Teachers are not accountable for any production because the UFT [United Federation of Teachers]
will protect them. This explains why 50 percent of the
school-age children are on the outside.

There were two public libraries in Brownsville; one of these
recently closed. Facilities in these libraries have never been adequate. The only alternative is a long bus ride to Grand Army Plaza
Library. Until recently, this bus ride required a double fare. As
a result, Brownsville children do not use the library.

There is virtually no recreation, public or private, in
Brownsville. The few parks and playgrounds in the area are not
supervised or maintained; school gyms are not opened in the evenings.
"Parks are not maintained and have become a hangout for winos and
drug addicts. Existing facilities here are being underutilized.
Facilities are outdated. The time involved from planning stage to
construction is so long that facilities become obsolete by the time
they are finished." Social clubs, movie theaters, and skating rinks
are memories to Brownsville residents. They must travel to
Flatbush to see a movie or to Crown Heights for skating or bowling.

While there are some day care and preschool facilities in
Brownsville, they can serve only a small segment of the population.
A large percent of Brownsville families are female headed, and
these constitute the bulk of welfare recipients. Many women with
children are forced to stay home and collect welfare because there
is no day-care facility for their children.

Children resort to the streets for recreation: "Many of our
children have excess energy. They have nothing to do with their
energy, so they get into mischief. This is definitely a cause of the
vandalism problems and the high rate of juvenile delinquency here.
The parks are so filthy and full of glass." Juvenile delinquency
rates and excessive vandalism substantiate this.

As for crime, Brownsville has always been famous, from the
days of Murder Incorporated to the present: "35 years ago, Brownsville had a high crime rate. But in those days you paid your dues
and you were protected. These days, you have no choice but to
live in fear of your life." "I was robbed and raped in a store on
Belmont Avenue. The only reason the man was caught was because
he threw the storeowner through the glass window." Residents
feel that part of the explanation for this high crime rate lies in
the inadequacy of the Police Department and deep distrust between
police and the community.

> It's unsafe to walk. There is no cooperation from police
> to keep this community safe and clean. In Brownsville,
> when people see a crime, they don't call the police, if
> anything, they try and see that no one gets hurt. Mean-
> time, we have more crime than we should have to put up
> with. The police don't cooperate—they want you to iden-
> tify. They make you feel like a criminal. Police simply
> don't feel pressured here. They seem to think they are
> running a camp here. Besides, how can we trust the
> police when we see them at night—going into trucks. We
> see what they are putting in there. They would arrest a
> citizen who goes in there and beat the hell out of him and
> then take what they want. Police know about drug drops,
> but do nothing about it.

> Crime—a move away from Murder Incorporated— is of
> serious concern. Crime has changed from organized
> crime to that which is one on one and is generated by the
> conditions. Much of the crime is done by outsiders who
> are under the impression that this is tolerated in Browns-
> ville. Police are not here to protect residents; they don't
> see themselves as a community service. They protect
> the Pitkin Avenue and Belmont Avenue Merchants Asso-
> ciations. Police do issue parking tickets, but they are
> selective in terms of this. They are especially active
> during community activities, according to race and
> political affiliation.

> Police harass residents and take part in things that are
> personal. Kids get harassed in the streets. There also
> was an employer/employee dispute over the employee's
> pay. These two guys would get out and fight every
> Friday. The employer was white, the employee was

black. The police busted in and termed this a racial
issue. He then roughed up the employee and locked
him up. Police chase children from corners and
shove guns in their faces. The mentality of the police
is as bad as that of the storekeepers. These people
don't understand the life style of the people. While
there are training programs, the attitude is still
present. This is the case, even with black policemen. Once they get that job and move to the suburbs,
they develop the mentality, just as those whites from
the suburbs.

The question of racial tension in Brownsville has been extremely overplayed. It seems as though any incident between two
racial groups is perceived by the press as a racial issue. Community leaders are irate over this; they feel that this "mass media
overplay" provokes anger and thus prevents the community from
organizing and improving conditions.

This is a calm area as far as racial problems. Every
so often you see a bit of tension between blacks and
Puerto Ricans. There was a problem during the riots
with whites coming into the community—especially
after Claude Reese [a young black boy] was shot and
killed. That issue became a black/white issue because
of a black community and a white police force. The
press exaggerates the racial tension. If the police
force was black, people would take to the streets the
same way. People say black/white, I don't pay it no
mind.

The tensions in Brownsville are economic tensions. With a 40 percent unemployment rate and total dependence on absentee decision
makers, the community is up in arms. "Tensions are caused by
decision makers who no longer live here. Tensions are caused by
inadequate services, houses, schools. Economic tensions—everybody is fighting over the same small piece of pie."

Tensions here are economic not only in relation to
jobs, but also because of the structure of the city.
We have 10 or 12 housing projects, they employ a
few hundred people. There are almost no resident
managers and staff is also from outside the community. The same is true for police, firemen, businessmen, and so on. None of the money used for the

community's needs is kept in the community in the
form of jobs.

The crime problem has become particularly severe on the
subways:

> Train stations are not safe nor are they clean. Miss
> Tucker was attacked and killed near a train station.
> One eight-year-old child witnessed the murder of his
> mother on a train station. We have decent transporta-
> tion facilities, some of the better facilities. Bus trans-
> portation has been improved after 30 years. We finally
> had the Pitkin Avenue bus rerouted. It used to cost
> Brownsville residents a double fare to get to Prospect
> Park because of inadequate bus connections. But the
> services that go with it—security, cleanliness—there's
> a lot of room for improvement. Streets and stations
> are not clean but they're cleaner than they used to be.
> There's sometimes a 20-minute wait for a bus on
> Pitkin Avenue.

> Train stations are not that safe, one woman was killed
> recently on Belmont Avenue near Junius Street. The
> train station steps are very hazardous. Brownsville
> has good access to transportation—buses, trains.
> Conditions of the facilities are not maintained properly,
> especially bus services. There are no police on the
> train stations. It's very lonely on the subway at night.

A revolving door prevails in the social structure of the black
slum in which those persons able (financially) to work for the community are soon shuttled into a middle-class world, leaving their
compatriots to fend for themselves. While there is evidence of
this transience in Brownsville, many resident leaders have a strong
sense of commitment to the neighborhood.

> I can move anytime. I want to stay! I'm here because
> I want to work and try to see change. I'm working
> toward that change. Brownsville is a part of my life.
> It's not everything I want it to be—I want to stay and
> work toward that goal. I identify with the neighborhood.
> I choose to be in the struggle to improve Brownsville.
> After all, I love Brownsville and when you love some-
> thing you say for better or for worse.

SAMPLE INTERVIEW NO. 1

1. To go back 20 years ago, it was more desirable in Brownsville. I still think, to an extent, it is still desirable. Landlords let their buildings deteriorate. Banks have moved out of the area. Businesses have closed down. The businesses that we have here close up at 6:00—we call it "Tin City"—all the gates come down. There's a lot to be desired.

The Community Action Program is one of the main forces working toward that. This neighborhood has changed a whole lot—in population, composition, and political and social climate. Twenty years ago you could walk down Pitkin Avenue and not be afraid of everything. The whole scenery changed. Famous politicians Stanley Steingut, Arthur Leavit, Benjamin Rosenthal, and Emmanuel Celler were all from Brownsville. The community has changed as we witnessed a turnover period. Today there is a struggle. Bedford Stuyvesant had its political base, it's different. We first have to establish ours. We had Pitkin, Loews, Jewish theaters—now they are all closed down. We have to struggle for cultural facilities.

No, this neighborhood is not a good place to live in. I would just say a flat NO. I am thinking of the factors—once they are determined, this neighborhood rates very poor. Some of those factors are good, safe, sound housing, good schools with education comparable to other areas. Good sanitation, police services, enough businesses so that people are not haggling across the city to get things they want. We have none of these things at a reasonable standard and so I will say that this neighborhood is undesirable. Prior to 1950-55, there was a different political, economic, and social climate in the community. It was Jewish, professionals and political people among them, with city, state, and national influence. The school structure was well organized. The community was well-organized. Demands for services were met.

2. No, but I see a lot of good points. I see a number of people going to college. This shows self-respect. In their anger, they still try to get ahead in life. The mayor is cutting services.

———————————

All of the Sample Interviews are based on answers to the Questionnaire at the end of Chapter 4. The interviewees for this interview were Ida Posner, housing specialist; Ronald Ward, housing specialist, Neighborhood Action Center No. 3; Bill Marley, public relations, Neighborhood Action Center, Brownsville Community Council.

They are supposed to be cut equally. We will be cut from two- to one-day garbage pick-up. Some areas now have four days. This is ridiculous!

3. I was born here. I moved out and moved right back. My roots are here in Brownsville. I can move anytime; I want to stay! I'm here because I want to work and try to see the change I am working toward. Brownsville is a part of my life. It's not everything I want it to be—I want to stay and work toward that goal. I identify with the neighborhood. I choose to be in the struggle to improve Brownsville and the nation. I choose to make Brownsville my front. I am here since 1960 and have seen certain programs start. I would like to see them completed. By 1955-60, the exodus was complete. There has been a 95 percent population turnover within the last 20 years. Many buildings here had to be torn down. Seven or eight projects have been built in the last ten years. I consider Brownsville my home. This is where I was born and this is where I plan to stay. This is where I choose to live and see it develop. When you love something, you say for better or for worse.

Twenty years ago when Howard, Van Dyke, and Brownsville Houses were constructed, I remember going up the stairs, my legs used to get caught between the stairs. There were sewer rats then! The biggest project area in the city is here. There are no services—they're building houses, but no parks, schools, municipal facilities. The projects are too high-rise, too cluttered. They claim that in New York it is space and construction costs, that's why projects are so tall. Van Dyke is 1,603 units, high-rise—the higher it is, the more crime we have. The smallest project has 1,326 units, and it takes up four blocks. The largest project here is Van Dyke. They're too close together. Criminals could get out without been seen. Planning for projects takes eight or nine years—a process of elimination when it comes to cost.

5. I have many close friends in this area but no relatives. I moved out of Brownsville for a short period of time (to Bedford Stuyvesant) and I moved back. My roots are here. I wanted to be here. Through my job as a housing specialist I have seen people move here from other areas. I try to face families in the Brownsville area. I came from Bedford Stuyvesant, where I lived in a run-down tenement. In 1960 I was offered an apartment in Tilden Houses. I did not know anyone from Brownsville at that time. I haven't consciously made an attempt to bring friends and relatives here. I was born here—a lot of my so-called friends moved out. All my relatives lived here once and have moved. They went up the ladder and moved out to Maryland, Long Island, New Jersey. My sisters moved to Long Island, my brother moved to Maryland, my cousins live in California and Florida, all over the country. My place is

here! I live in a development cooperative; at one time it was all
white, now it's 50 percent black. It is a nice place in which to live.
Many people moved out of Brownsville and cannot afford to keep up
their suburban houses.

Twenty years ago it was safe to walk the streets, now it is
unsafe. A lot of this is due to insecurity. There is a breakdown
in relations between the community and the police. There is deep
distrust between this community and police. There is no cooperation to keep the community safe and clean. Here, if people see a
crime, they don't call police; if anything, they try and see that no
one gets hurt. At the same time, police and community breakdown
is a major reason for the high crime rates that are higher than we
should have to put up with.

Police do not cooperate. They want you to identify the criminal. The police make all Brownsville residents feel like criminals.
The police do not feel pressured here. They are taught in school to
go to a ghetto area to discipline children, just to use the ghetto as a
training ground for a higher position. We cannot have confidence in
a structure that doesn't provide service that we need. Police officers come here from other areas. They seem to think they're running a camp here. Residents call for police protection only if they
have to. We don't need the police. We see the police at night,
going into trucks. We see what they are putting in there. They
would arrest a citizen who goes in there and beat the hell out of
them, then take what they want. Police know about drug drops, but
do nothing about it. The average income in Brownsville is about
$6,000, given the inflated dollar. People have to deal with problems
and organize around their incomes.

8. Public housing houses the majority of the population.
The private market is a transient area, temporary until you get an
apartment in public housing. There are a few homeowners here,
and they paid a lot of money.

What makes a piece of property valuable?—the property itself and the street on which it stands. Workmanship of the house
and facilities are also considered. Some houses in Brownsville
are sound as far as workmanship is concerned. They haven't been
kept up, services decrease, this is not a reflection on homeowners.
Conditions around the house cause the property to decline. People
here have problems from the moment they get up until they go to
sleep. They're wondering if their children will make it, and if they
do, parents are surprised.

Near the railroad tracks, there was an old decayed house.
We, as housing specialists, had to put people into this house at a
rental of $280 per month. When I touched the walls, they caved in.
People come here and wait to buy a co-op, go down South, buy a

home or get into public housing. Rents should have some relation
ship to service. We understand why they charge high rents on Park
Avenue. Here, Riverdale Houses, near the train that passes by
every ten minutes, police are inadequate, streets are filthy. Public services are at a minimum, rooms are very small, rents are
$236 per month for a one-bedroom apartment.

I don't understand rents, either. I live in Mitchell-Lama
and pay $150 for a one-bedroom apartment. Brownsville Houses,
a so-called low-income (low-cost) housing project, has higher
rents. The difference is in the method of planning.

The Marcus Garvey Building, they'll never rent it. They
raise the rents for existing tenants and force them to leave the area.
When they had demolition money, they went through this place.
They didn't examine structures, they just tore down entire blocks.
Sometimes they did the wrong blocks.

They are selling a few buildings these days, for $1.00—
another joke! But there is no money available to prospective homeowners to improve these buildings. Who has money to rehabilitate
these buildings? If anything, there is money for a cosmetic rehabilitation, never a gut rehabilitation.

Take a doctor who has certain responsibilities—he may earn
$40,000 to $50,000 a year. The income a person earns is not
based upon contribution, it is based upon privilege and power and
control. There's going to have to be another Civil War struggle.
As time goes by, banks are refusing to lend money to Brownsville
residents. Private housing is simply stepping out of Brownsville.
We had one of the biggest slumlords in New York City owning land
in Brownsville. He wanted tenants to take over Powell Street after
he milked the property and let it fall to the ground.

9. This is a calm area as far as racial problems go. Every
so often, you see a bit of tension between blacks and Puerto Ricans.
This problem was more severe during the late 1960s because of the
housing patterns in the community. There were also problems
here during the riots in the 1960s because of the whites coming into
the area. There was a problem here after Claude Reese [a young
black boy] was shot to death by a white policeman. That became a
black/white issue because of a black community and a white police
force. The press exaggerates the racial tension. If the whole
police force was black, people would take to the streets the same
way. People say black/white—I don't pay it no mind. There are
economic tensions—there's not enough to go around. Everybody is
fighting for the same small piece of pie, which is not much for
anybody. Tensions here are economic, not only in relation to jobs,
but also because of the structure of the city. We have ten or twelve
housing projects. They employ a few hundred people. Rents are

high in these buildings. People's incomes are supposed to generate rents. Almost all the project managers and staff are from the outside, not from the community. The same is true in police, fire, businesses, and so on. None of the money used for needs in the community is kept in the community in the form of jobs.

10. and 11. Public housing houses the vast majority of Brownsville residents. Most people who move into public housing stay there for at least ten years. It takes that long to move up educationally, financially. Public housing is a stepping stone. I once found an apartment in public housing for a client. She later came back to thank me. She said, "I no longer have to fight rats and roaches from attacking my child. I now see the benefits of heat and hot water, and I now can go back to school." Most of the projects here are low-income projects, low-cost in reality. They have attracted some problem families. The Housing Authority seems to send a disproportionate number of problem families to Brownsville.

Forest Hills has some problem families, but the community is a self-sufficient community and is able to absorb problems and make sure that they do not affect the community. Instead of having the dog wagging the tail, in Brownsville, we have the tail wagging the dog. If we had a stable resource population with 20 percent problem families, it would be O.K. Since it is the reverse, maybe 10 to 15 percent of the population trying to deal with the problems of 85 percent of the population, the situation is chaotic. In this way, public housing has affected the quality of life in the neighborhood. The project in Forest Hills is supposed to have the same tenant requirements as the projects here. We have too many more problems here, this is ridiculous. Rules are made to be broken. The one who speaks the loudest changes the rules. People who apply to Louis Pink Houses (a Federal housing project in Cypress Hills) are sent to Brownsville. We have more welfare people here than anywhere else in the city. Residents are not screened. We get all the problem families. If you are organizing, the problems of the community are yours, but a community should not have a disproportionate amount of problems.

We speak of scattered sites, but every time you try to build a house in Flatbush or other communities, the community goes up in arms. These people who now live in Canarsie and Flatbush came from Brownsville. They migrated to Flatbush and Canarsie as white people who were escaping—they don't want to live with black people.

If the garbage man doesn't pick up my garbage, I will call my councilman or senator. I will pick up the phone and make sure that these problems are attended to. But most people here are sick with apathy. This is a part of the deterioration of any community.

This neighborhood was never good! People came from Europe,
this is where they settled. There were always poor people here,
many welfare families. We had the highest prices and the most
inferior food, even then. Now, prices in Canarsie are far lower
than in Brownsville. This area was always a so-called ghetto.
It's just a matter of degree. We always had crime in Brownsville.
It used to be organized crime, now it's one-on-one crime. There
are advantages of organized crime, you pay for your protection.
If you pay your dues, you're safe.

12. People with cars don't do their shopping here, but
many of the residents have no cars and are forced to shop here.
I buy clothing outside the community. Many people buy clothing
outside the area. This is something you can carry. I buy appliances and furniture outside of the area. Brownsville used to be a
main furniture area, not too long ago.

There are very few playgrounds in Brownsville. Parks are
remote; maintenance is not there. One playground nearby, Lincoln
Terrace Park, is used by residents of Crown Heights, Brownsville, and East New York. It's the only real park we have. Betsey
Head Park is a terrible park. Facilities there would be adequate,
if they were maintained. There is a baseball field close by. In the
summer, pool water is filthy, your clothing gets tampered with—
there's no supervision. The little bit of available supervision
doesn't give a damn!

People who can afford to, go outside the community for
medical attention. The private doctors left the community for safer,
more lucrative areas. Although there are two doctors left, most
people are forced to use the clinics.

Banks in this area are few and far between. Most residents
here do not get a chance to do any banking.

All the facilities in this area are inferior. If I had a car,
I would do absolutely no shopping here! There aren't many supermarkets here and prices in the available stores are higher. There's
not much competition. We have mostly momma-poppa stores.
Puerto Ricans and Arabs are opening food shops on every corner.
The food is terrible. If you ever get to eat here, you will find that
the sandwiches are as expensive as they are in the city and the food
is stale.

I visited one local doctor and I wasn't too impressed. The
doctors are "having a ball" with Medicaid and Medicare patients.
They give too many prescriptions, almost always not restricted to
curing your particular illness. Three doctors left here after many
years in the neighborhood. There is one dentist in my development.
The doctors and dentists do not make any house calls. They charge
$5.00 to $6.00 for each visit. Not much at all, but most residents
cannot afford that small amount.

The medical centers are run by "rip-off" artists. They make you wait so long and then give you any old medication, and many varieties. Although this is a poverty area, they charge an awful lot of money. Most people from this area go to Kings County Hospital or Brookdale. Many times, when these hospitals have no beds for their patients, they send the people home to die! Just recently, Marcus Garvey's grandson died in Brookdale Hospital. I think this might be a bit political! Services must be improved. Hospitals have a shortage of help, some doctors have to work 24 hours at a stretch. They can hardly see while they might be performing a serious operation. There was a time when doctors came to your house. The professional population has now moved to better neighborhoods.

14. I go to Lutheran Hospital if an emergency arises. The emergency room in Kings County is much improved. I can compliment them on that. I remember when Kings County Hospital was a mad house. In those days, when you got someone to talk to you, they treated you like an animal. They separated adults from children. In Kings County, there is always a specialist on hand. This has been the case for the past four years. In the past, the board of directors consisted of politicians and philanthropists. We had to struggle in order to break this pattern. They gave the Brownsville community an advisory capacity, headed by Mr. Fuller. We do not yet have any power over decisions. So some services have improved but not enough.

15. Yes, recreation for adults is a problem. Day care centers, Headstart, Senior Citizens programs, and summer programs exist, but there are not enough! There are no programs for adults between 21 and 60. The taxpayers, the people who struggle to obtain all the recreational facilities, have nothing for themselves. My recreation release would be to go to the parking lot and talk to the fellas. There's nothing here for the working person. We are the supporters of other facilities here.

16., 17., 18. There is absolutely no recreation in Brownsville for teenagers nor are there any social clubs. All centers are closed on weekends. Teenagers and adults do not have the funds necessary to seek other amusement. One must leave the community to go to dances or the movies. Many of the children of this community have never been outside the community. Children have excess energy. They have nothing to do with their energy, so they get into mischief. Then we wonder why they get into trouble. This is a cause of the vandalism problem. Parks here are so filthy, and they are full of debris and broken bottles. When we complain to the Department of Parks, they say "yes, yes" but do nothing unless you keep after them. Many people here complain initially, and once the first bureaucrat says "no," they become discouraged and leave.

Existing facilities here are being underutilized. Facilities here are outdated. The time involved from the planning stage to construction to completion is so long that facilities become obsolete. Parents here must work, especially mothers. They cannot do volunteer work, as many mothers in other areas can do. Brownsville is advertised as a crime area and it is difficult to get the few available facilities because people read the newspapers and are afraid of Brownsville. The Brownsville Boys Club is one adequate facility that is being utilized by the boys from Brownsville and East New York.

19. Streets are being cleaned more often than they used to be, so this is one indication of a slightly improved service. They are giving more tickets than ever before. After the burning of garbage, a lot of services that we didn't have before became more evident. Broken telephone booths and abandoned cars create problems.

Streets have potholes aplenty! If you complain, someone comes down. People here just look; they say something has to be done, but they wait for someone else to do it. It wasn't always the case. When there was new construction, years ago, the problem was not as severe. We always did, however, have a problem with potholes.

20. Regulations for parking are strictly enforced.

21. Garbage is not being picked up properly! Garbage is picked up twice a week, which is simply not enough for a project population this size. Garbage pick-up was more frequent before the projects were constructed. Maybe I shouldn't say this, but I have a friend who works for the Department of Sanitation. As soon as the strike was over, the department neglected the black and Puerto Rican neighborhoods. The streets smell so bad! We have larger families, no facilities, more garbage. We occupy less space with more people. The Sanitation Department is very political. Besides the system being racist, it's also political.

When the borough total figures for voting were compared, the black neighborhoods had far less people registered. This lack of interest is due to so many ills. If you bother politicians and make sure they do their job, it will be done. But if a politician has a job, and no one pressures him to do it, it won't get done.

22. Day care facilities are inadequate in that I think we need more. I think they're doing a good job with what they have. If we had more day care centers, we would have less welfare. If the mothers could go out to work or school, this would benefit them tremendously. The government would save a lot of money if people could work for a living instead of staying home and collecting checks.

If there were jobs available, people would rather work. Brownsville day care centers are filled. There are many of them here but we need more. What we need even more is recreational facilities.

23. Train stations are not safe nor are they clean. Miss Tucker was attacked and killed near a train station. One eight-year-old child witnessed the death of his mother who was killed on a train station by a mugger.

The transportation facilities have been improved. We had the Pitkin Avenue bus rerouted after 30 years. It used to take two fares to get to Prospect Park because of the inadequate bus connections. We brought about that change. Buses and trains are adequate, but the services that go with them—security, cleanliness—have a lot of room for improvement. Streets and stations are not clean but they're cleaner than they used to be. There is sometimes a 20-minute wait for a bus on Pitkin Avenue. Most Pitkin Avenue buses have no air conditioning. They make sure to route the buses so that they pass through certain types of areas. The Pitkin Avenue bus, for example, goes through Brownsville and East New York. The Flatlands bus goes as far as Rockaway Parkway, a convenient spot since this is the Canarsie-Brownsville border.

24. Safety for children is a problem here. There have been many incidents of children being hit by cars en route to school. Some of the existing school guards are committed and this is a good thing.

25. Our schools are now underutilized. This in part is due to demolition, and many parents are sending their children to Catholic schools out of the area because the educational facilities here are horrendous. Parents try to see that children get adequate education. There is no chance of this in the Brownsville public school system. Educational facilities are poor. Buildings are old and not well maintained. Teachers are babysitting and our children are not learning. One man that I know has a child in the Brownsville public school system. He comes home with all A's. His father asked him to read a book, and he wasn't able to do it. His father went up to the school and inquired about this. The teacher told him, "Your son is well disciplined."

26. Schools are not generally opened during evenings and summers. There used to be a summer program here but it is no longer available. While a few facilities exist, they are underutilized. This, once again, is probably due to obsolescence. The existing facilities also need more staff. This is the first time I have seen the Neighborhood Youth Corps coordinate itself effectively.

27. There are two public libraries here but one was just closed down. Facilities are not adequate. They didn't have the supply of books necessary. This is why children never went to the

library. If the only alternative to this is to go to the main branch of the public library at Grand Army Plaza and pay a double fare, the children must do this in order to get the books necessary to complete their work. The city says that there's no demand for these books and that is the reason the local libraries do not have them. Our children are forced to go out of the neighborhood where the facilities are more adequate.

All the movie theaters in the neighborhood have closed down. In order to see a movie, you have to go to Flatbush. Some of the movie theaters have been converted to churches.

30. There are many churches in the neighborhood. There used to be many synagogues here. Many people are active in the church so that they can send their children to parochial schools. Some of the ministers in Brownsville are dedicated to the area. There are a few ministers, for example, Bishop Webb, who work with the youth. Unfortunately, accompanying the services and dedicated church people are rip-off artist ministers who sell their congregations down the river. There are many storefront churches in Brownsville that are run by these corrupt people. They preach all kinds of pleasant things to their congregations, take their money, and then let them down.

31. There are potholes in streets; streets aren't paved. Services aren't what they should be. Coming off Rockaway Avenue down from Fulton Street, the streets are paved pretty well up until about East New York Avenue, then everything stops. I don't know who is responsible for this but it is a problem. Manholes have increased because the main arteries are heavily traveled on by buses. The Committee to Save New York found that over $6 million is owed by realty. The slum landlords do not pay their taxes. Banks also owe the city a tremendous amount. We are paying for this via lack of city services. Parks are a main problem here. They are few in number and not kept up or supervised.

32. Municipal services in this neighborhood are poor.

33. Storekeepers do overcharge. They do not treat customers as they should. This comes, in part, from customers not demanding that quality service. Storekeepers are from other areas of the city and suburbs. When you have an upstate (suburb) mentality and you come into areas like Brownsville with this mentality, you are going to come to Brownsville with a derogatory attitude toward the people. It is the attitude! I stopped shopping on Pitkin Avenue a few years ago. I did this because I used to walk in, when they saw my face, they would say "We'll take care of you, there are some black and Puerto Rican people here too. We'll take care of them first and give them some merchandise. We want to give you something you'd like. So we'll just give them the other stuff and give you something

nice." I would say, "Look, I came here to buy something, show me what you have and that's all. Don't be bothering me about this nonsense . . . I live in this community and don't be bothering me."

A similar situation happened with a cab driver. Cab drivers drive me up the wall. Gypsy cabbies are also a pain in the neck, but not so bad as the others. When I get into a cab and tell the driver that I am going to Blake Avenue and Rockaway Avenue (where I work and a few blocks from my home), they start harassing me. "What are you doing there? How come you live there? I thought you were going to Canarsie or East Flatbush or someplace." I just argue with these morons and tell them to take me there and shut up! I've also noticed that the Puerto Rican gypsy cabbies charge me an arm and a leg. The other day, I took a cab on Utica Avenue to Blake and Rockaway Avenues. I got the same line of questioning from this cab driver. In most cases, the gypsy cab drivers are a little bit more cooperative, but there is tremendous variation in their prices. This is the type of thing you hear and you have to learn to cope with it. I look for gypsy cabs because I don't want to get annoyed. Storekeepers overcharge. Food here is horrible. Storekeepers certainly do harass me.

34. Children were getting roughed up a bit in the schools and some were arrested. Police harass residents and take part in things that are personal, for example, family disputes. Kids get harassed in the streets. There also was an employer/employee dispute over the employee's pay. These two guys would get out and fight every Friday. The employee was black, and the employer was white. The police busted in and termed this a racial issue. He then roughed up the black guy and locked him up. Police chase children from corners. One said to a child, "Run, run or I'll shoot you." He then shoved a gun in the child's face. Another policeman said, "If you run, you're as good as dead." The mentality of the police is as bad as that of the storekeepers. These people do not understand the life style of the people in the neighborhood. For example, cultural differences exist in different types of neighborhoods. Puerto Ricans have a tendency to shoot craps in the parking lots, while Cubans play dominoes. There are some training programs but the attitude is still present. This is the case, even with most black policemen once they get that job and move the suburbs. They develop the mentality just as those whites from the suburbs. I, for one, think that jobs like these and housing managers' jobs should go to people in the community.

These policemen and housing managers live well outside the area and don't understand how we live here. After 5:00 P.M. they can't be reached at all. It's still up to them. When the police come in and say they need a number of arrests, this is arranged. Another example:

I owned a gypsy cab. I couldn't find a job, so I bought a gypsy cab. I spent my last money, bought a car, got it insured and did everything I was supposed to do. There was a problem politically with gypsy cabs out here. There were too many of them, they were competing with the city cabs. But somehow, soon after, a law was passed stating that a cab had to be one color. I had my car painted three colors. They stopped me a number of times, gave me tickets. One day, in the pouring rain, I stopped and picked up a person (Puerto Rican) and a cop gave me a ticket for picking up this guy. When I asked him if he would do something had the passenger been his mother, he gave me another ticket. That, to me, is harassment.

35. There are no courts in this neighborhood, but courts for area residents are unjust.

36. Schools here, as said before, are poor. Teachers harass children.

37. Welfare workers do not visit this area. They harass clients in satellite offices.

38. Crime is a serious problem. I am in fear of walking the streets. It's much worse now than it has been, like any other area.

39. Yes, there are many fires in this area. The South Bronx beats us out, though! There are many fires because if you live in deplorable conditions and you have no way of escaping and you have five or six kids and the only way you are going to get housing is if there is a fire, you'll make sure one exists. I've talked to people and, while they never admit to setting the fires, I know they set some of them. They come in here and complain about lack of heat and hot water; the only way they can get out is if they set the fire. Fires are also often set by hungry landlords who own rent-controlled buildings in order to get their tenants out and rehabilitate the building, then legally decontrolling the apartment rents. Sometimes the landlords turn their buildings over to the city, especially if they owe back taxes for their real estate.

40. We always had the drug problem here. The police know where the drugs are but they allow this to persist anyway. Methadone clinics are here in large number. The once heroin addicts are now methadone addicts. In addition, many community residents are up in arms about the locations of these methadone clinics. They tend to be located right near liquor stores. The patients of these clinics hang around and create other problems. They urinate in the hallways, and so on.

41. This neighborhood is sometimes a very noisy place.

42. There are gangs here but their strength has decreased since the 1960s.

43. There is definitely a lack of places for children to play in Brownsville. This is not a good area to bring up children, but it's the best we can do.

44. Cluttered high-rise buildings perpetuate crime. The lower-rise projects have lower crime rates.

45. Burglary gates have been in existence since the early 1960s.

46. I have lived here 50 years; 15 years; 32 years.

47. Bad housing is a serious problem here. I think that if the housing problem was dealt with, a lot of other problems would be solved. Housing characteristics are bad—heat, hot water, rats, roaches, everything bad is in Brownsville. There was worse housing here 50 years ago, when I moved here, because there was no public housing. Housing was on the way out years ago and this recent transient population has made it crumble faster. Where I used to live, a cold water flat, we had no heat or hot water. We used to get water from fire hydrants. Another reason for bad housing is the extent of overcrowding. Because of the tremendous number of fires, people are forced to relocate. The supply of housing is low and the rents are high and so people are forced to crowd together and live in old, deteriorating buildings until they are burned to the ground. Then, if they are lucky, they will get into public housing.

48. People in public housing do not have a lease. The tenants do not know their rights. Tenants in private housing are usually not given leases either.

49. Let me tell you something about the homeowners in this community. We have had a tremendous turnover in homeownership over the past few years. They (black homeowners) put in their last dollar and they want to stay here. My advice to most people is, "Don't buy a house unless you know something about it." People have bought houses and because of bad advice have not been able to keep them up.

50. Complaints about the lack of service are like an endless cycle. You try and move elsewhere and you have the same problems.

52. Landlords do take advantage of welfare clients. They charge the maximum. The landlords have many sets of prices. Welfare clients are exploited and discriminated against. Public housing tries to screen out the large welfare families and these people are the ones who should live in public housing.

54. My bathroom, like most project bathrooms, has no window.

55. I have four rooms; I have three rooms.

56. Hallways and elevators are unsafe.

57. Rent control in Brownsville is almost nil. Landlords charge as much as $275 for a decrepit apartment. Rats, roaches, heat, hot water, a definite problem in public and private housing here.

Most people compete with each other. Agencies help enforce the discriminatory patterns. They refuse to take issue with problems here. Absentee landlords are slumlords. They live far outside and come in to collect rents. They provide minimum services and take maximum compensation.

59. Most older houses have no laundry rooms in the basement. Some projects have a laundry room but it generally serves a few buildings and tends to be a haven for criminal activity.

60. Tenants' associations are here and not as effective as they should be. There are strong block associations made up of homeowners and don't deal with rental housing.

61. Neighborhood improvement groups exist but are at the beginning stages.

62. We belong to the Gorman Tenants Council; Brownsville Community Corporation; Neighborhood Action Center.

63. Clubs are somewhat unified and help the community.

64. No, no, no, we have not received help. Major Owens is the only politician in Brownsville who is really _for_ the people. We try and work closely with him and others to better our community.

65. Yes, we have contacted Elizabeth Holtzman and Major Owens seeking help.

SAMPLE INTERVIEW NO. 2

1. Brownsville could be a good place to live in if people could be left alone to decide their own fortunes. Public subway systems and bus routes are fairly accessible. This is something on which you can build a community. But there are lousy schools, no recreation, no decent shopping facilities. The community has been asking for those for the past ten years. Little has been started, nothing completed. A degree of confidence has been shifted. Not much has happened in 20 years. A lot of documentation and that's about it!

2. The people who migrated to Brownsville 20 or 25 years ago had hope! They were young, strong, and worked hard trying to build a community. Many tried to work within existing organizational structures. Things started to change; people moved out and those who stayed attempted to take over, but this was not allowed. Schools, stores, and so on—everything is hooked up to politics. Abe Stark and his development came out of this area—it was the Democratic base of Brooklyn in the 1940s. In the past, Brownsville had resident owners. When they moved, they rented their houses and allowed

_____

Interviewees were Maurice Reid, W. Webster, and D. Devouse from Brownsville Headstart.

them to be abandoned. This caused others to move. Past owners
rented to Puerto Ricans where blacks were not accepted. That was
a piece of the evil. This created a division instead of unification
of a black and Puerto Rican community.

Even though old timers had moved, they still exercised control over the area. They couldn't control services, they took them
with them. There has been an increasing need for these services.
Young black children entered school. Parents were told they had
to be segregated, put into classes by themselves so that they could
reach the point where the other children were (even in kindergarten
and first grade). Brownsville produced some of the most educated
people in the country prior to World War II, in an essentially Jewish community.

3. Brownsville is the only home that I know. Although I get
frustrated and tired of the constant struggle, it seldom comes to
my mind that I can move. Brownsville is where I learned about
voting, politics, the educational system.

4. I would like to stay in Brownsville, and will stay!

5. I had no friends or relatives in Brownsville when I moved
here. I made friends while I lived here. I moved here out of need,
need for a place to live. They had just built the first housing project and my family needed a place in which to live.

6. The only thing the people in this neighborhood have in
common is the constant struggle for survival. There is a tyranni-
cal political system, a school system that cares nothing about the
children, and knows nothing about them. There are a lot of federal
and state plans that don't work. Everyone has something in common: higher cost of living, poor sanitation, bad housing, poor educational system, and so on.

7. There is an extreme lack of facilities that, I think, is
caused by the racial composition of this community. The white
structure doesn't really care about the community. There is a
sickness that causes blockbusting and has a bad effect on everything. This is what causes change in political climate in the community. People are blamed for the conditions, but if you look at the
services that disappeared when the neighborhood changed—and racial
trends—there is a definite correlation. Blacks and Puerto Ricans
tried to establish residences for teachers. This was stopped because it was a known fact that these residences were not for Jewish
teachers that were, at that time, leaving the area.

8. Marcus Garvey Housing rents for $300 to $350 for a two-
bedroom apartment. As the owner-tenants left, not only were they
renting in racist patterns, they were helped by the city—which collected high rents without maintaining property. Once the city no
longer picks up the tab, people who can afford it move on. The

community suffers from institutional racism and very conscious racism on the part of the people in government who make decisions.

9. The tensions in this area are caused by decision makers who no longer live here. They are caused by inadequate sewers, bad schools. There are economic tensions—all fighting over the same piece of pie. There are racial tensions caused by housing patterns. The conscious renting decisions cause stress between the blacks and Puerto Ricans.

10. The public housing projects are too large, too congested, and seriously affect the people in the area. The housing is neglected. There is no tenant education. There are no facilities for children or elderly people. The housing authority is the biggest slumlord in existence today. Fifteen to 20 years ago, talk was started about resident management, resident maintenance; we never got it! Resident maintenance is one of the biggest farces—it is so-called in existence but with such stringent conditions that the idea is negated. People cannot play an active role in community life. There is a 20-minute wait for elevators; congestion in the lobby. Public housing has a way of destroying the family unit. Many people did not want to leave Brownsville because they knew what it was like to be a part of the community. Many people fought bitter fights to be here. Because of income guidelines, people were forced to move. Children are in a position to be forced to lie about who is working in the household. There are no child care facilities in the three developments (L. Hughes, G. Plaza, Seth Low). We have brick and mortar slums, it's criminal. There is one community center and only one management office for the three projects. What can that accomplish?

11. This neighborhood, before the projects, was a well-run, well-organized small Jewish community. Facilities that were needed existed. There were adequate shopping facilities, small private homes, and small apartment houses. When you build high-rise apartment houses, facilities must be increased, but they weren't. How did it change? How did Europe change after World War II? It has subsequently become a disaster area. How did Europe change after World War II? It has subsequently become a disaster area. All the small private homes are gone, small apartment houses are gone, shopping facilities have closed. The children who go to school are not faced with teachers who believe they can't be taught—so in turn, they fail because they aren't properly taught. There is a tremendous fear of this neighborhood, and many people are afraid to move here because of the stories they hear. There were many more facilities here in 1955 than there are today, although there were less people.

12. We do our grocery shopping outside of the neighborhood. We purchase our clothing outside of the neighborhood. We visit doctors and dentists outside of the neighborhood. We bank inside the neighborhood. We don't have any movies or recreational facilities in this area. We have a park, but prefer the parks outside the area.

13. Good medical care is nonexistent. Brownsville has "Medicaid mills" that exploit the residents. We either use private doctors or the hospital emergency room when necessary.

14. In case of emergencies, we use the facilities at Kings County or Brookdale Hospitals. There are no private facilities.

15. There is absolutely no recreation for adults.

16. There is a definite lack of recreation for teenagers. The parks are inadequate and unsafe. We have one meeting room that is used for basketball, softball, and whatever!

17. The space designed for children has been turned into parking lots. There is absolutely nothing for younger children. As a pastime, they deface the property.

18. My children used the park within Van Dyke Houses. By the time they reached ten years of age, the center was in such a dilapidated condition that they refused to go there. The parks are not properly maintained and have become a "hangout" for winos and drug addicts.

19. The streets and sidewalks are in a deplorable condition. The phone booths are broken. We have a serious problem with abandoned cars. This has been the case for a long time.

20. Parking regulations are enforced, but the streets are rarely cleaned.

21. The garbage is not collected properly. The bags are placed outside on Friday and collected the following Tuesday. This causes mice, rats, and roaches. These are very unsanitary and very unhealthy conditions.

22. The day care centers are inadequate. Although there is an increase in population, the funds for the day care centers dwindle.

23. The train stations are very unsafe. There was a murder recently on the Belmont Avenue Station. The steps are broken and hazardous. Although Brownsville has the accessibility to the transportation (trains, buses) the conditions of the facilities are very poor.

24. We no longer have crossing guards; the streets are very unsafe for our children to cross. Lack of adequate street lights makes the crossing even more dangerous.

25. The educational facilities decreased with the increase in population. The schools are on a split session, making it very chaotic.

26. There is one school opened during evening hours for gym use. There were also very limited summer programs in a few schools.

27. There is a small library, not large enough for the number of children in this area.

28. The meat is of the poorest quality in this neighborhood, although the prices are high. If possible, the people shop outside of this area.

29. All the theaters have been closed since I moved here. There are none left.

30. There are many churches and storefront churches in Brownsville. They don't play a very great role in this area.

31. Services have decreased considerably, and in some instances have been cut out completely.

32. The public services and facilities in this area are poor. There is broken and defective equipment, litter is scattered in the street, and the overall appearance of the neighborhood is abominable.

33. Storekeepers overcharge because the people have no means of shopping elsewhere. They pay top dollar for the lowest quality. They have no regard for their customers and treat them badly.

34. The police are never around when they are needed. They don't feel that they have to protect the neighborhood, they are only around to issue parking tickets, especially when there is some kind of a community activity. The housing police are too few in number (24 officers for ten developments).

35. There are no courts in this neighborhood, not much justice either! Clear cases of collusion, especially with local school board and housing.

36. The schools are terrible. The parents should take a class action against the Board of Education for miseducating their children. Teachers physically abuse children and are never brought up on charges. They are merely transferred to other locations. Children are left to themselves. They are used for custodial services in the schools. The administration is corrupt and so are the policy makers. The school principal was replaced with a man who should be put to pasture. He merely had a political connection so he got the job. Teachers do not have to account for the lack of teaching. Fifty percent of the children who should be in school are on the outside.

37. The welfare workers no longer visit this area. They do their harassing down at the welfare office. If you work, you lose all benefits. This causes many people not to seek work.

38. Crime is a serious problem. It has changed from "organized" to gang warfare. Much unrest is due to the deplorable living conditions.

39. There are many fires in this area, and what has not been burned down should be!

40. This area is a haven for drug pushers and users. The methadone maintenance center brings many undesirables.

41. This area is extremely noisy.

42. Gang problems do exist. They have no other outlets.

43. There is no place for the children to play; they are exposed to many negative conditions and the environment doesn't help them to become solid citizens.

44. High-rise buildings create crime pockets. They are very unsafe.

45. Burglary gates have been on all stores since the early 1960s.

46. I have lived in this neighborhood 14 years; 20 years; 28 years.

47. Everything is bad: abandoned buildings, absentee landlords, new apartments have prohibitive rents. We are stuck in this ghetto. The neighborhood keeps getting worse, there's no way out!

48. I rent this apartment and pay $300 for four rooms, which is about 50 percent of my salary.

49. In public housing (one-year lease), there are no services, no repairs. There are no leases in private tenement slums, which are mostly owned by the city.

50. There are no lease agreements.

51. My rent is much too high. It has tripled since I moved in, and the services have gotten worse.

52. The landlords positively take advantage of the welfare tenants.

53. I have four rooms, two of which are bedrooms.

54. My bathroom has no window.

55. The elevator is very unsafe. There was a terrible accident where a child was killed by a falling elevator.

56. This apartment is not rent controlled.

57. We constantly suffer from lack of heat and hot water, rats, roaches, holes in the walls and ceilings, broken windows and pipes. I complained but it did no good.

58. The landlord does not live in this house.

59. There is a laundry room in this building, but this one room has to service 30 buildings.

60. There are some tenants' associations in this area, but they are very ineffective.

61. The local neighborhood improvement groups are also very ineffective. When they looked like they were going to accomplish something, they were taken over by the local politicians and the result was nil.

62. I, personally, belong to the Democratic Club, Tenants' Association, School Board, Commission for an Effective School Board, Block Association.

63. This is a way of demonstrating some kind of resistance to certain wrongdoings. We are able to rally if we show collective resistance. The clubs draw attention to certain things and educate people about their conditions.

64. We have asked for help from our politicians, but received none.

65. We would look to Owens, Chisolm, Holtzman for help if we could generate enough public pressure for them to respond.

NOTES

1. See Alter Landesman, Brownsville (New York: Bloch Publishers, 1971).

2. New York Herald Tribune, quoted in ibid.

3. Jacob Riis, How the Other Half Lives, Studies Among New York City Tenements, ed. Sam B. Warren (Cambridge, Mass.: Harvard University Press, 1970).

4. Milton Goell, Brownsville Must Have Public Housing (Brooklyn: Brooklyn Committee for Better Housing, 1941).

5. H. Savitch, "Powerlessness in an Urban Ghetto," Polity 1 (1972): 33.

6. Ibid.

7. "Nothing is Bright on Amboy Street," New York Times, September 22, 1974.

8. Ibid.

9. "The Decline of Brownsville," New York Times, March 7, 1968.

10. Quoted from New York City Planning Commission Master Plan, 1969.

11. Ibid.

12. Rae Glauber, "All Neighborhoods Change" (Brooklyn, n.p., 1963).

8

CROWN HEIGHTS

POPULATION

Crown Heights is adjacent to the slum areas of Bedford Stuyvesant and Brownsville and spreads out into white middle-class sections such as Flatbush. Crown Heights is a conglomeration of Jewish, black, Puerto Rican, and Chinese (to a lesser extent) elements.

> The newsstand at Utica Avenue and Eastern Parkway, one of Brooklyn's busiest intersections, tells the story of Crown Heights in a glance. Besides the city's mass circulation dailies, the stand carries thick piles of Jewish, Hebrew, West Indian, Haitian, black, Spanish, and Chinese newspapers, which are snapped up briskly by the polyglot population of the neighborhood. [1]

Eastern Parkway, the major thoroughfare, traverses the community and, accordingly, it divides the Hasidic south and black residential sections north of this line.

The neighborhood's development during the early part of the twentieth century was largely the work of its Jewish population. A move to Crown Heights was a step upward for Jews. Smaller numbers of Italian, Irish, German, and Scandinavian families also moved into the neighborhood.

After 1920 Crown Heights fortunes gradually declined until the 1950s when it was described as a lower-middle-income area. During this period the neighborhood transformation (from white to black) began.

After World War II a middle-income black group striving to move upward settled in the Children's Museum area (in the northeast section of the area). Among the first to arrive were blacks of West Indian origin (many of whom purchased homes north of Eastern Parkway and still reside there). Between 1950 and 1960 the black population in the Children's Museum area rose from one-third to about two-thirds of the total. While the great majority of the newcomers were tenants, there was a class of homeowners, some of whom later could not afford to maintain their homes. One real estate agent who has lived in Crown Heights for over 20 years explained:

> Post World War II Crown Heights experienced a rapid
> out-movement of whites, and in-movement of blacks.
> Many blacks who could not really afford to own homes
> were enticed into becoming homeowners. As a result,
> resident owners who couldn't afford to keep their build-
> ings in one family structure were forced to convert
> these buildings to multiple dwellings, that is, rooming
> houses.

Another group of blacks lives south of Eastern Parkway. Many of these residents settled in the area during the 1960s. "During the sixties, three-quarters of the residents of Crown Heights moved, with whites fleeing what they saw as a tide of blacks who brought crime and plummeting real estate values. The ethnic composition changed from 70 percent white to 70 percent black."[2] The remainder of the neighborhood is largely white, which, at present, is approximated at 25 percent.

During the 1940s, a community of Hasidic Jews came from Williamsburg to settle in the east central section of Crown Heights, immediately south of Eastern Parkway. This movement, referred to as the Lubavitcher movement, has since established itself in the community as increasing numbers of followers have been migrating to the neighborhood. The director of the movement, Rabbi Schneerson, has recently pronounced the permanent establishment of the worldwide Lubavitcher movement in Crown Heights with headquarters at 770 Eastern Parkway (near Kingston Avenue). Rabbi Schneerson said "the Lubavitchers will stop running!" This recent announcement has accelerated the in-movement of Lubavitchers from parts of New York City and other cities such as Boston and Philadelphia.

> In comparing Crown Heights with Dorchester, an old
> Jewish ghetto near Boston, Mass., well, there's
> really no comparison! Although there was an ortho-
> dox community in Dorchester, there was no real

community leadership. The strength and purpose of
Judaism is so much more evident in Crown Heights.

Many real estate agents point out the inflated housing prices
resulting from this recent population shift. One agent said: "You
can't touch a house in Crown Heights these days. The Lubavitchers
are taking over the neighborhood. They're bidding for every house
in the neighborhood and have caused prices to skyrocket!"

The Lubavitchers are the only Hasidic movement with a cen-
tralized power structure. There are eight Lubavitcher congregations in the Crown Heights area. Each congregation has its own
rabbi; however, guidance of the total movement is under the direction of one rabbi whose position is hereditary. He coordinates the
temporal and spiritual activities of the community and it is his existence that makes possible the geographic separation of the individual congregations. The remaining Crown Heights congregations
are made up of Hasidim of other European countries, mainly Poland
and Hungary. There is no cohesion among these individual congregations. When asked why he would prefer to move out of Crown
Heights, one long-term Jewish resident answered:

> The Lubavitchers make life unpleasant for other Jew-
> ish people in the neighborhood. They have their own
> friends, schools, and other institutions here and ig-
> nore the remainder of the community residents. I
> would like to move to Canarsie or Flatbush, as many
> of my friends who were residents here did.

Each congregation is derived from a particular locality in the country of origin.

The Hasidim of Crown Heights are mainly engaged in white-
collar occupations. A large percentage work outside the community
as jewelers, furriers, diamond cutters, postal workers, and operators of car rental services. Most of the Hasidic women of Crown
Heights are not employed.

Though their religious traditions tend to isolate them from the
community, the Hasidim of Crown Heights do take an active interest in civic affairs.

> The local antipoverty agency, the Crown Heights Com-
> munity Corporation, is controlled by Hasidic officials,
> who won their places in an election. The local school
> board has one Hasidic member even though most Hasidic
> children go to parochial schools. As many as 10 Hasidic
> residents have begun to take part in the Community Plan-
> ning Board.[3]

The blacks in Crown Heights are far less organized. As one black resident said: "If the black people in Crown Heights were as organized as the Hasidic Jewish population, this would be some neighborhood!"

RACIAL TENSIONS

The seething ghetto of East New York erupted in violence early Friday morning. In the aftermath of the violence, sparked by uncollected garbage, five people were jailed, a police car firebombed, an angry mob marched on a police station, and firemen were forced to call for police protection to fight the scores of fires set by the mob. While East New York was blowing up, a scant 12 blocks away, in Crown Heights, one of the most interesting and exciting examples of interracial peace and harmony was a reality.[4]

The question of racial tension in Crown Heights has been well publicized since the early 1960s. Many residents feel that racial tension is the only community problem in Crown Heights. However, newspaper accounts and residents' views are often conflicting. This section examines the question of racial tension among residents by comparing their views and the views of the press.

In 1964 a group of Hasidic rabbis, led by Rabbi Samuel Schrage, and other white residents of the area banded together to form an unarmed vigilante group, the Maccabees, to supplement and later aid the police. The initial consequence was an increase in racial tension because many blacks believed the Maccabees were aimed at them. There has been, since the 1960s, considerable apprehension; a small number of well-publicized crimes have disturbed the community.

Ten years after the Maccabee patrols made newspaper headlines, the neighborhood is thriving as an ethnic smorgasbord. Although in Crown Heights the Orthodox Jews and blacks live side by side, the contacts between these groups are rare and freighted with suspicion and fear.

On the corner of Albany Avenue and Empire Boulevard there is a candy store run by a black woman now. Friday night, a man who lived a few feet away was murdered. Did she hear about it, did she know the man?

> He was a Jew, said the woman, how would I
> know about him?
> The Jews refer to the blacks as the "schwartzes"
> and black children tell people that they hate Jews.
> Shortly after 11:00 A.M. yesterday, someone
> standing in front of Lefferts Junior High School yelled
> "Heil Hitler." The young man in the crowd of Ortho-
> dox Jews chased a black man down the block and began
> pummeling him. He was saved by the police. Then
> some of the children in a school window took up the
> chant "Heil Hitler!" A few of the demonstrators
> called back, "shame, shame, shame."

An Orthodox rabbi felt that the answer may be to pick up arms
and defend himself and his community. He points out the success
that Italians have in maintaining their stable neighborhoods.[5]
Many long-term black American and West Indian residents
see evidence of friction, caused by this lack of communication.

> Tensions arise because there isn't too much mingling
> of racial groups in the neighborhood; lack of communi-
> cation brings on tensions. There is no real out and
> out tension.
>
> (14-year resident, black American)

Another resident adds:

> The question of racial tension has been overplayed.
> There was a brief flurry in Rabbi Schrage's time.
> After the Jewish Defense League stopped being so
> active, all tension in the area seemed to dissipate.
>
> (30-year resident, black American)

The black West Indian population, which is primarily the home-
owning middle-income core of Crown Heights, is more scathingly
hostile, both toward the low-income black segment of the population
and the Hasidic Jewish population.

> We don't act as one community. They feel we don't
> understand them culturally and they don't understand
> us. The Hasidic community feels it has enough politi-
> cal power to deal with the people who control this city,
> so they don't have to deal with us [the West Indian popu-
> lation] on a local level.[6]

An angry real estate agent and resident explained:

> Hasidics are militant and politically sophisticated.
> Their demands on services could cause increased
> tension. For example, the area's police protection
> is inadequate. If they didn't load up 20 police to
> protect the Hasidics on one block, this wouldn't be
> the case.
>
> (25-year resident, black West Indian)

West Indian residents' complaints about the lower-income black American segment are almost always expressed within a housing framework:

> The welfare department exiles its clients here to
> specific buildings. The landlords then milk the
> buildings and allow them to deteriorate. This popu-
> lation, therefore, destabilizes the neighborhood.
>
> (8-year resident, black West Indian)

Black Americans are vehement toward the West Indian population:

> The West Indians move here in groups. They crowd
> into houses and have a destabilizing effect on the neigh-
> borhood. West Indians are very hostile toward others
> around here. They also think nothing of sitting outside
> and drinking on the church steps. The influx of for-
> eigners with a different value structure helps downgrade
> the area.
>
> (35-year resident, black American)

Although the white population belongs primarily to one central, organized religious community, the children's groups, ladies' groups, and so on, stratify the Jewish community.

> The Lubavitchers in Crown Heights do not mingle with
> other Jewish populations in the neighborhood, let alone
> the black people here. The mingling of people in Crown
> Heights is a memory. That's why a lot of white non-
> Lubavitcher are moving out.
>
> (14-year resident, Jewish)

A Lubavitcher rabbi explained the situation as follows:

> There are many sects of Jewish people here. They
> do not communicate. Each group attends its own
> temple and socializes only with those of his kind.
> (20-year resident)

The attitudes of Hasidic residents toward black residents are mixed;
some Hasidic residents recognize two classes of blacks, one as a
community asset, another as a detriment, while others view the
total black population of the area as being a stabilizing force.

> Crown Heights has two classes of blacks. There are
> some good, solid people moving from other ghettos of
> the city, trying to escape from undesirable surround-
> ings. Many of these people purchase homes and are
> committed to the community. There are also, unfor-
> tunately, the welfare element who come in with a lack
> of sense of permanence, feeling that they are tran-
> sients—they care less for other people's lives and
> property.
> (5-year resident, white Lubavitcher)

> Black homeowners (who generally are West Indians)
> beautify the neighborhood. The lower socioeconomic
> class, which resides in pockets of the area, causes
> the tension that exists.
> (15-year resident, white non-Lubavitcher)

> There's no real racial tension here, except perhaps the
> day after a major crime is committed. The black
> people in the community are more receptive to the
> Hasidic movement than were the Jewish population whom
> they replaced.
> (20-year resident, Lubavitcher rabbi)

> Crown Heights is today a model of racial harmony and
> integration. Simon Levine, executive director of the
> Crown Heights Community Corporation, says it is a
> ray of light in the darkness of racial strife. [7]

Despite this array of conflicting quotes, racial tension in
Crown Heights is present and has a destabilizing effect on the neighborhood. Continuous controversies arise concerning the world headquarters of the Lubavitcher Hasidic Sect. A police patrol is sta-
tioned outside the headquarters 24 hours a day, a symbol of the
group's political clout and a source of irritation among black com-

munity leaders. There has also been a long-waging battle over the barricading of an Eastern Parkway service road that runs past the Lubavitcher headquarters. "The corner of Eastern Parkway and Brooklyn Avenue was the scene of a clash Saturday night between 500 Hasidim and 200 police. Three Hasidim were arrested and eight policemen were injured." The clash took place because Dr. Rufus Nichols attempted to drive past the "Saturday barrier" with a patient and threatened to remove the barrier unless an agreement was worked out. Black residents of the community claimed that they were harassed when trying to use their cars on Saturday.

> Police have barricaded the street every Saturday for the last three years at the request of leaders of the Lubavitcher movement, a Hasidic sect whose head- quarters and synagogue are four houses away from Nichols's office, on the service road running parallel to Eastern Parkway. Hasidim spokesmen said the barricade was intended to protect both worshippers and in particular their children who congregate outside the synagogue during Sabbath services.
>   Nichols' wife, Janet, president of the Brooklyn Kingston Eastern Parkway Association, read a release issued by the group saying that "the arbitrary traffic restriction initiated at the synagogue must be relieved at once or we will be forced to take the law into our own hands."[8]

The Lubavitcher Rabbi Krinsky said the barricade was in- tended to protect his worshippers who attended Sabbath services. He claimed that several children had been hit by cars on the block during Sabbath.

Last year, black community members protested the establish- ment of an all-Hasidic, publicly funded day care center on Lefferts Avenue, complete with a kosher kitchen, and the planning board has refused to approve a Hasidic-sponsored drug abuse prevention cen- ter on Eastern Parkway.

But the antagonism between the two groups goes deeper.

> The scars of the Maccabees have never really healed, said one observer, referring to black resentment a decade ago at the formation of what was initially viewed as an antiblack vigilante group. Rabbi Groner, on the other hand, charged that some black community leaders were antisemitic, and Rabbi Lustig, the chairman of the antipoverty agency, said there was a natural competition

between the black oriented office of Neighborhood
Government and his own office. [9]

While there is serious disagreement from black community
leaders about the degree of "rapport," no one will argue with the
general sense of deep commitment each ethnic group has made to
preserving the area. "The determination of the people to maintain
the community is the greatest strength we have. They will scratch,
bite and fight, but they won't switch. We think this is the garden
spot of Brooklyn."[10] As a community leader summarized: "As far
as tension is concerned, 'a powder keg' is being suppressed by the
fact that people are in a superficial state of contentment. People
can't express their dissatisfaction and will eventually explode."

HOUSING

Housing in Crown Heights ranges from single-family dwellings
to high-rise apartments. Aside from a few old-law tenements, converted brownstones, aged frame buildings, and deteriorating four-
and six-story apartment houses north of Eastern Parkway, quality
housing is good. Unlike most transitional neighborhoods in New
York City, Crown Heights housing did not, to a large extent, suffer
from the usual consequences of blockbusting.

> Five years ago, the transition of Crown Heights from
> a practically all-white, Jewish community began.
> Every trick in the blockbusters' bag was tried to
> frighten whites into selling their homes for a song
> and running. They tried vandalism, threatening phone
> calls, the works! One real estate speculator even
> posed as an exresident to try to frighten a woman
> into selling her house.
> The people here, however, had roots in the com-
> munity—it was home to them. So most of them decided
> to stick it out and make the melting pot concept of
> America a reality.[11]

By 1971, New York Secretary of State John Lomenzo ordered
unprecedented controls over real estate operations in Crown Heights
and other communities:

> Through hearings, interviews with civic leaders and
> reports from the New York City Human Rights Com-
> mission Lomenzo had found improper and excessive

solicitation and harassment of homeowners generating fear and panic. . . . This renders impossible the orderly integration and preservation of the stability of the communities and promoted exploitation of minority groups.[12]

Two major public housing projects are north of Eastern Parkway: Kingsborough (1940) and Albany Houses (1950), which together cover about 7.5 blocks and contain 1,899 units. While some neighborhood residents feel that these projects have a somewhat destabilizing effect on the neighborhood—

Albany Houses is a sore spot, a breeding ground for crime, drugs, prostitution. It is the number-one target of the 77th Precinct since it has an increasing drug pocket. It used to be pretty safe in Kingston Park (near Albany Houses). Now, the park is unsafe as winos, methadone addicts, and prostitutes hang out there. While some project residents case parts of the area where two- and three-family homes prevail and burglarize and vandalize a few houses, the neighborhood as a whole is not affected by this—

they are first to realize that the problems within the projects are not dominant throughout the neighborhood:

Public housing always affects the quality of the neighborhood. For example, Albany Houses in this neighborhood has affected the quality of this area. Prior to the construction of Albany Houses, the site on which the project stands housed, at most, 120 families (60 two-family houses). Albany Houses contain 4,000 families in 21-story buildings, with ten apartments on each floor. These 4,000 families are provided with the same sewer, sanitation, education, and recreation facilities as the 120 families they replaced. The services simply do not increase to compensate for increased density of population. But, thank God there isn't enough public housing in Crown Heights to really affect the total neighborhood quality. The burden is on those who provide services in the area near Albany Houses.

A resident of Kingsborough Houses, a federal public-renter project consisting of an array of six-story buildings, explained the situation from a different perspective:

Public housing projects do affect neighborhood quality.
They can seriously upgrade a neighborhood. The
rules and regulations for tenants are strict and the
upkeep of the grounds is better than the structures
they replaced. The Housing Authority can't get so lax
as a slumlord could! It wasn't any better before the
projects were constructed. Private homes that were
falling apart were replaced by projects. One problem
with the projects is that the management has changed
over time, and with this is a negative change as far as
upkeep of the grounds and tenant screening procedures.
The management today simply has a lack of interest.

The Prospect Heights area near Grand Army Plaza, a prime
location for high-rise apartments, is one of the highest-density
areas of Brooklyn. Almost all the existing apartment buildings are
extremely well-kept and tenants generally have higher incomes than
elsewhere in the neighborhood. There is a slight problem in some
of these older buildings with rent-control tenants. Some buildings
in the area house extremely long-term residents. A Prospect
Heights resident explained:

Rents are too high and are extremely unfair. People
who are living here awhile pay absurdly low rents,
while those who moved in recently are paying exorbitant rents. These landlords are looking for money—
taxes are high, fuel costs have risen, and rent revenues
have increased only slightly. So the landlord simply
does not use discretion in screening residents. He pur-
posely takes in a few problem families, especially welfare families, to scare out some of the old timers.
These newcomers subsidize the remaining long-term
residents. Meanwhile, these newcomers are paying
ridiculous rents while services are still being cut!

Many of these buildings are becoming "tilted" with "problem families" and might eventually be abandoned by their landlords.

Many of the area's larger buildings have been allowed
to deteriorate, so that numerous charming blocks of
one- and two-family homes are framed by decaying
apartments, in the houses at their corners. The community has experienced an influx of welfare families
in some of these buildings.

North of the Prospect Heights apartments, the area contains a mixture of one-family homes and multiple-family walk-ups, some needing substantial repairs. In some instances, tenant organizations have been instrumental in securing building improvements. Brownstones and whitestones line the east-west streets; north-south avenues have a mixture of housing types. The conversion of some of the single-family houses and brownstones and whitestones into rooming houses has contributed to the declining quality of some blocks.

As mentioned earlier, the Children's Museum area, in the northeast section of the neighborhood (east of Prospect Heights and north of Eastern Parkway), was the first part of Crown Heights that received a substantial black population (during the 1950s). It was at this time that some of these newcomers were allowed to purchase homes in the area—homes that were being vacated by lower-middle-income whites as they escaped to "suburbia." One real estate agent and resident of Crown Heights for 30 years recalls:

> Post World War II—the Children's Museum area ex-
> perienced an out-movement of whites and an in-move-
> ment of blacks. Many of these blacks who couldn't
> really afford to own homes were becoming owners of
> single-family dwellings. As these people later real-
> ized, they couldn't afford to keep their buildings in
> one-family structure, so they converted these build-
> ings to multiple dwellings, rooming houses. The
> greatest culprits are the banks: those who refuse
> mortgages. Because of the financial institutions,
> people are hard pressed in finding money for renova-
> tion, rehabilitation, and in general upgrading the qual-
> ity of their buildings. In order to hold on to the house,
> an owner has no choice but to convert.

The trend in deterioration continued as the FHA stepped into the area. Although the situation here was not nearly as evident as in East New York and the South Bronx, it took its toll. A real estate agent explained:

> There has been bad housing here at an increasing rate
> with an increase in the number of FHA foreclosures.
> There wasn't much bad housing here 25 years ago and
> the area north of Eastern Parkway was a lot more de-
> sirable. Now there are deteriorated houses, FHA
> foreclosures, overcrowdedness in the existing struc-
> tures, because of tenant displacements—overcrowded

facilities and the high cost of property maintenance
which will result in further property deterioration and
abandonment.

Eastern Parkway, the "supposed" dividing line of the Crown
Heights area, is bordered by a variety of apartments, private homes,
institutions, and commercial enterprises, mostly in good condition.
Almost all of the housing south of this thoroughfare is well-kept.

Washington Avenue, in the western part of the area, overlook-
ing the Botanic Gardens, is one of the finest residential streets in
the community. The Ebbets Field section, immediately east of
Washington Avenue, has a concentration of apartment buildings, including Ebbets Field Apartments, Jackie Robinson Apartments with
1,321 units, and Tivoli Towers with approximately 700 units.

The section east of the Ebbets Field area contains "Doctors'
Row," the outstanding street of single-family dwellings. While the
surrounding streets are less elaborate, the housing is basically
sound, small yards are carefully maintained, and the streets are
clean. The Hasidic movement is a dominant part of this community.
Many of the private homes in this section are owned by the Hasidim,
the remainder are owned by black West Indians who have been in the
community for some 20 years. The property values in this part of
the community have changed drastically over the last five years.
One real estate agent asserted: "Prices of houses south of Eastern
Parkway and west of Utica Avenue are skyrocketing comparable to
houses throughout the state. The Hasidic are trying to buy back into
the area and their keen competition for houses here has contributed
to this." There are a few "trouble apartment houses" in this part
of the area, but some Hasidic residents have plans for the area:
"When we see a trouble building, we just buy the building." Unfortunately, along with the purchase of the buildings, the Hasidim will
displace the tenants and replace them with Hasidic tenants. This
will result in further deterioration and overcrowdedness in Brownsville and the northernmost part of Crown Heights.

The Lincoln Terrace Park section, immediately east of Utica
Avenue just below Eastern Parkway, has sound housing with some
deterioration. As one approaches Brownsville's border (which is
either defined as Rochester or Buffalo Avenue), the deterioration
becomes more evident.

The Wingate section, below Empire Boulevard in the south-
western part of the neighborhood, contains well-kept older single-
family homes. Previously an Italian enclave, this part of the neighborhood has changed most recently into a black middle-income home-
owning community. Black West Indians, some of whom previously
lived and owned houses above Empire Boulevard, own many of these

homes; native blacks own the remainder. There is virtually no deterioration in this part of the neighborhood.

The Crown Heights neighborhood is an area of great contrast
with some decaying and many well-preserved buildings existing side
by side. Although some of the apartments and houses aren't what
they used to be, the neighborhood as a whole still retains some of
its former elegance.

NEIGHBORHOOD

> Proof of the desirability of Crown Heights as a place
> to live in can be seen in the fact that there is a wait-
> ing list of 165 white families seeking apartments here
> and 43 more looking for houses.[13]

The proliferation of long-term residents of Crown Heights substanti-
ates this "positive feeling" toward the neighborhood.

Although most residents of Crown Heights feel that their neighborhood is a good place to live in, many point out declining features.
Many residents are appalled at the condition of some apartment
houses. One resident explained:

> There isn't much bad housing here, but the little we
> have is horrendous because of landlord neglect. These
> people are slum landlords in the true sense of the word.
> Upkeep is nil as landlords milk the houses. They have
> welfare tenants so they get top dollar; they have politi-
> cal clout, so they get away with violations.

A real estate broker explained this problem from a different
perspective: "Rent control has resulted in the abandonment of many
apartment buildings. Rents are inadequate to maintain buildings
properly and to give adequate services." The trend in abandonment
has been explained from yet another perspective: "Many people are
buying apartment houses here with unusually low down payments
and are charging exorbitant rents, giving no services whatsoever.
As houses become dilapidated, landlords eventually abandon them.
Many are eventually burned to the ground." Residents of these
apartment buildings suffer from lack of heat and hot water, roaches,
rats, holes in the walls and ceilings, and broken pipes. Tenants'
associations have been formed to bring some pressure to bear on
the landlords, but so far they haven't been too successful.

Residents consider the transportation facilities a neighborhood
asset. As one resident stated: "Access to employment or number

of hours spent traveling makes this neighborhood a very desirable one. While we are adjacent to Manhattan, and are just a few minutes away by train, we are not faced with the congestion of the city."

Crown Heights has always maintained an abundance of recreational facilities. The Brooklyn Museum, main branch of the Brooklyn Public Library, Botanic Gardens, and Prospect Park have served Brooklyn for many years. Recently, the addition of MUSE, an Afro-American oriented museum, and the reconstruction of the Children's Museum have provided additional facilities for the Crown Heights community. The only recreational facility missing in Crown Heights is the local movie theater. Approximately seven movie theaters have been closed down since the 1940s; many have since been converted into churches. One movie theater remains; its pornographic style, however, is not widely accepted among community residents. Movie theaters in neighboring Bedford Stuyvesant are attended by many Crown Heights residents.

> Motion pictures shown in Bedford Stuyvesant are almost always black movies, with distorted concepts and opinions. Notice how these black pictures come straight to Fulton Street. Children identify with Superfly, Shaft. Children are exploited and end up in jail. They learn, from these movies, to oppose, rather than to utilize, the law.

Crown Heights has always had an abundance of health facilities. Many established doctors live in Park Slope, near Grand Army Plaza, and along Eastern Parkway. Eight private hospitals and several nursing homes serve the neighborhood, including Lefferts General, Brooklyn Jewish, Kingsbrook, St. Marys, and Kings County. Brooklyn State Hospital, Downstate Medical Center, and Kings County Hospital form a large complex on the southern border of the neighborhood. When one observes the trends in health statistics for the Crown Heights area, compared to statistics of other minority neighborhoods in New York City, the availability of medical care becomes evident. Although some residents' complaints centered on the lack of drugstores in the community, most were in agreement that medical care was not, at present, a serious problem in Crown Heights. "There is no lack of good medical care here. We have many hospitals in this area and many good doctors. Unfortunately there are some people here who cannot afford to attend the offices of private physicians. But Kings County, a city hospital, is nearby."

Crime and, similarly, juvenile delinquency are not of serious concern to most residents of the area. While crime has been on the upsurge throughout the city, most residents feel that Crown Heights has not been hit particularly hard. The few residents who were in fear of crime were residents of the Prospect Heights and Children's Museum area. One resident remarked:

> Crime here is a serious problem, particularly mugging. When I come home from work and I have to walk one block from Atlantic Avenue to Pacific Street I am scared that someone with a knife will approach me. Crime here has changed significantly over the years. Muggings were not prevalent 10 or 20 years ago, as they are now.

It appears that existence of two projects in the area doesn't have any considerable effect on crime.

While the Crown Heights area does not have many fires, the area north of Eastern Parkway has more fires than its southern counterpart; the same holds true for vacant buildings. The infrequency of fires might be due, in large part, to the fact that the neighborhood is primarily a home-owning neighborhood, with a smattering of decaying apartment houses. One resident remembered: "There aren't many fires here now. But there were fires frequently around Rochester Avenue and Dean Street, where there was a string of abandoned houses."

Some residents of the neighborhood are disgusted with the services provided by the Department of Sanitation. They claim that garbage collectors harass them and, at the same time, avoid doing their jobs. One resident explained: "Some areas of the neighborhood have old sofas and mattresses lying around—in between infrequent garbage pick-ups. Things are so bad with the Sanitation Department that landlords have to hope that these items are picked up by people who need furniture." Another resident adds:

> If there are four garbage cans in front of my house, the garbage collectors will pick up one, if it is on the curb. If it is a few feet inward, he won't walk to pick it up. If some garbage spills out in the alleyways, it remains there. Dirty alleys, as a result, are a common thing around here.

In addition to this, there seems to be a problem with stray dogs.

> One problem here is the number of stray dogs that reproduce at a rapid rate. This place is like a Hitchcockian nightmare. Many dogs attack people on Crown Street. Every morning there's one under my car. The Sanitation Department and Police Department could do something to curtail this.

Shopping areas in Crown Heights are adequate. Major commercial streets include Utica Avenue, Flatbush Avenue, and Nostrand Avenue, but stores are scattered throughout the area, especially on north-south streets. The deterioration of some stores on Flatbush Avenue near the northwestern border of the area has worried residents and businesses.

The Hasidic Jewish population does its shopping both inside and outside the immediate area. Kingston Avenue and Utica Avenue have an abundance of kosher food facilities that serve this population. Most of these residents, however, leave the community to shop for clothing, furniture, and appliances.

The black West Indian population has a shopping convenience, since Nostrand Avenue has many Jamaican and West Indian groceries. Once again, these residents do the majority of their other shopping outside the community.

The native blacks, in general, do not feel that the existing supermarkets are adequate. One resident said: "We have poor-quality food here. Potato chips, cookies, crackers are often stale, cans are often swollen, meat and vegetables not fresh. I don't complain to the Board of Health. I have a car and thank God I can shop elsewhere."

Those who can afford the time and transportation to leave the community to shop generally do so. Among the most common shopping areas is the downtown shopping area, near Fulton Street. Some residents of Crown Heights do their shopping in the community because they feel that this adds to the neighborhood's stability, since many stores are owned by area residents. One resident stated: "One of the reasons Crown Heights is so stable is because of its self-containment due to the large number of resident-owned businesses. The money in the area circulates within the community as opposed to leaving the community."

The decline in the Crown Heights shopping district becomes obvious when one compares the 198 apparel stores that served the neighborhood in 1958 to the subsequent closing of almost half these stores. [14]

While most residents agree that the schools in Crown Heights have adequate facilities for neighborhood children, the bussing in of many children from outside the community overtaxes the schools and, as a result, causes many schools to function on split sessions. "School facilities are busting at the seams. They are extremely overcrowded. Many schools are on double session. Crown Heights public schools house a large segment of children from outside the community." Many residents have negative feelings concerning the schools: "Schools here are not good. Teachers can't teach. Their primary concern is their paycheck and how little they can work in order to get it."

The church in Crown Heights, as in most black communities, is the most important institution in the community. Aside from religion, the church serves the purpose of a meeting ground, a recreational and cultural facility, and a central organization for community efforts. Many families are active in the church so that they can send their children to parochial schools.

While the synagogue serves a similar purpose for the Hasidic residents, the emphasis on religion is much stronger. The Hasidic community is considerably more active in community affairs.

> Jews control much and are active members of the school board and restoration in Crown Heights. The white Jewish residents who have been purchasing property and doing rehabs, charging rents and causing many to relocate, are controlling the neighborhood. Poverty programs are under total control of the Hasidic community leaders. The School Board election is a perfect case in point. The majority of children in schools are black, the majority of residents voting at School Board elections are white Hasidic Jews.

Residents of Crown Heights are active in civic affairs. Among the most popular and effective organizations are the Crown Heights Board of Community Affairs, the Crown Heights Office of Neighborhood Government, the Crown Heights Management and Maintenance Organization, and the 77th Precinct Council. There are many block and tenant associations in the neighborhood that are somewhat active in combating problems. In short, the community looks upon social and political clubs and organizations as the organized, unified force in the community, that which brings the masses together to fight for community betterment.

SAMPLE INTERVIEW NO. 1

1. Yes, there were more white people in this neighborhood 10, 20 years ago, but no real difference in neighborhood desirability. I lived in three other locations, on the other side of Eastern Parkway and on this side of Eastern Parkway. There is no difference in this area between now and 20 years ago. Blacks who move in are just as harmless as those whites who left. The muggers are from

Interviewee was Lubavitcher Rabbi Spritzer.

other neighborhoods. When the Lubavitchers moved into this area in the 1940s, they encountered much resistance from other Jews.

2. This neighborhood changed from white to black. As a result, the sanitation department slackened off. Population changes haven't really affected the area. For the past 25 years, this neighborhood has remained stable. The crime problem is not too bad. There is accessibility to good transportation, and solid housing stock. There has recently been a slight rise in crime, and a lack of city services.

3. This is the place where I will live and stay, not a place I am at because of no alternative. I am looking to purchase a house in this neighborhood. If we move out, there will be another Brownsville coming right up because the black middle class will follow us out! There is neighborhood solidarity—one-family houses at auction are bid up to $40,000.

4. I would not like to move out of this neighborhood. I like it here.

5. My mother, brother, and sister live here. My parents came to this country from Germany when I was two years old. I helped bring friends and relatives to this country.

6. The Hasidic Jews from different dynasties (Lubavitcher, Ger, Belz) have nothing in common except for the fact that they are Jews. This neighborhood also has conservative Jews, black Americans (welfare to wealthy), and West Indians. The private homes are owned by middle- and upper-class people. Apartment houses are mixed. We hope to buy up all the surrounding properties, which are having problems, within one year.

7. I have never lived in any other neighborhood.

8. Property values were higher six or seven years ago, they leveled off, and they appear to be getting higher now. There has been a large demand for houses in the past few years.

9. There are some tensions and muggings from time to time. However, there has been no real tension in the last three or four years.

10. There are no projects in this area except for Ebbets Field. Any house that has more than 15 families requires more work. Keeping sanitary conditions and the neighborhood in good condition is difficult. When there is an absentee landlord, the house is not properly maintained and it deteriorates quickly. The absentee landlords would welcome welfare tenants because they can get higher rents and give less services. In addition, with a building of this size, a landlord cannot be selective in who he chooses as tenants.

11. The neighborhood was good and still is. Public housing can be good only if the management lives on the premises and if community organizations are active in the projects.

12. Our shopping is done as follows:
  Groceries—in the neighborhood
  Clothing—in the neighborhood
  Appliances and furniture—outside of this neighborhood
  Parks and playgrounds—we don't use them, we use the
     Jewish Center
  Banking—in the neighborhood
  Movies—outside the neighborhood
  Doctors or clinics—inside or out of the neighborhood

13. Lack of medical care is not a problem. We are surrounded with hospitals and clinics.

14. In case of sudden illness, I would go to Brooklyn Jewish Hospital or Brookdale Hospital. They have excellent facilities.

15. There is practically no recreation for adults, but we really do not require any.

16. There is no lack of recreation for teenagers.

17. For Jewish children, there is a great lack of recreation.

18. My child is only ten months old. He amuses himself.

19. The streets and sidewalks are in bad condition. We just had new telephone booths put on Kingston Avenue. The streets need repairs. We have limited problems with abandoned cars.

20. Parking regulations are strictly enforced, but the streets are not cleaned. When the street cleaners do appear, they merely spread the dirt and leave more garbage on the streets than they pick up.

21. The Sanitation Department picks up garbage but that is not its only responsibility. Kingston Avenue is literally filthy!

22. Day care facilities here are inadequate. There are two centers in the entire area with Jewish culture that are not sufficient for this community.

23. Train stations are safe and clean, transportation is adequate.

24. Streets are safe for crossing. The Yeshivas have their own guards since the mayor cut the budget and the city crossing guards were removed.

25. Most of our children go to religious schools, therefore, the existing public schools are filled with neighborhood children and many from outside the community who are bussed in.

26. Some public schools are opened during evenings and summer.

27. There are many libraries in this area. We also have the Brooklyn Museum, Botanic Gardens, Prospect Park, a magnificent zoo, picnic grounds, and a lake for rowing. We also have an ice skating rink. In the summertime, there are musicals, symphonies, and plays in the theater area.

28. The neighborhood groceries are adequate. We have Waldbaums, A & P, and a number of small Jewish groceries. There are also some small groceries that do not have the best quality of food.

29. There are no movie theaters in this neighborhood.

30. There are many churches and quite a number of storefront churches in the Bedford Stuyvesant area. South of Eastern Parkway, there are many synagogues. North of Eastern Parkway, there are some storefront churches.

31. Police protection is about the same as it was in the past few years. Sanitation services have decreased. The libraries are adequate.

32. Public services are good. They are maintained properly. The garbage is picked up fairly regularly. The street lights are adequate. Sidewalks and curbs are not cleaned properly but the condition is livable.

33. Storekeepers do not overcharge. The Jews are pretty good shoppers, they know how to stretch the dollar. Their customers are well treated since most storekeepers live in the neighborhood.

34. The police protection could be better. Instead of giving parking tickets, they should be in civilian clothes as decoys to catch muggers and purse snatchers. We are not harassed by police.

35. There are no courts in this neighborhood.

36. The Jewish schools are good. I don't know about the others.

37. Welfare workers do not visit.

38. Crime is not a serious problem. It is no worse than it has been for 10 or 15 years.

39. There are very few fires here. Most homes are privately owned and well maintained.

40. We have no drug hangouts here.

41. This neighborhood is not noisy.

42. We have no gang problems here.

43. There are places for children to play. Most children who go to religious schools do not come home until 5:00 P.M.

44. We have no cluttered high-rise buildings in this area. However, I do think that they are a key factor in ruining a neighborhood and the beginning of urban decay.

45. Some stores have burglary gates, but most of the stores and restaurants have the close-down gates. There are a few stores with no gates.

46. I have lived in this neighborhood for 25 years and have moved four times.

47. We have very little bad housing in this area. Some smaller apartment houses are being neglected but they are still habitable.

48. I rent this apartment for $175 per month.

49. My brother-in-law owns this house.

50. Mortgage money is available from Chase Manhattan Bank and there are some loans available for home improvements.

51. I don't think my rent is too high for this area and in comparison with other neighborhoods.

52. The welfare tenants automatically pay higher rents.

53. I have 5.5 rooms.

54. My bathroom does have a window.

55. This building has no elevator.

56. This apartment is not rent controlled.

57. We have no mice, rats, roaches, no broken walls, windows, and so on.

58. In the apartment houses, most landlords live elsewhere.

60. There are a few tenants' associations trying to improve the neighborhood.

61. The neighborhood politicians are making some effort to improve the area. Someday they might succeed.

62. I belong to the Planning Board, Jewish Community, Board of Directors for Jewish Survival, Block Association Consultant, United Block Associations, Housing Groups-Housing and Development Administration.

63. Each type of organization helps in another way to improve the neighborhood.

64. We have asked for no help from any of our local politicians, except for a signature needed for the local planning board.

65. We don't count on the politicians for help.

SAMPLE INTERVIEW NO. 2

1. This neighborhood has changed and is deteriorating in every way. The people changed, the stores changed, and the buildings changed. People live here because they have no choice. Ten years ago, this area was more desirable. Within the last five years, the neighborhood has turned around.

2. The transportation is adequate. The rehabs and two- and three-family brownstones are in excellent condition, although the

Interviewees were Gwenn Harman, Mrs. Lee, and Ed Parker from the Crown Heights North Multi-Service Center.

multiple dwellings are torn down. The people's emphasis is on obtaining instead of maintaining. The Jews control much and are active members of the school board. There has been a move to replace blacks in this area. There are some pockets of poverty in Crown Heights. We have many community resources, many more than Brownsville or East New York. The restoration is controlled by the whites. They are purchasing properties, renovating, and charging higher rents that would be cause for relocation. The city and state have discretion in subsidy policy decisions. Poverty programs are under total control and can be cut, resulting in rapid out-movement.

This area is overcrowded with many illegal aliens, which shows at election time. Services are being deleted such as police, sanitation, schools, housing, and so on. The community is in dire need and those are the ones with severe cutbacks.

Crime is not reported properly. The Police Department is reluctant, the Sanitation Department is negligent. Hospital services are inadequate. Emergency rooms are terrible.

The teachers are incompetent, they don't even teach the basics. Students are not properly prepared. The motion pictures shown in these areas have distorted concepts and opinions. Black pictures come straight to Fulton Street. There is a false image—children identify with Superfly and Shaft. Children are exploited and usually end up in jail. Opposing, rather than utilizing, the law comes in large part from identification with black movies.

Illegal search and seizure had been going on in the ghettoes for years. Legal Aid doesn't see the client until a few minutes before the criminal approaches the judge. The law is different for the rich white than it is for the poor black.

3. This is my real home. There is no other place for me to go. People move because they are unhappy with the conditions, they move where they think things are better. There is a large turnover in registration of students.

People are demanding and aggressive. Almost all of the illegal aliens are pregnant. $5,000 must be put up by a sponsor (the legal minimum). The movement here is from one rathole to another. Environment creates nomadic attitude. Newcomers create an air of despair and this affects the longer-term residents. Transient population with uncaring attitudes causes people to want to move. Ten to 12 years ago, this area was better than Flatbush. The large apartment houses have dropped living rooms and spacious closets.

4. I would not move from this area. It is worth fighting for!

5. I have many relatives and close friends in this area. This is the case of the Caribbeans and Haitians because they don't feel like a part of the community unless they have a group to represent them.

6. The people in this area have an "I don't care attitude," which comes from despair. They have lost their sense of values—parents are not active in the PTA. Values are put in materialistic perspective. People live from day to day and accept the things as they are, not making an active move to change them.

7. The influx of foreigners with different value structures helps to downgrade the neighborhood. People are interested only in self-betterment, as opposed to community betterment.

People in this community are in an economic bind. The wages are low, and they are being exploited for services, consumable goods, and so on. They need extensive education in all areas. The system is geared to exploit the poor man and protect the wealthy.

8. Apartments are leased, in two-family houses, for parties, gambling, and many other illicit purposes. They house as many as six families in 11 rooms. Landlords buy houses to make some money and live elsewhere. Haitians sit on the steps in nightgowns and drink beer; 11 people live in three rooms. Store owners don't even have to sweep their store fronts or use garbage cans. Tenants are being exploited. Property values and rents are ridiculous.

9. There is tension. "A powder keg" is being suppressed by the fact that people are in a superficial state of contentment. What is in store is a continuation of the 1960s, but worse. People cannot express their dissatisfaction and will eventually explode. They have not yet reached the breaking point. This is not necessarily pertaining to this neighborhood, but a general attitude.

10. There is not enough public housing to affect the quality of this neighborhood. The crime element in the project affects the neighborhood. People from projects have come to parts of this area where the two- and three-family houses prevail and burglarize and vandalize them.

11. It used to be pretty safe in Kingston Park (near the Albany Houses), but now we have winos and methadone addicts. There is a lot of drugs and prostitution. The project is a sorespot for crime, drugs, and prostitution. Albany Houses is a no. 1 target of the 77th Precinct.

12. We shop in and out of the neighborhood:
   Groceries—in because of the lack of carfare to go else-
      where
   Appliances and furniture—outside the neighborhood
   Parks and playgrounds—outside the area
   Doctor—in the neighborhood
   Banking—in the area
   Movies—outside the area; there are no theaters in this
      vicinity

13. Yes, definitely, medical care is a problem. But it has not always been this way. Doctors used to make house calls when they were safe to make.

14. In case of sudden illness or accident, I expect to "croak." I dread getting ill or having an accident because of the long delay in services. We are harassed, abused, and frustrated. Services are performed predominately by Caribbeans at St. Johns, Brooklyn Jewish, and St. Mary's Hospitals. We are constantly aggravated by their attitudes.

15. There is a tremendous lack of facilities for adult recreation.

16. There is a lack of recreational facilities for teenagers, but this poses no serious problem.

17. There is also a lack of recreational facilities for children in this area.

18. My children use the streets for recreation; Prospect Park in the summer. Crime makes it unsafe for children to go off their own block.

19. Streets and sidewalks are in bad condition. It was not always this way.

20. Parking violations are not too noticeable since parking regulations are not enforced, especially near schools. Alternate-side parking should be enforced for streets to be cleaned, but people are not acknowledging regulations and are not receiving summonses for disobeying the regulations.

21. Hell, no! Garbage pickup is deplorable.

22. Although they are increasing the number of facilities, the day care facilities are still inadequate.

23. Public transportation is adequate, although the train stations are dirty and unsafe.

24. It is not safe for children to cross the streets going to school. There are no crossing guards.

25. The schools are not equipped to handle the influx of new students. Educational facilities did not increase with the increase in school-age population.

26. The public schools in this area are not opened during evening hours nor do they provide any summer programs for the children.

27. There is a public library in this vicinity and it has adequate facilities.

28. The neighborhood groceries have very poor quality of merchandise: rusty cans, swollen cans, rotten meat, rotten vegetables, and so on. Complaints are made but go unheard.

29. There is only one movie theater left in this area, which shows only porno flicks. Seven movie houses were closed down, some have been converted to churches.

30. Churches—oh yes indeed! If churches had as much impact as synagogues, this would be some neighborhood!

31. Yes, all municipal services have decreased considerably.

32. The general quality of public facilities and services in the immediate vicinity is poor. There is broken and defective equipment, litter scattered on the streets, inadequate street lighting, and so on.

33. Definitely, yes! Storekeepers are not generally from this area. The stores have high prices and low-quality merchandise.

34. There is inadequate police protection. Police are <u>now</u> reluctant about harassing people.

35. There are no courts in this neighborhood.

36. The schools are certainly inadequate. This is a Title 1 area; schools are in a target area. Teachers might teach themselves out of a job.

37. No welfare workers ever visit this area.

38. Crime is a very serious problem. Pocketbooks are snatched, apartments burglarized, children robbed while going to the store, and so on. Crime has gotten a lot worse since the 1950s. People used to leave their keys in the doors or their doors opened. Not any more!

39. There are more fires in the area than there used to be. There is an overload of current, poor wiring, neglect, and so on.

40. This has been a hangout for drug users and addicts, and this has always been true in pocket areas. The pocket has increased tremendously over the years. Drugs dropped in the area as a form of exploitation. Every ghetto area has been affected by drug users and addicts.

41. This neighborhood is noisy—day, night, all the time! Calypsos make a lot of noise. People, as well as music, contribute to the extreme noise in the neighborhood.

42. Gang problems—40 thieves! There are Caribbean gangs, Mohawks, Outlaws, and a few others that are used as a point of identification or association with people.

43. There is a definite lack of places for children to play in this area. It is positively not a good place in which to raise children.

44. Tenants are now trying to prevent crime in large apartment buildings.

45. Not only the stores in this area have burglary gates, but most apartments have some sort of protection on their windows.

46. I have lived in this neighborhood 21 years; 15 years; 1 in transit.

47. Bad housing is a very serious problem; not so much the outside of the buildings, but the insides are dilapidated. The housing in this area was good in the 1950s.

48. I rent this apartment and pay $270 per month for rent.

49. Families usually receive three-year leases in rent stabilized and subsidized housing, but multiple-dwelling landlords tend to give short-term leases to secure transiency.

50. Banks in this area give mortgages to the residents.

51. My rent would be considered fair market for this apartment.

52. Yes, tenants on welfare are a much better source for profit and exploitation.

53. I have six rooms.

54. There are no windows in my bathroom, only air vents.

55. This building has an elevator, but it works very poorly in my section. Sometimes all the elevators do not work. Tivoli Towers has a nice lobby, large bathrooms, but the hallways are not safe, the elevators are unsafe.

56. This apartment is not rent controlled.

57. Thank goodness, my house is free of problems. We have sufficient heat, hot water, no roaches or rats, and no holes in the walls or ceilings.

58. Although most landlords live on the premises, their interests are only monetary. There are no locks on the doors and no extra services.

59. The laundry room is a problem. In most apartment houses, there are no laundry rooms. Many laundry rooms had to be shut down because of crime problems.

60. There are many tenant associations and they are effective as long as they hold that interest in affecting change.

61. Yes, and I belong to some clubs.

62. There are many neighborhood improvement groups such as Crown Heights Board of Community Affairs, Better Block Association, 77th Precinct Community Council, Price Advisory Commission, 1200 Dean St. Block Association.

63. Clubs help through community interests. They work with the offices of neighborhood government, give advice and counseling in an advisory capacity. They also give assistance in problem solving.

64. People in this community are not politically oriented. There is a definite lack of knowledge on the part of the residents as to political services available to members of the community. The political situation is tense; politicians fight among each other.

65. There is a lack of communication between elected politicians and community people. People have lost faith in the politicians. Many residents of the area are apathetic. The Hasidic Jews show up at election time and are active school board members. More emphasis should be placed on education so that people recognize their voting power.

NOTES

1. "Crown Heights Ethnic Smorgasbord," New York Times, August 1, 1974.

2. Ibid.

3. Ibid.

4. "Crown Heights—An Example of Racial Harmony," Sunday News, June 14, 1970.

5. "Racial Troubles in Crown Heights," Newsday, September 30, 1975.

6. ". . . Ethnic Smorgasbord," op. cit.

7. ". . . Racial Harmony," op. cit.

8. "Hasidim and Police Clash in Crown Heights," New York Post, June 5, 1973.

9. ". . . Ethnic Smorgasbord," op. cit.

10. Ibid.

11. ". . . Racial Harmony," op. cit.

12. "Blockbusting in Crown Heights," New York Times, June 16, 1972.

13. ". . . Racial Harmony," op. cit.

14. New York Mirror, New York News, New York Times, General Outdoor, unpublished circular, New York Market Analysis (New York: N.P.C., 1961).

9
EAST NEW YORK

THE TRANSFORMATION OF THE
EAST NEW YORK COMMUNITY

East New York's boundaries are Atlantic, Van Sinderen, and
Fountain Avenues and Louisiana Avenue and Linden Boulevard.
Transformed in a short span of years from a middle-class Jewish
community into a neighborhood with a large number of abandoned
buildings, deterioration, and severe racial problems, it now needs
major public investment to be reestablished as a viable residential
community.

Until the 1950s, East New York was a stable, flourishing
middle-income neighborhood. The area grew up at the end of the
nineteenth century and the beginning of the twentieth century. By
1940 almost the entire northern half of East New York, above New
Lots Avenue, had been occupied by Jewish, German, Russian,
Polish, Italian, and Lithuanian immigrants and their descendants
who moved in from Brownsville, Bushwick, and other crowded
localities.

After World War II, new homes were built south of New Lots
Avenue and along the eastern part of the area. A few long-term
residents began leaving the oldest tenement buildings west of Pennsylvania Avenue, but the influx of blacks and Puerto Ricans remained
slight until the late 1950s.

Within ten years (from 1956 to 1966) East New York became
one of the city's worst slum areas. Adjacent Brownsville had already been transformed into a crowded slum. When many of
Brownsville's residents were displaced by public housing projects,
thousands of them were forced into East New York. By 1966 the
area west of Pennsylvania Avenue was predominantly black and

186

Puerto Rican. Between 1960 and 1966 the population west of Pennsylvania Avenue shifted, from an estimated 85 percent white to 80 percent black and Puerto Rican. As Jewish families moved, residential buildings, community centers, synagogues, and stores were left abandoned.

Italian-Americans and other groups of European descent also left, but more slowly and reluctantly. As blacks and Puerto Ricans moved eastward into solidly European-American sections, racial tensions mounted. By 1966 the area was smoldering. The move to East New York brought no benefits to the minorities. They found themselves in a spreading slum. Change had occurred too fast for the community to absorb it. Competition for crowded housing, lack of jobs, inadequate recreation facilities, and youth gangs defending "turfs" inflamed racial tensions. The community exploded in riots.

In the aftermath of the riots, some sections resembled ghost towns. Accumulated debris lay untouched. Disabled cars and shattered glass blanketed the streets. There were dozens of vacated, burned out, and destroyed homes and stores, their doors ajar, their windows smashed. Families moved into the area and out again. The rates of juvenile delinquency, crime, and fire soared.

The situation in East New York has, since the 1960s, been one of transition and instability. Judging from statistics showing medical pathologies and welfare caseloads in the area, the current situation indicates further deterioration. In East New York the rate of juvenile delinquency has risen rapidly during the past 25 years. Juvenile delinquency rates for health areas in East New York averaged 10.0 per 1,000 youths in 1950, 40.0 per 1,000 in 1960, and 150.0 per 1,000 in 1970. Crime rates have soared as East New York ranked 30 (from a possible 150) in felonies in 1960, accounting for 1.39 percent of the city total, and jumped to a rank of 6 by 1970, accounting for 2.54 percent, almost double the percent of the city total.

The trends in fire statistics substantiate the problem of vacant houses evident in the area. As of August 1974 there were 959 abandoned structures in the area; this number has since increased significantly. In such areas as East New York, the malignancies feed on themselves.

Early in the analysis of East New York's conditions and needs, the community presented its view that East New York was a step-community, lacking in desired services and facilities. Existing facilities were either poorly equipped, difficult to gain access to, understaffed, or staffed with hostile and indifferent people. One community resident stated: "The Welfare Department no longer visits the homes of its clients, welfare workers do their harassing in the satellite office." Those new facilities that were built neglected essential services and equipment (new schools without gymnasiums or equipment for hot meals, for example). "What do they expect us to do?" asked one community leader, "play in these filthy rat traps they won't tear down?" Another leader complains: "Portable classrooms, portable welfare centers, portable libraries, portable pools. Everything in East New York is portable. When are we going to get some real attention?"

A good deal of the community's ire is directed against the way services are now provided, particularly police and sanitation services. As the needs and the dependent population have increased, the services have deteriorated. The community is bitter over the neglect; its morale has suffered deep blows because of it.

If there is an obvious lack of communication between the community and the Department of Sanitation, the breach is, if anything, wider between the community and the police. While the Sanitation Department is accused of lying down on the job, the police are accused, in addition, of harassment. One long-term resident claims:

> Twenty years ago, when I first moved here, the neighborhood was predominantly Jewish and there was police protection to speak of. Now that the population composition of the neighborhood has shifted—it is now a black and Puerto Rican ghetto—the only time you see a policeman is when another policeman is in trouble! Sometimes policemen protect storekeepers and teachers, but they don't give a damn about the residents.

When irate community residents called the Sanitation Department about overflowing garbage cans in front of absentee landlords' houses, the matter was referred to the police, who promptly ticketed cars parked in violation of alternate-side regulations, and nothing was done about the offending landlords. One resident complained that

> because of the buildings owned by absentee slumlords, and FHA, there accumulates filth which breeds rats. There is a lot of rat poisoning on these blocks. This is not taken care of—as many people get bit and poisoned— some die! Nobody lives in many of these houses but the rats. If garbage was ever collected properly here, the rats wouldn't have an incentive to congregate.

When a citizen complains about poor police work, he is likely to be harassed by visits from other officers.

Both police and sanitation staffs are mostly white and appear to be as prejudiced against blacks and Puerto Ricans as are the landlords and storekeepers. They look for failure and see it in the filthy streets and the high crime rates and rationalize that there is no need or reason to extend themselves on behalf of this population. This dulled desire to protect the area leads to greater community dissatisfaction with the police and to poorer police work. When policemen are seen drinking beer in their patrol cars by citizens who have tried in vain to get police to respond quickly enough to stop vandals the week before, bitterness and cynicism are likely reactions.

Complaints of inadequate protection are heard throughout the community; fear for the safety of persons and property is great. Industry hires guards to protect premises and worries about employees getting safely to and from work. Many companies have security parking lots for their employees. Some landlords live in fear of vacancies since they are almost certain to attract the vandals who rip out the plumbing and fixtures and terrorize the tenants. Parents worry about their daughters walking in the streets or in the schoolyards in broad daylight; stories of muggings and rapes are common.

Neglect of Linton Park is a complaint of the residents. In this park there are stanchions for swings, the grass has been stamped down, and there is no outline for a playing field.

I have learned from data regarding School District 19 that the mean transiency rate for the area is 81 percent. Human Resources Administration estimates that there is a population turnover rate of 18 percent each year. "The ministers of several churches in the area have indicated that they have been unable to organize effectively because no one stayed around long enough to become a leader." The entire population in this area is in a constant state of flux.

There are no publicly sponsored day care centers within the East New York core area. There are some centers in surrounding areas: the Sylvia Klein center more than 20 blocks away from Pennsylvania Avenue, the Louis Heaton Pink Center more than 20 blocks away, the Community Day Nursery in Van Dyke Houses in Brownsville. This information documents the community's belief that East New Yorkers either have no facilities or that their needs are considered with Brownsville's (now changed to Community Services Administration) Headstart classes. There are no Headstart programs in East New York.

Community people, youth, patrolmen of the 75th Precinct, youth board workers, and recreation workers in the few existing facilities all call attention to the lack of recreation facilities in East New York, particularly for teenagers. There is a scarcity of parks and playground spaces in large parts of the community. Although there are adequate park and playground facilities in nearby Cypress Hills and Highland Park, black and Puerto Rican children are discouraged from using these facilities.

East New York, a region of misery, is made up largely of old frame and brick one- and two-family dwellings, either attached or with tiny yards, and three- and four-story red brick and dirty yellow brick buildings. Many of the old houses, built 50 or 60 years ago, barely qualify as homes. There are also several hundred empty, mostly two-family houses foreclosed by the FHA in the past few years. Their tinned-up doors and windows and rickety porches are a depressing legacy of lost hopes. This ironic impetus to the abandonment problem came about, according to local critics, because the FHA's effort to help low-income families purchase houses was flawed by incomplete investigation of rundown properties and consequent inflated appraisals and mortgages.

The low landscape is marked by lots, even blocks, filled with ragged piles of old bricks and timbers and half-demolished structures. The vacant houses in East New York are now burned-out, vandalized, shattered, filled with old shoes, smashed furniture, forgotten dogs, and a sour effluvium of neglect and despair. Professional "strippers" often brazenly drive up in trucks in broad daylight and remove the copper, brass, and lead plumbing, the sink, and the radiators for sale to scrap-metal dealers. Windows and doors are sealed with tin or cinderblocks or left open and broken. Scores of buildings have had the tin coverings or the metal gates, which uselessly guarded empty stores, ripped away and the interiors ransacked, gutted, and heaped with rank debris.

The sidewalks and streets are littered with garbage, wind-whipped newspapers, and rotting mattresses. Broken glass is always being crunched underfoot.

Behind many of the shabby doors in the decayed inhabited houses, ovens burn day and night with their doors open in a desperate attempt, whatever the cost, to warm unheated overcrowded apartments. Families endure without heat or hot water, occasionally without water.

"There's no vest pocket badness" says the director of East New York Housing Services, an agency of the antipoverty East New York Community Corporation. "It's just all bad. East New York is not a sound community. There's too much turnover. It's a constant struggle for survival, that's what it's become."

In a neighborhood described by residents as desirable as late as 1960, whites panicked at the influx of poor minorities and homeowners feared their property values would collapse. Blockbusting, with its tragic catalog of onerous second mortgages and rapid foreclosures, was rampant in the early 1960s, accelerating the neighborhood's change. Black and Puerto Rican homebuyers, anxious to escape their surroundings, became victims once again of what a consultant to the City Commission on Human Rights called a "debtors' treadmill." The population in the area changed to more than 80 percent black and Puerto Rican; the remnant was made up mostly of elderly whites, either unwilling or unable to move.

The vicious, dreary cycle of expectation and fact commenced as welfare tenants arrived in greater numbers and landlords, in general, fearfully certain that their properties would be wrecked, collected all the rents they could and let the buildings run down. There were victims and villains on both sides. The tenants' attitudes became: the landlord doesn't give a damn; I don't give a damn. Mutual self-destruction prevailed. Convinced the neighborhood was sliding into the lower depths, the banks gave up on block after block, and mortgage money became scarcer and scarcer. Decay and abandonment proliferated.

> Overflowing garbage cans out on the sidewalk in front, broken windows, mailbox doors ripped off in the lobby, no front doors, the usual sour run-down building smell, peeling paint, chunks of fallen plaster on the floor, a leaky roof over the stairwell and scraps of old food on the stairs. The apartments were full of cracked and peeling paint, gaping holes where the plaster and boards had fallen away, leaking pipes, complaints of roaches and rats, faulty toilets and, most important, repeated angry claims by many tenants that there had been no heat or hot water for at least seven months.[1]

As the "dolorous" 1960s wound down in East New York, landlords found themselves caught between what housing experts assert was insufficient rent-controlled income and soaring costs for maintenance, heating oil, taxes, insurance, and mortgage payments—if they could get mortgage renewals at all. Fearful of property damage and city-ordered rent reductions for housing violations, burdened with poisonous landlord-tenant disputes, unable to sell, they let go. The final and perhaps most significant factor in the complex process of abandonment was a failure of confidence by the landlords, not only in the building, but in the block, the neighborhood, even the city, which went beyond economic reason.

It is within these boundaries that a scenario called "End Game" is played out with Beckettian irony, states George Sternlieb, a Rutgers University urbanologist, who produced a study of rent-controlled housing for New York City.[2] In "End Game," according to Sternlieb, the landlord skimps on repairs, taxes aren't paid, the building is milked for maximum rental income, essential services such as heat and hot water end. Finally, the landlord walks away. In a given situation, he has gotten all he wants out of the building; he doesn't wish to invest any more on the chance of future gain. The tenants move or survive amid junkies, drifters, fires, muggings, thefts, vandalism. Ultimately, the building is vacant and the city takes over a gutted shell for tax delinquency, foreclosing in an in rem proceeding.

In 1974, 959 buildings had been vacated in the survey area. One Model Cities fireman estimates that the total number of vacant, boarded up FHA-owned buildings is probably in the vicinity of 2,500, many of which have been boarded up for five years.

In 1967 it was estimated that a 15 percent vacancy rate existed in the area west of Pennsylvania Avenue. By 1968 this vacancy rate was wiped out. It was instead replaced by overcrowding, hotel placements, doubling up, squatting, and living in hazardous and uninhabitable conditions.

As the number of abandoned buildings soared, and the East New York area has not had a substantial loss in population (578 persons from 1960 to 1970), it can be assumed that the remaining parts of the area have absorbed the population, resulting in serious overcrowding.

Public housing projects went up in Brownsville, uprooting residents there, and they, together with other displaced people from Central Brooklyn, Harlem, and the Bronx, moved to East New York. Many were welfare families for whom the city found apartments in the area. This has led to the criticism by many East New York residents that the city "dumped" welfare clients in the community, dragging it down. Many irate community residents strongly suspect that there is collusion between welfare investigators, landlords, and speculators. Welfare investigators are supposed to inspect each vacant apartment rented to a welfare family to insure that it is standard, but in practice the only apartments checked out are voluntary moves by tenants. At the least, the system favors exploitation; at the worst, there is collusion.

Infant mortality, venereal disease, pneumonia, influenza, and other disease rates are as high in East New York as in other slums, but the situation is more critical than in most; existing facilities are further away and more overcrowded. There are no hospitals in the area; there are only a few public health facilities, which residents avoid because of corruption and exploitation.

The rate of infant mortality has traditionally been utilized as a major determinant of the quality of medical care in any given area. Areas with the lowest percentages of out-of-wedlock births

are almost always those with the lowest rates of infant mortality.
East New York fares extremely high in both categories: in 1970 the
average health area rates per 1,000 births were 52.8 and 49.6,
respectively.

Recently, increased attention has been given to the area of
venereal disease, which appears to be approaching endemic proportions in the nation. Rankings of the health areas suggest that the
East New York area demonstrates extremely high venereal disease
rates: in 1970 it had 520 cases of gonorrhea and 149 cases of
syphilis. These figures are well above the city average.

While the incidence of tuberculosis among the population appears to be low compared with other diseases, its existence, even
in small numbers, represents a continuing danger. East New York
health areas, in 1970, had 46 cases of tuberculosis and six deaths
due to tuberculosis.

The East New York area has no public housing except for
Pennsylvania-Wortman and the limited efforts by Model Cities to
construct low-rent apartments, many of which are intended to serve
the senior citizen population. Surrounding the area are an abundance
of federal and state public renter and urban renewal projects. Most
of this housing is located near the southern boundary, Linden Boulevard; the remainder is located east of Fountain Avenue, in Cypress
Hills.

Blight continues to spread, and the number of burned out
buildings is increasing. West of Pennsylvania Avenue, 60 to 80
percent of most blocks need extensive rehabilitation or clearance.
Here the nineteenth-century frame dwellings and tenements are in
appalling condition, many subdivided into tiny apartments. Many
buildings have already been abandoned in large numbers by both
landlords and tenants. In others, landlord-tenant friction is in-
tense, and there is no hope of salvaging the buildings without change
in management. There are many abandoned buildings that are
shells. Neighborhood teenagers continue to set fires. They say
they hope that the buildings will one day burn to the ground and be
replaced by new housing.

THE RUINATION OF EAST NEW YORK'S
HOUSING STOCK VIA THE FHA

There is a part of Brooklyn called East New York, which
visitors, in awed voices, compare with the bombed-out cities of
Europe after World War II, and later of Vietnam. Most of the
houses on any given block are boarded up with plywood squares.
The gutters hang, rain washes in through the holes in the roofs.

Ruined by the elements, and gutted by the thieves, the houses seem
to be disintegrating like the stumps of rotted trees. Fires at night
cremate the remains. The next day the family moves out of the
house next door and another house is abandoned and eventually destroyed. Almost all of these boarded-up houses are U.S. government property via the FHA scandal.[3] "The neighborhood has been
FHA'd. To be FHA'd is to be ruined."

In addition to this, HUD in 1972 ended FHA mortgages for New
York City and had red-lined the area as effectively as the old policies of economic viability that existed up until 1968. Then, to com-
plicate matters still more, on January 4, 1973, the Nixon administration ordered the end of subsidized housing—an order that effectively ended the FHA resale of its repossessed houses, since the
only way the government can sell foreclosed houses in central
cities is to give away a subsidy with them.[4]

There is a further catch: black-listing FHA mortgages in the
slum areas means that homeowners, who live there and faithfully
make their mortgage payments, will not be able to resell their
houses, at least not if they bought their property from the FHA.

The East New York core area market became dominated by
the FHA:[5]

FHA foreclosures have ruined the neighborhood, making the value
   of the area's houses far less than the 1968 level.
To sell a house FHA costs the owner a great deal of money because
   he must pay to bring the home up to FHA standards for a homeowner sale.
FHA has stopped mortgages anyway!
To resell, they must either price their property at no more than
   50 percent of what they paid for it, or pay high costs for FHA
   mortgages to new buyers (who, in many cases, are no longer
   available).

Conscientious homebuyers must abandon their property if they
ever want to move, letting it foreclose, further ruining the neighborhood, adding to the FHA inventory, and keeping in motion the
economic wheels that make the man next door abandon his property.

If you seem to hear a roaring sound, don't worry! It's the
bulldozers and wrecking cranes going about their busy work of
destroying houses, some of them in sound condition, smashing
walls and pushing away the debris of houses every day.

The crackling sound you hear comes from fires in the abandoned houses—about 5,500 fires a year in 1971 and 1973. Approximately half the fires are set by children playing with matches.
One in five is set by professional arsonists to collect fire insurance.
One in ten is lit by tramps, thieves, and drug addicts.

The grunting and thumping sound comes from the increasing number of families who are abandoning their FHA houses to the arsonist, the vandal, and the thief. The hammering comes from the workmen nailing sheets of plywood over the windows and doors in a fruitless attempt to keep disaster out of the empty house. The whistling sound comes from the wind as it blows through 2,500 empty houses.

Finally, there is the babble of the many refugees who lived in these houses and lost them, and then somehow got lost themselves. Where do these people go? Nobody knows, but they seem to have disappeared. Have they doubled up or fled to nearby slums to live in public housing or other dilapidated private dwellings?

One warm day in late August 1975, after long hours of discussing the FHA and East New York, I was taken on a tour (by a New York City fireman) of East New York. We got into his car and went to see what he was referring to. For an hour we drove up and down the shattered streets, counting deserted houses. The total finally rose into the thousands and we lost count while he explained which group of speculators dominated this ruined area and which firm had destroyed that one.

There may have been thousands of ghost sales in East New York but nobody will ever know how many because it is nearly impossible to track down the people who once lived in the abandoned houses. It's even more difficult to find them if they never existed, because a ghost buyer is just a signature on a mortgage and a phony job and credit report. The phantom real estate business may be the easiest way to make money in the history of crime. The speculator can purchase a house for $3,000 and have it appraised by the FHA for $12,000. He signs the purchase offer himself and assembles credit and job information, either by forging the documents or by getting them for a person with the same name as the ghost. The information is forwarded to the mortgage company, which gets FHA underwriting and approves the mortgage. The mortgage company does not investigate the job and credit information: none of the mortgage companies did in Detroit because the FHA never required them to. The FHA never investigated the information either, because it assumed the mortgage companies checked them out as they do for conventional mortgages. But the mortgage firms felt checking was unnecessary because even if the house foreclosed, they were paid by the FHA. So the mortgage for $12,000 is granted, and the speculator is paid $12,000 for the house. His profit is $9,000. The house is deserted, no payments are ever paid, and the mortgage is foreclosed. The abandoned house now belongs to the FHA.

A variation of this technique is one in which the speculator rents out the house after a ghost sale and collects rent from it until the government comes to board it up. But in no case does the government get any of its money back.

Inter-Island Mortgage Company of Hempstead was the major mortgage company involved in the East New York FHA scandals. The disclosure involved false statements submitted to the FHA by a mortgage company about the completion of required repairs. Other violations included: concealing the identities of home buyers who had previously defaulted on another mortgage; listing the names of fake buyers in cases where real estate companies collected rent payments and made no mortgage payments; taking money deposits higher than the property amount; and lying about the source of the down payment.

One major reason for the East New York scandal was the manipulation of capital. Basically, none of the problems in the neighborhood could have developed without the active participation and profitable involvement of mortgage capital sources. The mortgage companies and, behind them, the banks, insurance companies, and pension funds provided the bulk of the money.

In most cases, the speculators didn't have enough capital of their own to carry out the widespread buying and selling that the scandal was built on. Although initial purchase prices of houses from private owners were low, many speculators still had to borrow the money from mortgage bankers. Then, to buy more houses, more money had to be borrowed.

It was to the financial advantage of the mortgage lenders to make the loans and then allow, if not actively encourage, buyers to default. Although some of this windfall went to the secondary mortgages, the mortgage bankers prospered as FHA was gutted and the neighborhood ruined.

Because FHA insurance protects the mortgage lender in the case of foreclosure, the mortgage companies abdicated their traditional role and responsibility for screening potential home buyers and ensuring that the property was structurally sound and valued fairly. It didn't make any difference to the banker what the house was worth, or if the owner stopped payments. In fact, it was to his benefit if the house foreclosed.

"The government comes in the night to turn people out of their houses and to board the houses up so that nobody but criminals, addicts, and rats can use them." Furthermore, "the government works with real estate men to put you into 'trick bags,' to promise you something and then throw you out in the cold and bulldoze it down so you can't get it." "I often think of the rich landlord roasting in his fourteen-room mansion in Scarsdale or Great Neck after an arsonist torched houses he owns in this neighborhood." This was the view of one long-term resident of East New York as he described the FHA housing scandal:

What will finally astound me is the day the government
that ruined this neighborhood writes off and tears down
all the houses that are left and backs the real estate
men and mortgage bankers in their new city project on
the cleared land.

I would be happy if I could live there, of course,
but there's no chance of that. The clean, sturdy,
room units are for the middle class who has always
appreciated the convenience of living close in. The
apartments won't be for me. I'm too poor. Too ig-
norant, they say; too careless with property; too
angry to behave properly in school.

What the FHA scandal actually is, is the most
expensive urban renewal project ever attempted. It
seems like an ass-backward way of going about it,
but it works—thousands of families are coerced to
relocate.

SAMPLE INTERVIEW NO. 1

1. This neighborhood wasn't designed to have as many people
as it does. There are too many multiple dwelling houses with
large families and too many small children. The two-family
structures were built in the 1930s and the design does not fit the
needs of the people today. Cost of renovation and repairs are
overpowering to most homeowners and many have to neglect the
property because of this. Tenants have the attitude that "it's not
my property, so who cares!" They say it's the landlord's responsibility. It is the landowners who bleed buildings, exploit tenants
and merchants, so that very few have stayed and kept their stores.

The cost of merchandise is higher and they blame it on the
high cost of insurance, many fires, and vandalism. The people
must leave the area to purchase the necessities and those without
cars are forced to shop in the neighborhood where the merchandise
is inferior and the prices exorbitant.

Transportation is excellent except for Starrett City. There
is accessibility to buses and trains. The situation was similar 15
years ago, and during the last five years, due to the planning, the
area has been built up.

Interviewees were Lily Martin, East New York Multi-Service
Center; and Harding Bowman, East New York Community Corporation.

2. Fourteen years ago the community was predominately Jewish with some blacks and Hispanics—not too many children! Most temples had children in day care centers. Planning and facilities were for Jewish children only. PTA was controlled by the clique of long-term residents. When the neighborhood got mixed, the PTA worked together (blacks and whites). The transients in the area cause an uneasy situation that is difficult to work with. The attitude of the police department changes as the neighborhood changes.

3. I consider this neighborhood my real home, a part of my life.

4. The attitudes in Harlem are different from Brooklyn. It is more friendly in Harlem, more distant in East New York. I would like to move to Virginia or North Carolina.

5. I have no relatives or friends in this neighborhood.

6. This neighborhood has many large families who are working hard to make a living to support their families.

7. (Covered earlier.)

8. It's disgraceful! Value of property is supposed to be higher. $40,000 for a house, taxes are increased; fuel costs vary in different neighborhoods. Electricity costs are $63 to $75 per month as opposed to $43 in Hollis. The rate of delinquent payments is so high that the bills are adjusted to account for allowances for doubtful accounts. Rents vary from $250 per month to $350 per month.

9. There is no racial tension at the present time, although there was quite a bit of tension in the past that died away.

10. The public housing-clustered type of living STINKS! They are institutions where everything is like prison with "Keep off Grass" signs, guards. The attitude of people is that they are a bit better than their neighbors. Projects are totally devoid of ideas. Turnkey 2,3 is a good idea.

11. This neighborhood was never good before the projects, it was outdated and deteriorated. The building of the projects, so to speak, improved the area; however, the necessary facilities were not provided. Model Cities was designed to model a livable environment. Poor management and lack of funds resulted in inadequate programs.

12. We do most of our shopping outside the area; this includes groceries, clothing, appliances and furniture, and movies. We use the doctors and clinics in the neighborhood.

13. The lack of proper medical care is a serious problem. We have Medicaid mills and now have facilities to handle overnight operations. There is private and public coordination of health facilities.

14. In case of sudden illness or accident, we go to Kings County Hospital.

15. There is no recreation for anyone in this area.

16. No recreation for teenagers.

17. No recreation for children.

18. My children use the backyards and the parks for amusement.

19. Plenty of abandoned cars in East New York.

20. Streets are not cleaned, although parking regulations are enforced.

21. The garbage pick-up was better, and is constantly getting worse.

22. Day care centers are O.K.

23. Graffiti and trains drive me mad! Riding the trains can drive me to Bellevue.

24. There are no more crossing guards.

25. The educational facilities are not equipped to handle the influx of additional students.

26. The public schools are not opened in the evenings, nor are they opened during the summer months on this side of Linden Boulevard. They are, however, opened on the south side of Linden Boulevard.

27. There is a public library in the immediate area.

28. The neighborhood has a very poor quality of food. The meat, vegetables, and fruit are of inferior quality.

29. All three movie theaters have been closed. Isn't that a damn shame?

30. Yes, yes, church is very important!

31. Police, fire, and sanitation have decreased. Phone calls don't bring any policemen unless there is a policeman in distress!

32. The quality of public facilities and services is poor, very poor!

33. Yes, the storekeepers are very nasty to the customers and they overcharge on every item.

34. The police protect storekeepers, school teachers, not residents. They do harass the people, however, and make sure the ghetto remains a ghetto.

35. The courts treat people like cattle.

36. (Covered earlier.)

37. No caseworkers visit the area any more. They harass you by mail now.

38. Crime is a serious problem. Breaking into your home, and robbing the hell out of it, fire bombing, rape, and so on—crime is up 200 percent.

39. This place is a regular bomb-fire. The Fire Department is the only department that earns its money in East New York. Landlords burn the abandoned homes to collect insurance. There is a conspiracy to destroy and rebuild and move people out of the area. There are some electrical fires. People also set fires to escape deplorable surroundings.

40. This area is a hangout for drugs and drug addicts.

41. People can't sleep—rats and roaches keep them awake. Loose pipes, garbage in and around walls. I don't know how the people get the certificate of occupancy.

42. There are gangs in this area, but they are lessening.

43. The teachers come to the schools to do their field work, and then they cut out!

44. High-rise buildings with little or no facilities cause crime.

45. Most stores in this area have been burglarized.

46. I've lived here 16 years; 14 years.

48. I don't rent. I moved here because of urban renewal.

49. Don't know!

50. There was an FHA scandal in this area.

51. The rents are much too high in this neighborhood. The welfare system feeds from state to city.

52. Landlords take advantage of the tenants who don't know any better.

54. The bathroom in my house has a window.

55. God forbid! Hallways are not safe, the elevators never work.

56. Most apartments in multiple dwellings were rent controlled but not in the two-family homes.

57. I own my home.

58. There is an absentee landlord here. He lives way out in Suffolk County.

59. People are robbed and raped in the laundry rooms. We use the laundromat in the stores.

60. There are no tenant associations. Everyone has their own idea and does nothing.

61. Some neighborhood groups are effective, most are not.

62. I belong to political and social clubs.

63. Clubs are not effective because they were singling out the people and not caring about the community.

64. We have asked for help for the schools, bussing, and more police protection, but received none from our local politicians.

SAMPLE INTERVIEW NO. 2

It was a more desirable area 10, 20 years ago. I know from experience, since I've lived here 24 years. When you see black and Puerto Rican people moving into a neighborhood, it's an inter-racial neighborhood, Jews move first and then Italians follow. When the real estate companies see this, they step in and they bring in any kind of people that they know will make the building dilapidate. Of course it was more desirable 10, 20 years ago.

We didn't have so many runaway landlords 10 or 20 years ago. The surrounding area was nice. We didn't have so many people moving in and moving out; we had a more stable population. People are forced to move out of apartments. The landlords put them through a lot of nonsense. They don't maintain the buildings, yet they raise the rents in the apartment. It's getting worse and worse and worse every year. If you want to live in a better place with your children, it is impossible to get a decent one in this neighborhood. I know a lot of people who don't want to rent apart-ments in these lousy buildings with garbage lying outside, but they have a vary hard time finding apartments and are stuck here. There are a lot of vacancies here.

Real estate companies in East New York have set many of the fires in this neighborhood. I would estimate this at 45 fires. All these buildings belong to the same real estate company. The taxes are very high, a lot of landlords couldn't afford to keep up the buildings, because prior to the neighborhood change, which brought with it transience, the rents were low and costs of taxes and fuel were rising. In this area, before the neighborhood changed, most of the landlords were living in the buildings. These people (tenants) had been living there for 10 and 15 years and their rents were hardly increased because of rent control. When they moved out, the landlord could get only a 15 percent increase. Because of this factor, old-time residents would move out only so fast. Once they move, it is the intent of the real estate company (who is gen-erally the landlord) to move in and move out as many families as possible so as to legally obtain rent increments. Many landlords

---

Based on the Questionnaire in Chapter 4, the questions were not answered in order. Interviewees were Anna Heath and eight coworkers from the East New York Anti-Poverty Program.

who own the smaller buildings have left their buildings and then
FHA steps in and takes buildings over and they board them up. On
my block, we have six FHA-owned buildings that are boarded up.
I was living in this neighborhood when it was just a few blacks and
just a few Puerto Ricans and there was much more police protection. Our children had much more police protection when going to
school. On each corner there was a crossing guard and policemen
were evident on certain corners. Now, we can't get one policeman,
not one, to cross our children in this neighborhood. But if you get
in your car and drive out further into another neighborhood, you'll
see a policeman on every corner. And this is really not fair! We
don't have a school crossing guard because the mothers can't afford
to work, if they are lucky enough to have a job. Many mothers
cannot live on $18.00 a week, which is what some jobs are paying,
and, therefore, they are forced to remain on welfare. Their hus-
bands are not making enough money to support them. So those who
can work, have to do so at whatever salary they are offered and, as
a result, our children are unprotected.

Public housing is not in the core of East New York. The way
they rent apartments is extremely unfair. I see families coming in
this area from other areas and getting into public housing. But I
have been trying to get an apartment in public housing for years and
they won't rent me one. I have been living here a long time and I
have lived in the same apartment for many years, so why won't
they rent me an apartment? In this community the residents get
nothing. When you go down to apply for a project apartment, they
talk down to you and give you a blue or a pink card and they run
you around. As for the private landlords, they live outside of the
area in Queens or Long Island. Excuse my expression, but the
landlords don't give a shit about the property or the tenants. Like
last year, I knew a family who had no heat or hot water for six
weeks. The landlords don't do anything. Sometimes they come
down here once a month to collect the rents, but they never make
any necessary repairs. I don't think this is fair. The people who
are from this community get pushed aside when it comes to public
housing. In the private housing, I know people who pay as much
as $250 per month for horrendous apartments. I don't understand!
The majority of the landlords here live out in Queens and Nassau
County. Somebody I knew got sick and had to be sent to the hospital
because of lack of heat and hot water. You walk down the streets
and you see dirt and vomit. The apartments aren't worth half the
rents being charged for them. In addition, the people in this
neighborhood are hard pressed for money and jobs, they can't
afford $250 for rent. Many of them can't pay $100. The city allows
the landlords to charge any rents they want to.

The little children today are exposed to so many bad things. I know my little grandchild, she is six years old, was asked by a little boy to get undressed in front of him. She said "no, go away." The children have no supervision and are not brought up right.

Property values! I bought a house six years ago for $20,000, now if I am lucky, I can sell it for $10,000. Twenty-three years ago, I paid $18,000 for my house (it was hard to get that time). I asked around and found out that in the Model Cities area, all the houses that had recorded violations were owned by blacks and Puerto Ricans, the houses in the worst condition were passed by when inspectors from the Building Department were here examining buildings. The houses that belong to the real estate companies, which are the worst around, are never inspected! Violations are never corrected; poor people have to sit there and suffer. The landlords don't care, especially if the tenants are black and Puerto Rican, because they know that these people can't move and, if they do, conditions elsewhere are the same for them!

I had a little problem in my house, with a light in the vestibule. The building inspectors made a big stink about this, while on my block there are some horrible houses that are owned by real estate companies and the inspectors passed them by. The inspectors ask you for money and they tell you if you give them some money, they won't come back! They ask for $15.

Conditions are getting worse and worse. I would like to move but things are not better anyplace else for us! The schools, streets, and everything else is horrible here. The bus drivers here are women drivers. They have a very nasty attitude toward our children. The same is true for ambulance drivers. They come here and harass the families of sick people. One day a man was bleeding and losing a lot of blood. When the ambulance came, they told us they were going to take him to Brookdale, which was very far away. We demanded that he be sent to Kings County, a better hospital that is much closer to here, and they told us to shut the hell up. P.S.: they took him to Brookdale and he died.

When the neighborhood changed from white to black and Puerto Rican, the services followed this change. Police protection decreased and so did sanitation and all other social services. This isn't fair— we pay taxes too! The streets are broken up here but they don't care. You should see how they pick up the garbage here. They don't pick it up, that's what's so sad! Sometimes they pick up a can or two, but most times they leave so much garbage on the curbs. They have no consideration for the area residents.

This is the first time I saw a rat in my house. I've lived in this house 26 years and I never saw a rat. Mice, yes, but never a rat! I have the exterminator come in twice a month to make sure of this.

But this month I saw a rat in my house! Behind my house are some FHA-owned buildings. That's where the rats are coming from. When FHA takes over, they do not spray rat poisoning, they do not keep these houses clean. I called the Health Department and they won't do anything. I would say that we have had 25 children bitten by these rats and nothing has been done. Many of these children died. At Kings County Hospital there are 125 cases of this. One lady from Fountain Avenue died! Another lady is in the hospital now and will have to get her leg amputated. This is all because of the filth that piles up behind the FHA-owned buildings. They never send exterminators to exterminate houses. Nobody lives in these houses but the rats. The rats are breeding and I can just imagine that they have a ball because there's no one to interrupt them. You can look through your window any afternoon and see a big fat rat. It's disgusting.

Transportation is not good. We are somewhat close to trains but the buses are slow as hell!

Medical care is in this area worse than poor. There is one medical center on Pitkin and Pennsylvania Avenue and in this place the people are treated like cannibals.

There are not many day care facilities here. Working mothers have no place to leave their children during the day. Many of these mothers are forced to stay at home and remain on welfare.

Public transportation in this area is not a problem. The train stations are not safe or clean but the trains are adequate.

The schools in this neighborhood are horrible. Teachers are not there to teach and the result is that the children don't learn. The gym is not open during the evenings and children have no other recreational facilities besides the streets.

The library in this area is far away and many children are afraid to travel to it. Besides, this library has so few books, it really doesn't pay to make the effort.

The neighborhood groceries here have the worst food at the highest prices. We do not have any supermarkets here; we have those rotten bodegas and they are a royal "rip-off"! These stores are run by Puerto Ricans but owned by ex-residents of the community.

There are no longer any movies in this area. They all closed down when the neighborhood changed. The closest movie theater is in City Line, and East New York residents are afraid to go there. We are not wanted in that area and the residents there make sure to tell us that. Children are especially scared to go to that area— they might get beat up.

There are many churches in this neighborhood and many storefront churches at that. The storefront churches steal from

the residents; the other churches are attended often and are a good
thing in this area.

The levels of public facilities and services have changed with
the neighborhood. The police used to be cooperative, when I first
moved here. Now they don't care about the residents. They protect the teachers and storekeepers. Sanitation is just as bad.
They leave so much garbage on the streets, you wouldn't believe it.
There are problems with potholes, lights, and just about everything!

Storekeepers in this area overcharge and give you lousy
merchandise. They know that residents here are too poor and too
tired to shop elsewhere, so they really take advantage of them.
Storekeepers (owners) are not residents, but they hire residents
to run their stores.

The police in this community are the worst. They do not protect the residents; they often sit in their police cars and drink beer.
A person could get killed around here and they wouldn't bat an eye-
lash. As far as their emergency services, this is a frightening
thing. I once had to wait an hour and a half for the police to send
an ambulance over here to pick up a man who had a heart attack.
They take their sweet time, you know. In the meanwhile, this man
got so sick he almost died. I was so nervous, but the first thing
the ambulance did was ask me for $200. If I hadn't had this money
with me, they would have left him on the street and he would have
died.

There are no courts in this area, but the people here are not
treated fairly.

The schools here are terrible. They are old, crowded, and
functioning on split sessions. There are annexes on wheels but
these are terrible. I have a son who attends the public school here.
He is not learning but he is being promoted every year. I wish I
could afford to send him to another school. His teachers say he is
good, but I know he cannot read, and he is in the fifth grade.

Welfare workers never visit here. They just send their
clients here to rent these horrible apartments with all the rats,
roaches, and mice. You could imagine! They pay high rents for
these apartments—they really keep the landlord in good business.
Why should a landlord fix his house if he could rent it to a welfare
family and get a high rent?

There are so many fires here. The Fire Department does its
job. Some fires are set by drug addicts who often hang around in
abandoned buildings. Some are set by residents who see no other
way out of their misery. Most of them, however, are set by the
hungry real estate and insurance brokers who would like their
properties to burn down so they can collect insurance. There were
not always so many fires in this neighborhood. This came in with

the FHA housing. Many people were forced to abandon their houses and once these houses were abandoned, someone set fires to them. Some fires here are caused by the electrical system because many people live in a small house, but I would guess that not many occur this way.

There are drug addicts up and down Liberty Avenue. They always take old ladies' pocketbooks and ask everyone for money. They carry knives and sometimes they have guns. They scare us and our children. The drug addicts have been in this neighborhood for a long time, but things are getting worse.

There is a gang problem in this neighborhood. There are gang wars here all the time. The real problem is with the gangs from the next neighborhood (Highland Park). If East New York residents go over there, there is a big fight!

There is no place for children to play. They must use the streets. The only park near here is in Highland Park-Cypress Hills and those residents do not want our kids there—they always beat them up!

High-rise buildings cause more crime. Thank God we do not have many of these. We have enough crime here. The stores have burglary gates and even bullet-proof glass. This has been the case since the 1960s.

I have lived in this neighborhood for 18; 24; 20; and so on, years. I have lived in the same house for 18 years; I have rented an apartment in the same house for 10 years; 12 years; and so on. (There are eight people in this interview.)

Bad housing here is one of our biggest problems. There wasn't much bad housing here when I moved here. The residents were Jewish and they lived in their own houses. Now they rent the apartments out and let the buildings fall apart.

Rents are much too high for the heatless decrepit apartments here. Landlords charge the highest rents to welfare clients. There is no rent control here. Landlords secure transiency by making life so unpleasant for tenants that they keep moving. There are always holes in the walls and broken pipes, but it does no good if you complain.

The tenant and block associations here are unorganized. There are a small number of community leaders, but the community is so transient that they cannot be effective. Politicians are not concerned with East New York residents. They work north of Atlantic Avenue.

NOTES

1. "East New York—Shacks and Hovels," New York <u>Times</u>, March 28, 1971.

2. See George Sternlieb and I. B. Indik, <u>The Ecology of Welfare and the Welfare Crisis in New York City</u> (New Brunswick, N.J.: Transaction Books, 1973).

3. See Brian Boyer, <u>Cities Destroyed for Cash</u> (Chicago: Follett Publishers, 1973), for a detailed account of this process. Much of the description of East New York that follows is described in this study.

4. Ibid.

5. Ibid.

10
SOUTHEAST QUEENS

The area referred to in this study as Southeast Queens stretches south from Archer and Jamaica Avenues to Baisley Boulevard, on the east Farmers Boulevard, on the west the Van Wyck Expressway to Foch Boulevard, and south through 143rd and 144th Streets to Rockaway Boulevard.

Southeast Queens consists of two distinct communities: St. Albans, which has been a black middle-class community since the 1940s, and South Jamaica, a lower-income black area characterized by extreme pockets of poverty with poor housing, sanitation, and all other indications of a powerless population. These two communities merge at Merrick Boulevard.

That patterns of residential differentiation are little affected by the impact of racial change suggests the presence of class segregation in the black community. Powdermaker, however, observed that

> Side by side live the respectable and the disreputable,
> the moderately well-to-do and the very poor, the
> pious and the unsaved, the college graduates and the
> illiterates, the dusky blacks, the medium browns, the
> light creams all thrown together because they are
> Negroes.[1]

This chapter analyzes the transformation of South Jamaica and St. Albans via the population composition, housing stock, and neighborhood quality and the effects of interactions between the two distinct communities.

SOUTH JAMAICA: POPULATION AND HOUSING

A South Jamaica resident recalled:

When I moved here, the neighborhood was 90 percent
white and 10 percent black. As the neighborhood population transformed, I have observed the rapid decline
in all services. However, I do not want to move, I am
not financially able. Besides, there's no need to move
into any other black area, the same lack of services
always follows you.

In South Jamaica, defined as the area west of Merrick Boulevard, the population changed greatly after 1940.

In 1900 the population of South Jamaica was 4,500. It
already included Negro settlements. Since that time,
there has been continued black in-migration. Extensive
expansions of the Negro community occurred after the
depression and after World War II. From 1950 to 1960
the Negro population doubled while some 25,000 whites
left the area. Today, black residents constitute approximately 95 percent of an estimated population of
77,000. [2]

Just after World War II, a few blacks were able to buy houses
beyond the Atlantic Avenue section to which they had previously been
confined. "There was too much bad housing when I moved here, but
this neighborhood was better than Harlem. We were able to buy a
new home." Panic selling by white homeowners set in (with much
help from real estate speculators), and the area by now has become
predominantly black (98 percent of the population).

Most of South Jamaica's existing housing was built during the
post-World War I real estate boom. The developers did not follow
a regular street pattern and many blocks were small and irregular.
Intersections were often poorly aligned, with streets coming in at
regular angles. Many streets were left impaired and irregularly
graded. The houses themselves were of small and medium-sized
two-story frame construction, free standing on minimum-sized lots,
often with 16- to 20-foot frontages. [3] Many of the streets lack public
sewers and many houses still rely on cesspools.

Housing is the most critical issue facing the community.
There is extensive blight due to the severe deterioration
of the aging housing stock, much of which was speculatively

built as low priced single family frame dwellings more
than 40 years ago. Since that time, many of the houses
have been converted to multi-family use. Tree lined
streets and superficial exterior renovations can give a
false impression. The structure behind the facade is
often in serious decay. Foundations have settled, wiring and plumbing are obsolete and many units have been
illegally converted to multi-family use. Trash and
abandoned cars can be found on sidewalks and streets;
vacant lots are frequently littered and filthy."[4]

South Jamaica Houses were built by the New York City Housing
Authority in two stages, the first completed in 1940 and the second
in 1954. The project is built on 24 acres in the South Road-160th
Street area, replacing badly deteriorated housing on that site. "The
projects here improved the appearance of the site and the immediate
area. The neighborhood was not a good one before the projects were
constructed. The South Road area was called 'the area with houses
not fit for human occupancy.'" A second public housing project,
Baisley Park Houses, was constructed on vacant land along New
York Boulevard in 1961.

While the existing housing stock of South Jamaica is dilapidated,
rents and, similarly, property values have been rising. The situation is particularly acute for welfare families. A housing specialist
describes:

90-20 169th Street, South Jamaica, New York. . . .
Walls have been ripped out to expose water pipes.
Exposed wiring and unsafe, exterior wiring substitute
for insulated cable in most of the apartments. Water
damage has caused ceilings to buckle and fall, walls to
become discolored and, in one apartment, left water
ankle-deep on the floor. Residents have been without
hot water for seven days. Many small children had
found mice in their cribs. Addicts come to the building at night and use the halls as a public bathroom.
Rents are as high as $280 per month.

Rents are too damn high in the South Jamaica area.
The Welfare Department pays more than I can afford.

Welfare clients—slumlords gouge these people! Welfare clients are generally emotionally limited and not
the brightest—they pay outrageous rents.

Many residents feel that these rents can be charged since the area contains a preponderance of single- and double-family homes and very few rent-controlled (or stabilized) units. With limited exception, the only high-rise buildings (apartment buildings) in the area are the projects.

> Rents here are more expensive than a congested area. We have little or no rent control because of the one- and two-family houses. As a result, people pay through the nose, especially welfare clients.

> Property values are rising, rents are rising far too high. Because this area has virtually no apartment houses and no rent control, landlords in the one- and two-family houses can charge as much as they want . . . and believe me, they do!

When asked how this "exploitation process" can persist, one resident explained:

> One of the reasons rents are high is because landlords take advantage of welfare families, especially large families. Urban renewal and public housing displace many large families. Since the projects are constructed in such a way that they cannot house these families, these people are forced to live in private rental housing. Projects, supposedly built for the poor, tend to reject welfare tenants. These two groups (which are often one) are forced to accept the housing offered by the private landlords. The landlords of these houses realize this and invite welfare clients so they can skyrocket their rents.

Home values are also greatly inflated when compared to similar houses in other communities. There have been few single-family houses available to blacks in the metropolitan area. Where such houses have been available, a sellers' market (and real estate speculation resulting in highly inflated market prices) has existed. In addition, the rate of default has been significantly higher among these groups.[5] This has allowed owners to set prices at the highest level prospective buyers will pay, and many purchasers find themselves paying 30 to 40 percent of their income for housing.

The "no down payment" is a practice found to be necessary to "move" the houses on the market. It most often encourages families to buy, even though they do not have the financial stability to follow through.

> There wasn't any bad housing when I moved here, but
> there sure is a lot now. South Jamaica real estate op-
> erators allowed people to buy houses with a no down
> payment policy with knowledge of their lack of ability
> to pay off mortgages. The result has been that many
> people had to convert their homes and many had to
> abandon their homes, both causing the area to de-
> teriorate.

An estimated 40 percent of the one- and two-family houses
are owned by absentee landlords. [6]

> There are many money hungry landlords in this area.
> Houses are bought and sold every day. Landlords dis-
> possess their tenants by claiming that they are moving
> back into the house, but in fact these landlords evict
> tenants and either skyrocket rents or sell the buildings
> to other unscrupulous brokers.

> We have a large degree of absentee landlordism in
> South Jamaica. Many of these landlords live in Florida.

It is the opinion of most residents of the community that many of
these absentee landlords are black buyers of 10 and 20 years ago
who have moved on to more affluent communities to the east and
who keep their old houses for rental income. This situation causes
sharp comment among former neighbors, who complain of poor
maintenance and unacceptable tenants—conditions that depress the
general neighborhood character. There are also numbers of buildings owned by slumlords.

In one such house several toilets were inoperative, some
radiators were disconnected, and the heat had been turned off the
previous day by the Fire Department because of the hazard of a gas
flame out of adjustment. [7] While many welfare families are tired
and poor, they accept such conditions passively; others take out
their resentment by destroying fixtures and dumping garbage indis-
criminately.

The homeowner who has difficulty in meeting his mortgage
payments will probably neglect maintenance and permit the building
to deteriorate. He may take in roomers or relatives for extra income, which in the past has resulted in overcrowding and damage.
The tenants in these buildings generally have no leases.

Landlords simply increase rents when they want to evict tenants. This process secures a transient population, which contributes
to the deterioration of the area.

In the few apartment houses, most people have leases.
In the private houses, virtually nobody has a lease.
The landlords jack up the rent when they want to get
rid of a tenant.

There are a considerable number of month-to-month
tenants in this area.

The absentee owner, finding that his income is inadequate for both
payments and maintenance, neglects his building, making the tenants suffer. These economic pressures put a premium on finding
tenants and roomers who can regularly pay high rents and who are
not in a position to criticize deplorable housing conditions. The
welfare family fills this bill all too perfectly.

SOUTH JAMAICA: NEIGHBORHOOD

South Jamaica has long been a neglected area of the city and
now it shows the result of the neglect in dilapidated and overcrowded
housing, inferior education levels, poor sanitation, high crime rates,
unpaved streets, inadequate transportation, and other indexes of deterioration and decay.
A low level of municipal services is always an indication of a
deprived community, resulting in health and sanitation hazards and
low morale and apathy on the part of many inhabitants.[8]

I've seen people dump dead dogs in back of my house
and don't mention rats to me! Empty whiskey bottles,
broken glass, dishwashers, broken toilets for weeks
decorate the area. And . . . stripped and abandoned
automobiles, their insides burned out, lie in various
positions. The neighborhood was bad 10 years ago,
but it's getting worse.[9]

The need for sanitation services in South Jamaica far exceeds
what is currently provided by the city. The condition of vacant lots,
littered streets, erratic bulk garbage collection, and the prevalence
of rats are of major concern to residents of the area. Trash is collected on a biweekly schedule and in a haphazard fashion.
Vacant lots are found in every section of the community, and
most are covered with trash, weeds, and bushes. Illegal dumping,
junked cars, and littering produce quantities of refuse. Much of it
blows from the lots into nearby streets and properties. There are
places in the community that harbor rats living in loose garbage.

Lack of systematic inspection and action by responsible agencies is of great concern to residents. Decrepit and unattractive streets contribute to an atmosphere of decay, which must be altered before any overall improvement in the physical environment of South Jamaica can take place.

Inadequate street sweeping is another major complaint. Residents claim that when the streets are swept, much of the debris is not collected. At present, there is no alternate side of the street parking in South Jamaica and, thus, street washing is almost, if not entirely, nonexistent. Uncollected refuse on the streets also clogs sewers and causes flooding after rain.

Sections of South Jamaica, particularly in the "pit" to the north and along New York Boulevard, are slums afflicted with poor health, many families needing public assistance, and high crime and juvenile delinquency rates. Blocks of small one-family and two-family houses, many of them illegally converted to multiple dwellings, have become crowded slums. Many residents feel that this is the main reason for the increasing rate of structural fires.

> There are a lot of fires here. Some houses are frame, overcrowded. They house large families. Many have been illegally converted into 2, 3, 4 . . . family houses. There is simply too much pressure on the electrical system.

> There are many fires here. There have always been many but it's getting worse. The combination of illegally converted single-family houses and faulty wiring causes these fires.

One planning and community development consultant and resident of the area explained: "Fires here are a part of the urban renewal process. Buildings are intentionally overtaxed and unimproved. Fires have become common around here. The conversion of houses and overuse of current causes fires."

Although a few trees line the streets, low density of population and a limited amount of public housing are the only characteristics that distinguish these areas from the worst parts of Harlem, Brownsville, or Bedford Stuyvesant. Most residents of South Jamaica feel that the projects have had a positive effect on the surrounding area. "There isn't enough public housing here to really affect neighborhood quality. Baisley Houses have been well kept and have not contributed to any decline in the neighborhood." One official from the Jamaica Office of Planning and Development added: "The projects in this area certainly didn't affect the area in a negative way. Projects here improved the appearance of the site and the immediate area. Projects here are well-run." Although some residents feel that public housing projects are a stabilizing force because of the "limited number of projects," others see this as limited effort by the city to upgrade the area.

> The city has not given the South Jamaica area a particularly high priority except for the early construction of a public housing project. Urban renewal effort has been minimal in the area. A lower population might be a causative factor of the low priority of South Jamaica.

While the residents of the South Jamaica area see the projects as a stabilizing force, residents from neighboring St. Albans feel quite differently: "Projects themselves have problems of homicide, muggings, and so on. The stringent income limits for tenants also help destroy the stability of the area. Once a family gets on its feet economically, it has to move out of public housing."

There has been no urban renewal in the South Jamaica area, but the construction of York College (which will probably not be completed for a long time because of the city's financial condition) poses a threat to long-term residents who feel that they will be displaced from the area:

> Because of York College construction, much relocation will go on here. Many black residents are afraid that they are being ripped off in selling their properties. These people feel that after they are dislocated, they will not be able to buy back into the improved area. This construction almost resembles the effects of urban renewal.

Health conditions of South Jamaica's population are seriously deficient. Infant mortality is twice that of Queens as a whole; the tuberculosis rate is four times that of the borough. The South Jamaica area has virtually no hospital or related facilities. Community residents are irate over this fact.

> Lack of good medical care is a serious problem here. Most doctors and all hospitals are well outside the community. The ambulance service is also deplorable. One lady got cut in the park and I had to call the Fire Department for an ambulance. By the time the ambulance arrived at the hospital, the lady was dead!

The drug problem is evident in South Jamaica, as pointed out by residents: "We have had drug users and addicts here ever since poor black people realized that there was such a thing as drugs."

There is a serious crime problem in South Jamaica. The 103rd Precinct fares #1 in felonies for New York City. Juvenile delinquency rates are also high:

> One of the bad points in this neighborhood is the commercial strip—there is a lot of loitering, liquor stores, bars—guys gang out in the streets. This is definitely a cause for mugging, robbing. A lack of police service doesn't make the situation any better.

> There is "black on black" crime here. Kids go into people's houses and take televisions, and so on. I am in fear of being heisted after dark, having my car stolen, being burglarized.

The most serious points of crime are along Sutphin Boulevard, at the intersection of South Road and 150th Street and on New York Boulevard and South Road. [10] In addition to the problem of inadequate police protection, there has been increasing tension between black residents and white police. A similar situation prevails with respect to storekeepers. "There is a tremendous amount of tension between white police and black residents and between white storeowners and black residents." While Jamaica Avenue is a long-established shopping street, residents are disgusted with existing shopping facilities, particularly groceries.

> Neighborhood groceries have poor quality merchandise, to say the least! We have complained to the Board of Health about rats and rodents—you can see their feet in the shelves, and in the boxes at Key Food, Mets, and so on.

> Poor, very poor quality merchandise in the neighborhood grocery. Last week my wife bought flour and it was full of worms.

Residents complain about the exploitative prices they are forced to pay when shopping in the area:

> South Jamaica is an isolated, exploited ghetto area. Residents are plagued by poor housing and education and not enough money. Merchants exploit customers

by charging higher prices for clothing and food than
merchants in other parts of the borough.

> Yes, most storekeepers here do overcharge. Store-
> keepers treat people with disrespect. Storekeepers
> are not area residents. They take the money with them.

Residents who own cars (very few) do the majority of their shopping
outside of the area. For those who must remain, prices are high
and merchandise is inferior. The poor transportation networks in
South Jamaica (double fare zone) tie more residents to Jamaica
Avenue for shopping.

> Transportation is poor in this area, and expensive! It
> costs you $2.00 to take a train to the city and back.
> Sometimes you have to wait one hour for a Green Line
> bus. There is no train station in the area, so you have
> no choice but to wait for the bus.

> Storekeepers here do overcharge. They blame this on
> high rates of pilferage. They have older merchandise
> and no cash flow. This, in part, causes storekeepers
> to increase prices. Most of the price increases, how-
> ever, are a result of plain exploitation on the part of
> the storekeeper. The neighborhood is accustomed to
> this type of treatment. People can be exploited be-
> cause of poor transportation. Storekeepers here do not
> treat people very nicely. That's why those who can,
> leave the area to shop. One store on Merrick Boule-
> vard has bullet-proof glass enclosures—most imper-
> sonal service. Storekeepers come and exploit the area
> and then go to the suburbs.

South Jamaica lacks indoor and outdoor recreation facilities.
Prohibitive transportation costs tend to prevent children, teenagers,
and adults from leaving the community for recreation.

> There aren't many parks or indoor recreation facilities
> in the area. The total environment can contribute nega-
> tively to the bringing up of children.

> Movie theaters close down? Are there any left opened?
> Easily five or six have closed down since I've been
> here.

Several movie theaters in the area have closed down,
with the advent of television. As the character of this
neighborhood changed, the theaters closed down. The
only movies shown here now are pornographic. Most
people here can't afford the double fare to go to other
areas for movies, so they stay at home.

Schools in the area are inadequate. Many parents bus their
children elsewhere, to Flushing and Bayside:

Schools in this area are not good. So many things are
wrong with them. Teachers are somewhat of a problem. They cannot handle unruly children, which we
have plenty of. The teachers write these children off
as not being able to learn. I send my children out of
the area.

While the church is an important institution in the South
Jamaica area, the proliferation of storefront churches as a side
business has reduced its value markedly.

We have plenty of storefront churches in this area.
There are 17 storefront churches in a ten-block radius.
Every time a store goes out of business it is replaced
by a storefront church.

We are besieged with churches; every week a new
storefront church appears. The church acts as a form
of recreation. A small church can provide a sense of
identification for people who are not aggressive. However, in the South Jamaica area there are hussle bangers in the church. The shoe cobbler is a storefront
preacher on the side. Established churches stay
where they are. Pentecostal Churches, Church of
God, and so on, rise and fall throughout the year.

The church in many neighborhoods acts as a stabilizing force. Active community leaders congregate in the church and organize themselves in an attempt to solve the social ills in the community. This
type of situation does not prevail in South Jamaica. While many
residents recognize and understand the community's problems,
there is no collectivity among residents. "People here have the instruments and know how to work to make change, but they work
separately and are not at all consolidated."

There are some tenants' associations and neighborhood improvement groups, but residents don't see these groups as being too effective.

> We have a whole slew of tenants' associations and neighborhood improvement groups. They have a little party and let off steam. Efforts are not coordinated. These groups tend to be internally oriented, like a motorcycle club.

> There is a lack of collectivity in this area. There are too many groups fighting for their own selfish interests. . . . We have not received a dime of any section 235 or section 236 money.

As a result, the community's needs have not been attacked in a constructive manner and the problems in the area have remained and in many cases have worsened.

ST. ALBANS AND ADDESLEIGH PARK: HOUSING

> Almost no new housing is available to the Negro in new areas of Long Island and other suburban metropolitan communities. The result is that the 1,300 Negro families in New York who are qualified to buy new housing press against any single area opened to them. If all builders opened their sales to Negroes, the housing supply for these families would be filled without any noticeable pressure in any area.[11]

The residents of St. Albans followed the same patterns that other suburban-bound groups did in seeking escapes from the increasing number of problems they were encountering in inner city neighborhoods. But as blacks, they found that their opportunities, at the end of World War II, were limited by housing market discrimination.

For those who had lived mostly in Harlem (and the Bronx to a lesser degree), one escape was Bedford Stuyvesant. But the central Brooklyn area, with its own stable middle class, offered only a limited number of homes and a brownstone environment that too closely resembled the neighborhoods most people were more than anxious to escape.

Queens was considered the promised land. There were tree-lined streets and an abundance of parks and open land. Some inroads had been made into the Jamaica area when a handful of black families set off panic selling by whites, but discriminatory real estate rules tended to protect the better neighborhoods. One St. Albans resident recalls: "When I moved here, this neighborhood was desirable, a dream come true! One of the main desirable features was that there was an opportunity for homeownership."

A court case challenged traditional racial restrictive covenants that forbade the sale of homes to blacks in the Addesleigh Park section (located east of Merrick Boulevard and centered around Linden Boulevard). A victory in 1946 brought in many middle- and upper-income black families.

Long associated with the affluent and prominent, St. Albans has been the promised land for New York City's emerging middle- and upper-class blacks. The first blacks to make the breakthrough into St. Albans were show people, sports figures, and professionals, including Lena Horne, Brook Benton, Fats Waller, Jackie Robinson, Roy Campanella, Ella Fitzgerald, and Count Basie. Most of these people moved into the exclusive Addesleigh Park section. The Basie home, located at 175th and Addelaide Streets, still stands as a monument to black affluence. Behind it is a large swimming pool surrounded by an acre of land known for exclusive garden parties in New York City.

Unlike the breakneck exodus of whites from nearby South Jamaica, change in St. Albans was more deliberate. As is the case in areas that open up to blacks, the cost of houses was much steeper than the market value for whites and the influx of blacks was slow.

Blacks paid dearly for the suburban-style charm of St. Albans. Lawrence Corbier, owner of the Ebony Oil Company, which services the area, remembers:

> The whites would sell their homes for $6,000 or $7,000; then the real estate speculators would sell them to us for $20,000 to $25,000. Naturally the blacks would be forced to work two and three jobs and even take in boarders in order to pay off the immense mortgages.[12]

Nearly all the sports and entertainment celebrities have left St. Albans. Most of the homes have been purchased by upper-echelon black civil servants and working people. "Middle and upper income blacks are moving further into Long Island."

Middle-class status in St. Albans and other black neighborhoods has often been a state of mind rather than a reality. To maintain their homes, both husband and wife have had to work, a situation that has not yet changed. Caught in the squeeze of wage and promotion freezes, inflation, rising fuel costs, and property taxes, a lot of belt tightening is taking place. A St. Albans resident commented:

> When we came out here it was a little steep but we
> scraped and paid $20,000-$25,000 for our house. Now
> many of the homes are worth $40,000 to $50,000, and
> the exclusive residences even more. There are many
> expensive homes on Murdock Avenue and Linden Boule-
> vard that seem to lack a coat of paint or the minor re-
> pairs that would return them to their original conditions.
> Many of the newcomers cannot afford the upkeep. Some-
> one like myself, I couldn't move in here now. I bought
> this house by putting $1,000 down on the G.I. bill.

As one drives past row after row of neat little homes, one is hard-pressed to believe that life in St. Albans is anything but wonderful. But behind some of the brick and stucco lurk some serious community problems. Just when many families had almost paid off their mortgages, crime and urban blight started to creep into the area.

While the FHA scandal was not of paramount importance in St. Albans, it left its marks. One resident explained:

> This neighborhood is now typical of black so-called
> middle-class neighborhoods, certainly far different
> from a white middle-class neighborhood. Real estate
> speculators did not encourage the right type of mobil-
> ity. They instead encouraged people who could not
> afford houses to buy in, resulting in these people hav-
> ing to take in roomers. Scare tactics were used by
> real estate operators. They invited anyone here who
> had $200 down, and encouraged them, when necessary,
> to take second mortgages and roomers. As a result,
> professionals and welfare recipients live in this area,
> side by side.

Another resident remarked:

> Black people who are middle class unfortunately can-
> not live in a middle-class area, that is, one that re-
> mains as such. Our city fathers will not permit this.
> They insist on mixing levels of society in black areas.
> This practice is rare in white neighborhoods. In this
> area, vacant areas are immediately filled with welfare
> clients.

This mixture of economic classes in St. Albans has led to tensions among residents. "Tensions arise between old stable families and the new welfare tenants. There is also tension between the youth and older people." More recently, there has been another problem: the reemergence of real estate speculators who have sprung an extended form of blockbusting on the black middle class. A number of homes bought by the speculators have been rented to welfare families with the full cooperation of the Department of Social Services. Others, originally constructed as single-family homes, have been converted into rooming houses for welfare recipients. This has had a deteriorating effect on the community.

> The Social Services Department refuses to accept its responsibility. The results: chaos, wreckage, ruin amidst decent communities. The same atmosphere invades the schools. Many parents refuse to send their children to public schools. This in-movement of welfare families also affects businesses. Many businesses in this area have closed down because of robbings, muggings, burglaries—we have so many vacant stores here. This used to be a good shopping center, especially Linden Boulevard near Mexico Street,

said an active community leader.

Because of rising property values, the St. Albans community presently houses a diverse population; there still remains a class of old stable homeowners and a newer class of welfare renters. There are very few younger families in St. Albans. Despite the absence of young couples, a great number of young children roam the area. They are foster kids taken in from city agencies by older people who have raised their own children and now have the room. An alternative to taking in foster children is to rent an apartment. Some rent to relatives or friends, but some St. Albans residents say others have taken in welfare families, and that the result has been vandalism and crime, a resultant depreciation of property, and an overall decline in neighborhood quality.

ST. ALBANS AND ADDESLEIGH PARK: NEIGHBORHOOD

> They call it the Forest Hills of Southeast Queens. And though it may be a little ragged around the edges now, the St. Albans area, with its luxurious single-family houses and manicured lawns, is still the showcase it was when blacks first moved there nearly 30 years ago.

Its picture-postcard attractiveness belies the
stories told about blacks by the real estate dealers
who panicked the whites out of St. Albans after
World War II. [13]

The nature of the black community adjacent to the area just
inside the South Jamaica line is important because it consists of
middle-income, stable, home-owning black families. The lots are
bigger, the yards better kept, the houses larger, in better condition, and more expensive than those occupied by the people living
adjacent to them. One would assume that there is relatively little
crime in this part of the neighborhood, and consequently little spillover of South Jamaica's problems. However, long-term residents
of the area perceive the St. Albans situation quite differently:

The pockets of poverty in South Jamaica have carried
over into other communities, namely St. Albans and
Addesleigh Park. In the past, when blacks moved up
the socioeconomic ladder, they moved out here. More
recently, since the late 1960s, welfare clients have been
moved here. As a result, the neighborhood is far less
desirable now.

Residents feel that the Social Services Department is exiling its
clients in large numbers to St. Albans and contributing tremendously to the transformation of the area.

The fire which took the lives of nine children and two
adults living in a one-family house on Mexico Street,
St. Albans, July 18th, may be an example if ghettoization continues to spread, almost 100 homeowners
charged last night. It may be that the man who created
the ghetto may have the same color skin as I, said a
St. Albans civic leader, but I worked for what I got
and you people [Department of Social Services] are
the ones who are creating the ghettoes here. [14]

The Welfare Department feels that its clients are incapable
of handling money, so the landlords receive their checks from the
Welfare Department. Sixteen people lived in the house that burned
down, and although the Welfare Department says they were related,
the fact is they weren't. An investigation was never taken to prove
their relation. One Social Services Department official responded:
"The position of this department is that every man has a right to
determine for himself where he wants to live and we will not tell

him where to go. We will help them find apartments, but our resources are limited."[15]

Many St. Albans residents who, until recently, saw the problems of crime and drugs as an outside phenomenon, from South
Jamaica, realize that the borders of South Jamaica and its social
problems are expanding into the St. Albans community. Residents
remember when they could walk a couple of blocks away from Merrick
Boulevard, and the quiet safety of St. Albans seemed miles from the
everyday problems of the poor.

The cheap lounges, bars, and grimy storefronts and the closed
stores that point out the flight of white businesses to the more affluent suburbs are evidence to long-term residents that their neighborhood is taking a turn for the worse.

> We no longer have good shopping here. There used to
> be a nice small shopping center on Mexico Street and
> Linden Boulevard, but ride past there now and you will
> see the vacant stores. With the changing character of
> the population, the storekeepers picked up and left the
> area.

Residents are appalled at existing shopping facilities in St. Albans,
especially for groceries: "As far as neighborhood groceries, there
are a damn few here that are satisfactory. Small grocery stores
simply don't exist. Supermarkets are filthy." As a result, many
St. Albans residents travel far outside the community to do the bulk
of their shopping, to Elmont or other parts of Nassau County. Some
residents, particularly the elderly and welfare families, are forced
to shop in the community and purchase inferior merchandise at exploitative prices.

> Neighborhood groceries have poor quality merchandise,
> especially meats and vegetables. Some of this is due
> to poor refrigeration. A new refrigeration system was
> supposed to be installed but it never was. The store-
> keepers are in no hurry to upgrade their stores, they
> have a sense of security. Elderly and poor families
> have no access to cars and since public transportation
> is so expensive (double fare) and inefficient, these
> residents are forced to shop inside the community.

Public transportation is a problem for residents of St. Albans.
"We have no cross transportation here. One has to ride 35 to 40
minutes on a bus to arrive at a dirty, unsafe, train station."

Inadequate **roads** is another major complaint. Streets and sidewalks are often in bad condition, abandoned cars dot the curbs. While residents admit that this problem is not novel to the community, they feel that the problem is getting much more severe.

> Oh yes, streets and sidewalks are absolutely in bad condition. Some streets have no sidewalks. Bus stops have a lot of graffiti. Many abandoned cars appear throughout the community. While the streets were never great, 15 years ago they were taken care of. Since the population of this community shifted, the city shifted its services outside the community.

Some residents feel that the increased density of population explains the conditions of the streets: "Streets are not as clean as they were 20 years ago. Abandoned cars lie around for a long time. The incoming of too many people has caused saturation, congestion, and has a negative effect on the neighborhood." Others feel that the city has withdrawn such essential services as the economic structure of the community has changed.

While nearby South Jamaica has a high structural fire and false alarm rate, this problem is not as evident in St. Albans. Residents feel that the predominance of owner-occupied single-family homes explains the difference.

The crime problem has recently been of paramount concern to St. Albans residents.

> Practically every house has an alarm system and a dog. I am in fear of robbery, burglary, intimidation of my young children, vandalism, pocketbook snatching. Crime against person and property have increased, increased tremendously. The 103rd Precinct has the highest rates of many individual crimes and, as expected, the highest unemployment rate in New York City.

> Crime is a most serious problem here. I was held up right in this building [NAACP building, Jamaica Branch].

The increasing awareness by St. Albans residents of the crime problem in the area has caused increased tensions between stable long-term homeowners and more recent migrants. Old-timers blame the high crime rates on these newcomers.

> Are there tensions here—yes! The other side of the
> area, west of Merrick Boulevard, houses drug addicts
> and alcoholics, sick people. These people have a lot
> of problems, economic in root [unemployment]. Re-
> cently these people have been allowed to move into St.
> Albans and this has created our crime problem! In
> this neighborhood, you see black people turning on each
> other, like rats in a cage. There are too many and
> they have to survive. In addition, increased tension
> arises because of the awareness of police brutality—
> the disregard for the citizen by the police force.

As in South Jamaica, the drug problem is evident in St. Albans.

> A bright shiny front does not guarantee what is within.
> Just last week, one of my neighbor's sons was ar-
> rested for selling hard drugs. I later found out that
> this young man had been selling drugs to support his
> own habit. This young man came from a middle-class
> family. The drug problem in a black community sees
> no income level. I don't think the problem is as
> severe in a middle-income white community.

The state of community health in St. Albans is deficient. The
rates of communicable diseases, while above the borough average,
are far less than those of South Jamaica. Residents feel that many
private doctors have left the community as the population shifted.
"Lack of good medical care is a serious problem now but it hasn't
always been." There are no hospitals in the immediate area.
Jamaica Hospital is the closest hospital facility.

St. Albans lacks recreation facilities. The few parks in the
area are not well kept and are understaffed. "Parks have winos
and stuff. There is no supervision in the parks, children cannot
use facilities as a result. Parks are few in number and are not
used by many children because parents are in fear of sending their
children to them." Virtually all the movie theaters that served the
area are gone. The St. Albans Terrace, on Linden Boulevard, was
at one time a movie theater. Because of the expense of public transportation, many resident children and teenagers are forced to remain in the community. With limited parks and playgrounds and no
cultural recreational facilities, children are forced to use the
streets for recreation. Many residents feel that this is one of the
main reasons for the unusually high juvenile delinquency rates.
The increasing number of foster children in the area is also of considerable significance.

In the past, the public schools in the area were of a high caliber. At one time, teachers were residents of St. Albans and had a stake in the community. Students were also of a much higher caliber.

> Schools in the area are not good. Students' reading
> levels are well below par. Part of the problem stems
> from the lack of interest of the parents. A child's be-
> havior is reflective of the home from which he comes.
> As a result of the people who moved in recently—the
> welfare element—the learning process has deteriorated.
> While teachers do play a role in problems in the schools,
> they would hesitate to harass children if they felt
> threatened by the parents.

The vulnerability of areas like St. Albans lies in the lack of political power. St. Albans is pretty much a "bedroom community," people come home to sleep. There is no general feeling of community.

Reverend Robert Ross Johnson, pastor of the St. Albans Congregational Church, chides the traditional conservatism of the black middle class and its unwillingness to get involved in solving social problems. "They're blind to it," he says. "They're not ready to move others along. They'd like to think it isn't there. It's what white society has done to them in terms of the poor. People have a tendency to stay to themselves and not be involved. The only way they will act is if they are physically threatened." Johnson finds that many St. Albans residents are still tied emotionally and politically to their old neighborhoods. "Some of these people go to Harlem and Bedford Stuyvesant to go to church. I ask them: do you do your shopping there and send your children to school there?" While the answer to both of these questions is no, residents don't shop in the area or send their children to neighborhood schools unless they are faced with no other choice. "This is not the best place to bring up children because of lack of facilities. The high school [Andrew Jackson] is terrible. Part of the commitment to this area includes finding an alternative school system." Many residents are active in the church so that their children can attend parochial schools.

In a sense, the lack of involvement in St. Albans may not be different from the attitudes of the black middle class elsewhere. Historically, people are moved to action only when they feel directly threatened. A recent example of this type of community concern was the issue of closing down six libraries in Southeast Queens. One active community leader said:

I warned these people that our libraries were being
underutilized and that this might result in the closing
down of some of them. I told residents to make an effort to take out books, even if they weren't planning to
read them, just so that circulation would be increased.
But nobody listened and now, six libraries in Southeast
Queens will be closed down as of November 1, 1975.

On October 23, 1975, approximately 250 St. Albans residents attended a meeting "in protest" of the closing down of these libraries.

Complaints about poor municipal services and crimes are not
satisfied by stopgap measures like the private guard service hired
in Addesleigh Park. The fact that St. Albans probably has the
largest concentration of black professionals in the city adds to the
frustration of many residents and leaders.

SAMPLE INTERVIEW NO. 1:
SOUTH JAMAICA AND ST. ALBANS

1. Yes, yes, at the present moment it is still a good place to
live in; needs must be attacked in a constructive manner. There is
a need for a rehabilitation plan that takes into account characters
other than physical. The human quotient is needed in planning.
Tenant councils are necessary to maintain high stability. Some of
the present things were less apparent 10 or 20 years ago. There
is an influx of welfare tenants in one- and two-family homes. The
deterioration isn't as bad as other neighborhoods. Social patterns
predominate, but not any more than 10 or 20 years ago. Population
characteristics are the same for the past 10 years. Fewer children, less juvenile crime, more children, more juvenile crime.
Schools are way below the city norm for reading levels.

2. Foster-care children are rejected in the schools. Many
people (renters) use foster-care children for supplementing income.
The lack of many high-rise houses is a positive thing. This neighborhood has many individual homeowners who lack the resources to
keep their property in good condition. The city has not given South
Jamaica a particularly high priority except for the public houses
constructed earlier. Urban renewal efforts are minimal in this
area. Lower population might be a causative factor of low priority
in South Jamaica.

Interviewees were William Lucas, a planner; and Reverend
Johnson.

3. I consider this neighborhood to be my real home. I've lived here for 20 years and moved here because of need, not desire; I've lived here for 35 years and consider this my real home.

4. I might move, possibly to get a little further away from the job. I don't want to pioneer in other areas where the blacks are rejected, such as Rosedale. I will remain here for economic reasons; I can't afford to move.

5. Older friends have moved away and we are trying to encourage relatives to move here. I influenced many people to move into this area.

6. People have a tendency to stay to themselves and not be involved. Physical threats are the only way there is any action. There is a great diversity of people who share only the racial background, they do not share the same educational and financial background.

7. Bedford Stuyvesant had a similar situation. There was nice housing on the block but the neighborhood was slowly being deteriorated.

8. We are appalled! Rents remain pretty much the same while property is run down. Banks will not lend mortgage money necessary for upkeep. There is a transition from older established families to younger established families. We have young executives and teachers in this area. Property values are down and rents up while we attract more blue-collar and welfare people.

9. For a long time, we had class tensions, not racial tensions. There was much frustration due to lack of organization. The increasing Puerto Rican population might tend to cause racial tensions. There are economic tensions, crime, drugs, and educational tensions.

10. Public housing has no direct impact, although we find negative elements coming from the projects. South Jamaica II did not have a negative impact on the area. Part of this is due to the fact that it was constructed across the street from a co-op.

11. We have limited public housing. Scattered sites are optimal.

12. Shopping

Groceries: outside the neighborhood
Clothing: outside the neighborhood
Appliances and furniture: outside the neighborhood
Parks and playgrounds: outside the neighborhood
Doctors and clinics: outside the neighborhood
Banking: outside the neighborhood
Movies: outside the neighborhood
We shop in either Elmont or Nassau County.

13. There is a glaring lack in delivery of health services and health care problems do exist and always have. Proposals have been drawn up, but not much has been done about them.

14. In case of sudden illness, we go to hospitals outside of the area. Services are fair.

15. There are no recreational facilities for adults. People have to go outside of this area and are reluctant to go elsewhere for their amusement. Facilities for seniors have increased. Private facilities are lacking. A young swinger has nothing to do! All we have are commercial bars, pool halls; there are no bowling alleys and only three tennis courts. There is absolutely nothing to do in this area.

16. There are no teenage centers and they hang out for lack of anything else to do, which, eventually, leads to destruction.

17. There are virtually no facilities for children. We have one playground, no school programs, no little league, no Four H clubs, or football—no all-American sports. We do, however, have a few Boy Scout and Girl Scout troops that are widely scattered.

18. Our children use the streets for recreational facilities. They would use parks if they were available and were safe from crime. Years ago, there were empty lots in which to play, but they have been filled with houses.

19. Merrick Road is atrocious; Main Street is in bad condition, but the side streets are all right. No telephone booths, many abandoned cars, although that's not a major problem.

20. There is no alternate side of street parking. People are afraid to park on the streets. The side streets are pretty clean but are in poor condition.

21. The garbage collections are getting better. It is collected twice a week and has been consistent for the past 35 years.

22. The day care facilities are improving. The quality of the programs leaves much to be desired.

23. Public transportation is a big negative—a great hardship for residents. It costs $1.00 to get to the city and $1.00 to get back. The bus ride is terrible and there is graffiti all over everything.

24. Crossing guards did exist; police also assist children.

25. The schools are not equipped to handle the influx of new students and the quality of the education is poor.

26. The schools are closed during the evenings and during summer months.

27. There is a new library in this area, although it is not well utilized. They do have adequate facilities for school-age children.

28. The produce and meats are of poor quality. We do have an A & P but it's not very clean. People tend to shop elsewhere if they can.

29. All the movie theaters have been closed.

30. We are besieged with churches! Every week, a new storefront church is opened. Church is a form of recreation. A small church provides a sense of identification for people who are not aggressive. There are many hustle bangers in the church; the shoe cobbler is a storefront preacher on the side. West of Merrick Boulevard there are not as many new storefronts as the eastern part of the area. Storefront churches are for the West Indians; the first group from the British West Indies came in the 1930s and early 1940s.

31. One would think that with increasing population, services would increase. But instead what we have is a diminution of services. There is no hospital or any child stations in the immediate area. Drug stores are all closed during evening hours; within a three-mile radius there isn't a drug store opened after 6:00 P.M.

32. Public facilities and services are generally good west of Merrick Boulevard. Street signs and lights are in good condition. East of Merrick Boulevard the situation is just the opposite. Many streets are in bad condition and there is a lack of street lights and signs.

33. Storekeepers overcharge in this area. They blame this on high rates of pilferage. The truth is that they have older merchandise and no cash flow, which causes them to increase prices. This is plain exploitation. The neighborhood is accustomed to this type of treatment. People can be exploited because of poor transportation. Storekeepers do not treat people very nicely, that's why people leave the area. Some stores have bullet-proof enclosures—most impersonal service. Storekeepers come and exploit the area and then go to the suburbs.

34. There are no foot patrolmen. There are five cars that serve the sectors and a few motor scooters between 8:00 and 4:00 P.M. Efforts are extremely limited in main areas. The crime problem here is limited to household robberies. Police goof off by staying in safe areas, heavy traffic areas.

35. There are no courts in this area. The available courts are so jammed. This area supplies lots of clients. Courts contribute to the problem of crime—there are two standards of justice.

36. Unqualified no! The schools are poor. The caliber of teachers is a problem; facilities, parents, programs, are a problem. There is also a discipline problem in the schools. Many children are bussed out of the area. There is a lack of community concern on the part of the teachers; they live elsewhere. They do not harass students, students harass them!

37. Welfare workers—in the eastern portion—they don't visit too much. People go to the centers, become a number; welfare

workers are very callous and, in some instances, harass the
people. Very few of them do a full day's work.

38. Practically every house has an alarm system and a dog.
We are in fear of robbery, burglary, intimidation of young children,
vandalism, pocketbook snatchers. Crimes against persons and
property have increased, increased tremendously. The 103rd Precinct has the highest rates of individual crimes, especially felonies.
The people in this area constitute a high degree of unemployment.

39. Fires are a part of the urban renewal process. Buildings are overtaxed and unimproved. Fires have become more common. Conversion of houses and overuse of electric current causes
fires.

40. Drug problems exist both east and west of Merrick Boulevard. A bright shiny front does not guarantee what is within. Non-
minority areas, with homes of similar value, will have less of a
problem.

41. There is noise sometimes: hot rodders, motor bikes,
trucks, violate residential streets.

42. Gang problems have existed for at least 35 years.

43. This is not the best place to bring up children because of
the lack of facilities. The high schools here are terrible. Part of
the commitment to the area includes finding an alternative school
system.

44. We do not have a problem of high-rise buildings.

45. Stores have burglary gates; there are security systems
in all homes and stores.

46. I have lived here 35 years, 6 years in a new house; 20
years in the same house.

47. There is virtually no bad housing west of Merrick Boulevard. In some instances, housing has been improved. There is a
problem in the eastern part of the area with many illegally converted
houses. The Neighborhood Housing Services Corp., which consists
of local residents and banks, is involved in administering mortgage
and home improvement loans.

48. I do not rent this apartment.

49. Most tenants do not have leases or formal agreements.
Many renters are transient, younger, single people. Most people
who can afford to rent will buy; $250 a month rent can translate into
a $20,000 home with mortgage and taxes. Repairs and services are
not handled in a business-type fashion. Lumber is of poor quality
and extremely high priced. A lot of people are involved in home
repair situations. Business practices are deplorable. Jack Leg
Home Improvement Companies do a job, and do a job on you in the
process.

52. Welfare renters are seriously exploited.

53. I have 8 rooms; I have 11 rooms.

54. The bathroom in my house has a window.

58. West of Merrick Boulevard the landlords rent apartments in one-family houses. East of Merrick Boulevard, there are many absentee landlords. Anything that approaches ten units, the landlord does not live in the house or the area, the house is an investment.

59. Most apartment buildings have laundry rooms in the basement.

60. There are some tenants' associations, but they are not too effective. Fights are concerned with rents, have done nothing to control the crime problem. They are primarily concerned with maintaining the building and have no effect on the surrounding area.

61. There are a whole slew of neighborhood improvement groups. They have a little party and let off steam. The efforts are not coordinated.

62. Initiated civic organizations and clubs.

63. Clubs in this community tend to be internally oriented like a motorcycle club.

64. No.

65. No.

There is not any one reliable measure today of the percentage of income used for housing. There are tremendous variations in the percentage of income spent for housing. I spend 35 percent of my income for housing. Discrimination in housing causes blacks to allocate more of their income toward housing.

In this new Section 8 program, finders, keepers is the name of the game. The property owners are really being subsidized, not the tenants. Since federal programs call for small apartments, large families will be exploited under Section 8. Any standard that is used for housing costs should be individual and be related to costs in the neighborhood, not in the city as a whole.

SAMPLE INTERVIEW NO. 2: SOUTHEAST QUEENS

1. This neighborhood is not a good place in which to live. It was more desirable 10 or 20 years ago.

2. The good points of this neighborhood are that it has a suburban atmosphere, and it is not too far from the city. The bad points

---

Interviewee was Anna Thompson, a civic leader from Hollis, St. Albans.

are poor transportation and continual deterioration of the business area. Farmers Boulevard, Hollis Avenue, and Linden Boulevard have limited shopping conveniences, especially supermarkets. There has been a decrease in the number of pharmacies, an increase in crime, muggings, and burglaries. The long-established residents have been moving out and the influx of people with limited resources for home investment were forced to bring in roomers. There is an erosion of middle-class families, who are being replaced with welfare families. The schools have deteriorated. Civic organizations that were active at one time are hanging on by bare threads.

3. I consider this neighborhood not as a real home, but a place where I happen to be living.

4. I would love to move out of this neighborhood and into Jamaica Estates, Belrose, or Holliswood. I am not there because of prohibitive interest rates. I do intend to make the move at some time in the future.

5. I have no relatives in this area, but I do have a few close friends. I came in following close friends because they helped me to look for a house.

6. There is diversity, which is typical of black so-called middle-class neighborhoods; it's not the same type of mobility as white middle class. Real estate brokers did not encourage this mobility. They encouraged people who cannot afford houses to buy them, resulting in these people taking in roomers. Scare tactics were used by real estate operators. They invited anyone here who had $200 down, and encouraged them, when necessary, to take second mortgages and roomers. In this area, professionals live side by side with welfare recipients.

7. I lived on Saratoga Avenue and Broadway 15 years ago when the area was very nice. I moved to purchase this home. I see this area as resembling the deterioration of my prior neighborhood. The same thing is happening with businesses moving, poor quality of people taking in roomers.

8. The area is deteriorating with lowering property values. It is frightening because the values are not fair market prices.

9. There is no racial tension here because everybody is black. There is, however, tension between youth and older people, a form of class tension.

10. Public housing is not the same as it was years ago. Requirements for occupancy are not as stringent. It deteriorates the neighborhood by making it more crowded. The schools have not been increased to allow for the influx of new students. The projects bring in people of lower educational levels.

11. The neighborhood was a good one before the projects were built.

12. We do our grocery shopping and buy our clothes outside the neighborhood. We do, however, bank and use the doctors and clinics in the neighborhood. We have to go outside for our movies and we don't use the parks at all.

13. Lack of good medical care is a serious problem and has always been a serious problem.

14. We use the Brooklyn Jewish Hospital or the LaGuardia Hospital.

15. We have no recreational facilities for adults in this area.

16. There is a lack of recreation for teenagers and this causes crime.

17. There is no recreation for children in this area.

18. When the schools were opened in the evening, the middle-class parents would not send their children because of the crime problem. My children belong to the Drum Corps, Girl Scouts, take piano and karate lessons.

19. The streets are in very poor condition. Some blocks have no sidewalks. There are graffiti marks on the bus stops, and many abandoned cars. Fifteen years ago this was a beautiful neighborhood, but the streets were never great. There are no telephone booths in the area and the telephone company knows the reason they are not being installed.

20. There is no alternate side of the street parking. People complain about moving their cars.

21. There has been a marked improvement in the garbage collection due to the activities of the Civic Association and the block associations who have been breathing down the necks of the Sanitation Department.

22. We could use more day care centers to accommodate the middle-class children.

23. Public transportation is an absolute problem. There is no cross transportation. There is a 35- or 40-minute ride to the trains, and the stations are unclean and unsafe.

24. Crossing the streets is not a problem for the children.

25. The schools are not equipped to handle the influx of children. Thousands of families are brought into the neighborhood and no additional schools are being built to accommodate their children.

26. The schools in this area are not opened in the evening nor are they opened during the summer months.

27. There are adequate library facilities in this area that are underutilized. Both libraries in this area are being closed down.

28. Neighborhood stores have poor quality merchandise, especially meats and vegetables. Some of this is due to poor refrigera-

tion. A new refrigeration system was supposed to be installed.
The storekeepers have a sense of security because the elderly have
no means of transportation and must shop in the neighborhood.

29. The one movie theater we had in the neighborhood was
closed down.

30. There are too many storefront churches with insincere
ministers in this neighborhood. These churches are of no value.
The regular churches with the white ministers actively participated
in problems of the community and tried to help solve them.

31. Sanitation pickups have increased. Street repairs and
neglected sewers were always a problem in Queens, because they
were never included in the capital budget, as promised. Police
protection has decreased considerably—it started to improve with
the Lindsay administration.

32. The general quality of public facilities is good. Garbage
is not scattered around, although some equipment needs replacement.

33. Storekeepers overcharge in this area, but they do not
treat the people badly. The storekeepers used to live in the neighborhood, but they don't any more. There are not many stores left
in this area.

34. We do not have adequate police protection. The situation
has improved because of the civilian patrols, block associations,
and community relations. The police do not harass us. All precincts have active community affairs departments or police precinct
councils.

35. There are no courts in the immediate area.

36. The schools in this area are not good. The reading levels
of the students are below normal. There is no interest on the part
of the parents, and the children reflect the negativeness of the home
from which they come. The learning process has deteriorated.
Teachers would hesitate to harass children if they were threatened
by their parents.

37. Welfare workers do not ever visit this area. They do not
even appear when they are asked to come out. They don't know
what's going on in the welfare homes. There were 22 people in a
home, 11 died—welfare didn't know of the situation.

38. Crime is a serious problem, particularly mugging, crime
against my children. Crime has increased tremendously. When I
moved here, we could walk home at 3:00 in the morning, keep doors
open, and there were no burglar alarms or bars on the windows.

39. There are a considerable number of fires, and a tremendous number of false alarms. Jamaica/Hollis had one of the largest
number of false alarms in the city, the largest in Queens.

40. This area is a hangout for drug users and there are a few
methadone clinics in the area. This has not always been the case.

41. The neighborhood is noisy, much noisier than it used to be. Too many young kids are "hanging out." There is too much permissiveness of residents who allow for sextets, or a combo of musicians, who will unresponsibly play until all hours of the night.

42. There are gang problems in this area and it has gotten worse in the past three to four years.

43. There are no safe places for children to play. Children need a constructive kind of environment that is supervised and has an educational type of recreation. This is not a good area in which to bring up children.

44. High-rise buildings perpetuate crime.

45. Most stores in this area have burglary gates and this has been the case for about five years.

46. I have lived in this neighborhood for 15 years, and in the same home.

47. Bad housing is not a widespread and serious problem. Boarded up houses are, however, a serious problem. They become vacant after an FHA or Veterans Administration foreclosure and then vandalized. There was no bad housing 15 years ago.

50. Local banks loaned money to the builders, not directly to us.

52. Landlords are ripping off welfare tenants.

53. I have 7.5 rooms: 4 bedrooms, living room, dining room, kitchen.

54. The bathroom in my house has a window.

55. This is a private house, no elevator is necessary.

57. I have my own house so I don't suffer from lack of heat, hot water, rats, roaches, or broken walls.

58. Landlords live outside the buildings and outside the area.

60. There are too many local neighborhood improvement groups—and they are all ineffective. There are too many large civic associations and they attack the problem on an areawide basis, not on a local basis. There are too many small groups, and each one tries to be the leader.

61. There are not many tenants' associations in this area.

62. I belong to the Civic Association, Political Club, Black Association by necessity.

63. Clubs, if they address themselves to areawide problems in a unified way, can be very effective in combating problems. Politicians and people in city hall respond to unified community organization.

64. We asked for help in removing a methadone clinic and building a hospital. We tried to get jobs for minority-owned companies. We asked for help to alleviate the influx of welfare recip-

ients. We asked for help in maintaining our hospital and servicing our veterans.

65. We know all of our legislators and are in constant contact with them.

NOTES

1. See H. Powdermaker, <u>After Freedom</u> (Toronto: Macmillan, 1939), for an analysis of class segregation among blacks in the south.

2. "What Is South Jamaica," Long Island <u>Press</u>, October 3, 1968.

3. See Hoberman and Wasserman, <u>South Jamaica Community Development Study</u> (New York: Hoberman & Wasserman Architects and Planners, 1969).

4. "What Is South Jamaica," op. cit.

5. See Hoberman and Wasserman, op. cit.

6. Ibid.

7. Ibid.

8. Ibid.

9. "The Borough's No. 1 Eyesore Is South Jamaica—Lots Abound with Large Assortments of Junk and Garbage," Long Island <u>Press</u>, August 9, 1971.

10. See Hoberman and Wasserman, op. cit.

11. "St. Albans Opens to Negroes," Long Island <u>Press</u>, May 29, 1956.

12. Illusions of the Black Middle Class," Sunday <u>News</u>, June 16, 1974.

13. Ibid.

14. "Disaster on Mexico Street," Long Island <u>Press</u>, August 14, 1968.

15. Ibid.

11
THE ROCKAWAYS

Many Rockaways residents perceive the peninsula on which they live as a city within, but apart from, the city. As one resident said: "Rockaways is my real home. I relate to the Rockaways. We are so physically isolated from the rest of the city that we must be a community." The major change that occurred in the Rockaways in recent decades was the transformation from a resort to a year-round community. Population density has soared and, for the first time, high-rise buildings silhouette the waterfront. The bulk of these high-rise buildings are public or publicly aided housing.

These changes have created tensions among the residents. They have argued that development occurred without adequate infra-structure. Many residents were opposed to the proliferation of public housing on the peninsula, especially since this caused a tre-mendous increase in population that was not followed through by an increase in municipal services. The lack of planning has been felt by Rockaways residents, who must contend with backed up house drains, flooded streets, and unhealthy conditions resulting from the absence of storm sewers and adequate roads. The lack of infra-structure extends to other areas: social services, health services, and recreational and educational facilities that have failed to keep pace with the growing population.

Two neighborhoods, Arverne North and Edgemere North, have deplorable housing conditions. This has been the case since the early 1950s:

> Crumbling, ramshackle boarding houses, rookeries
> jammed to the hilt with families living in one- and two-
> room cubicles. . . . Dirty kids playing in litter-
> strewn streets and in rubble-laden backyards. . . .

239

> Dank, crusty cellars used as living quarters, where
> an adult can't walk two steps without bumping into
> overhead pipes. . . . Shattered plaster walls, ex-
> posing "live" electric wiring . . . in three-story
> wooden buildings with no fire escapes.[1]

Many apartments in these buildings lacked bathtubs and some
had only one toilet. For these decrepit apartments, families paid
as high as $45 per month for one-room apartments (in 1954). The
cost to these families was almost double that during winter months,
for tenants had to keep their ranges burning constantly to keep warm.

The one- and two-family houses in Edgemere are converted
bungalows and vacant lots exist on nearby land. Deterioration and
large sections of neglected, marginally developed land in Arverne
are a constant reminder of the transitional nature of this neighborhood.

Community residents are opposed to the provision of clusters
of nursing homes and other health—related facilities for the aged.
The situation is even more acute with regard to domiciliary care
facilities for adults. The Rockaways would contain 72 percent of
the Queens county total if all such beds now planned or under construction were built.

The poor and the elderly on the peninsula are particularly
handicapped by the double fare zone (initiated in 1956 and recently
abolished) and geographic isolation, which place an intolerable
burden on the morale of those seeking jobs, health care, social
services, and contact with those not living on the island. Residents
are burdened by the long costly journey to Brownsville, where the
closest income maintenance center is located, and Kew Gardens,
where Queens General Hospital and the nearest vocational training
school are located.

NEIGHBORHOOD

The Rockaway Peninsula is an 11-mile finger of land, separated from the southern shore of Long Island by Jamaica Bay. It
contains some of the most beautiful and desirable land in the city
with a magnificent beach and the cleanest waters in the metropolitan
area. Air pollution is minimal, even on the worst of days. Despite the natural resources, the Rockaways, in the past decade or
two, have been going downhill.

Although the peninsula still has strong residential communities (in the east, Far Rockaway, Wavecrest, and Bayswater; and
in the west, Rockaway Park, Belle Harbor, Neponsit, Breezy Point,

Fort Tilden) the Rockaways have been converted into a depressed area. The peninsula is the location, today, of some of the worst poverty pockets in New York City.[2]

Several factors have been involved, first and foremost among them being the exodus of business and professional communities from the peninsula. Taxes have imposed a greater hardship on the community's depressed economy, especially in view of the concomitant diminution of services. Soaring crime rates have taken their toll on the area.

As businesses closed and shopping became worse, the high cost of living added fuel to the fire. The most important factors can be boiled down to two: the near impossibility of making a living in an area where there are almost no jobs, with inadequate public transportation to areas that have jobs; and the city's determination to turn the Rockaways into a welfare peninsula.[3]

The fact that the Rockaways are, historically, a seaside resort community has some effect. A declining summer market was beginning to manifest itself after World War II. When the automobile came into its own, after World War II, Long Island's beaches were accessible to the city dweller. The widespread use of air conditioning obviated the necessity of going out to the seaside to cool off, and television tended to confine people to their homes. However, these factors are highly overrated. After all, why didn't the car, television, and air conditioning ruin the New Jersey shore community? A much more important set of factors is New York City's policies and lack of policies in the community.

When the Long Island Railroad trestle across Jamaica Bay burned down in 1950, the city stepped in with a promise to incorporate the Rockaways into the subway system and provide low-cost, dependable rapid transit. While the city did build a mass transit connection to the mainland, it is not dependable or low cost. In 1956 the city instituted a double fare. The inequity of the double fare coupled with the poor service prompted many residents to move out of the area, closer to the labor markets.

As the market for summer rentals declined, owners who were desperate to meet financial obligations found they could maintain a reasonable profit by converting properties to year-round usage and renting to welfare tenants. At the time the diminishing market began to reach its peak, relocation from the Hammel area was instituted. There was blockbusting, speculation, and the preying upon of minority families. Hence, what was a seasonal slum gradually became a year-round slum as the advent of minority-group families curtailed seasonal marketability.

The city's first answer to this crisis was enactment of the Treulich Bill, which precluded conversion of bungalows by installation of heat unless they could comply with the provisions of the administrative code. The next step was the introduction of an Area Services Program.

As the community began to slide downhill under the weight of bureaucratic immobility, the city took drastic action: it removed 310 acres from the tax rolls by declaring them a slum clearance area—the Arverne Urban Renewal Site. In the opinion of many people, this is when the Rockaways' troubles began in earnest.

The Arverne-Edgemere Urban Renewal Project seemed to be a well-intentioned, good idea. Its purpose was to eliminate half a square mile of slums, encumbered with decrepit, obsolete, old beach bungalow housing. But it got weighted down in bureaucratic red tape. The plans were adopted, then changed, then contested, then disapproved, then canceled, and the cycle was repeated again and again. The original half square mile of slums grew to several square miles. In places garbage is piled ten to 12 feet deep. Why doesn't the Housing and Development Administration (HDA) contact the owners, make them clean up the mess and fence the lot, as the law requires, to prevent dumping? Because HDA, our stalwart enforcers of the law, the nemesis of scofflaw landlords, finds it inconvenient to cite itself for violations. HDA isn't set up to harass the landlord when it is, itself, the landlord.

Of course, this has a deadening effect on the surrounding property. Neighboring property owners, chilled and revolted by the sight of what their community has become, move out, leaving more abandoned houses to add to the vacant, unsealed structures that dot HDA's never-never land. There are now some 300 vacant abandoned structures, many of them vandalized and/or burnt out, between the renewal site and Jamaica Bay.[4] It is like a cancer spreading through the community, to the east, north, and even west.

The Rockaways desperately need parking for visitors. Not only is parking being squeezed off the peninsula, but the tolls on the bridges linking the Rockaways to their sustenance—the beach-goers during the outdoor recreation season—have been increased from $.10 to $.50. The rationale supposedly behind this is to discourage use of the private car and to encourage the use of mass transit. The only feasible way to encourage people to use the IND "Toonerville Trolley" would be to borrow some manacles from the Correction Department and chain people to the car straps.[5]

If the city were really interested in promoting the use of mass transit, it would change this line into a low-cost dependable rapid transit system, by the simplest expedient of following up on the plan it adopted when it acquired the right of way between Liberty Avenue and White Pot Junction. This line was to connect the Rockaways to Manhattan via the Long Island Railroad's forgotten spur. The forgotten spur had been brought up again, as a possible route for a high speed connection to Kennedy Airport. Recently, this train began operating between Manhattan and Kennedy Airport. This is a great idea, but it would serve a lot more people if it connected with the Rockaways.

Into this transit limbo, which the middle class is abandoning at full speed, who dares to tread? Only those who are told by those with the power to tell them where they must live. HRA, overjoyed at the prospect of a gaping vacuum, sends its welfare clients out much faster than the subway trains could ever carry them.

The tragedy is that the poor are, themselves, the losers. They are relocated from a slum in the Bronx, Brooklyn, or Manhattan into an instant slum, no better than where they came from. From there they could ride a train for one fare to a job market in a matter of minutes; from the Rockaways, there is no place to go, no way up, no way out!

A survey of residents of developments under the jurisdiction of HDA revealed that almost 50 percent came from Brooklyn, largely from Flatbush. This survey indicated that 56 percent of the labor force is employed in Manhattan, while 22 percent and 15 percent are employed in Brooklyn and Queens, respectively. Only 4 percent of these residents worked in the Rockaways.[6] Incontrovertible evidence of the city's policy to exile low- and no-income people into the Rockaways are the 11,000 welfare checks sent there in every mailing.[7]

Business is addicted to purchasing power and follows it where it goes. As the city drives middle-income people out, it replaces them with welfare clients. The purchasing power in these areas, in the long run, is never replaced.

Isn't it more decent to transplant disadvantaged people to a viable, functioning community, rather than banish them from one slum to another? Worse, to a slum in a double fare zone, with neither the hope nor the incentive to find a job. Yet the bureaucracies insist on swamping the community with the unemployed, knowing that there are no jobs, no hope, and no future for them here. As one community leader said: "Pick up a lot of people, pack them in large houses, give them some money; you instill illness in them—you entertain present illnesses and create additional ones."

But what of other city services? The obvious reasons for living in a city rather than in the country are legion—police protection from crime, paved streets, piped gas, water and sewers, and so on. The crime rate, of course, is an endemic problem in all urban slums, worst of all in the slum that the city has created in the Rockaways. Police protection is inadequate, as one member of the community states:

Police protection is adequate in number. The number
of policemen on the force for this population is adequate. But police are inadequate in the performance
of their duties—in respect to abandoned cars, trespassers, responding to calls, stray dogs—their attitude on the job is wrong. But 12:00 midnight police
are going around with flashlights and checking cars.

Streets are absolutely deplorable. Naturally, the city's offi-
cialdom has explained that New York City's climate is rough on
asphalt, and that it is difficult to maintain passable roads. "The
Highway Department is extremely negligent. There have been
many cracked sidewalks and potholes here for the longest time,"
adds one active community leader.

Garbage collection in this area is highly inadequate. Garbage
pick-up has occurred twice each week (the same, by the way, as
when this was a summer bungalow community). This is simply
too infrequent for a project population of this size. As one community resident stated: "Garbage is not picked up as often as it should
be. Garbage bags often hang around for days and then the dogs get
at them. This causes the neighborhood to get filthy."

Sewers are another matter. The first new business built on
116th Street in two decades was a diner at the corner of Beach
Channel Drive. It was delayed six months in getting its building
permit. One resident adds: "Due to the high tide and inadequate
sewers, many floods occur in basements of houses near the beach-
front. Water often remains for 52 hours after the rainfall."

Special things, like the Rockaways beaches, are another
matter. About five years ago, the sand was washed out to sea.
For five years, waves have been beating against the boardwalk,
and the visitors in search of beaches have headed toward Montauk.
Although the Rockaway Peninsula has what some consider to be a
nice beach, there is a tremendous lack of indoor recreational facilities. Almost all movie theaters that, at one time, served the
peninsula's population have closed down. Children from the neighborhood must go far outside their community for any indoor recreation. One resident claims: "My children have to go to Flushing
Meadows or Elmont for any roller skating, bowling, or other
recreation."

There is also a problem with library facilities. Until recently, the peninsula housed two libraries, which serviced a population of 100,000. Due to the recent budget cuts, one of the facilities was closed down.

In short, the city is aware of the Rockaways problem. It has
done virtually nothing to remedy these problems; in fact, it has

further exacerbated them. The city has attacked the urban rot that the mindless indifference of the bureaucracies has nurtured by bringing the Arverne-Edgemere Renewal Site to a complete standstill, destroying both Arverne and Edgemere. It has flooded the peninsula with public housing, resulting in tremendous population increases, while services have not been increased. It has promoted a glut of nursing homes and domiciliary facilities on the peninsula and exiled welfare clients there in droves. It has prevented a housing market from being developed by its policies of prohibitive transit fare, circuitous routes, and exorbitant bridge tolls. By placing the power to zone the peninsula into the hands of people with no knowledge of, or interest in, economics or construction, the result is that what they don't prohibit, economics does. At the same time, it has neglected the beach, the boardwalk, and existing recreational facilities, as well as the highways and streets, and even the land and houses it owns. The cancer is spreading from its 310-acre garbage dump throughout the community. To make things worse, the city has raised taxes so precipitously that the middle-class and business communities have been decimated.

One can readily see, from this analysis, that the public housing projects on the Rockaway Peninsula were constructed in an already existing slum area. At the time of construction, many converted bungalows had been deteriorating; many more were left abandoned (some of which were demolished to make way for projects). Residents of this area were faced with limited shopping facilities and a double-fare dilemma. In addition, streets and sidewalks were in bad condition, sewers were neglected.

Most important of all, the city has crowded thousands of people into Arverne, Edgemere, and Hammels and services including police, sanitation, fire, and so on, have been provided at the same levels as when these areas were summer resorts. Due to the lack of necessary municipal services, the neighborhood has deteriorated further.

HOUSING

The Rockaway Peninsula is the location today of some of the worst housing in New York City. The percentage of dilapidated housing in Health Area 37 (roughly Arverne) is 43.9. A Rockaway Community Council leader explained: "Bleak, weather-beaten dwellings face the ocean in Arverne. They are called home by the poor on the peninsula. Mosquitos breed where the pavement cracks, and trash litters the alley in the background." Many of the peninsula's poor are housed in ocean-front rooming houses and summer bungalows that have been converted to year-round use. He continued: "This is poverty in its worst form. Not even a rat would want to live in those Arverne cottages, but people are paying double the rent that many of us are paying in the Jamaica area."

This is the way it is today for Arverne residents, but it wasn't always like this. Thirty years ago the area represented one of the best seaside resorts in the New York metropolitan area. But the once glamorous ocean-front playground was allowed to fall into decay and now it has virtually crumbled.

The true origins of conditions in Arverne actually go back more than 22 years when the city built its first housing project in the Redfern area of the Rockaways to replace a slum. At that time, Redfern was considered the "tobacco road" of New York City and the municipality's worst slum. The persons affected in the Redfern condemnation were primarily black. Though this particular development held forth promise of decent housing conditions for the site tenants, this promise was never fulfilled. Instead, most of the residents of the area relocated to the Hammel area on the north side of Rockaway Beach Boulevard, an area of dilapidating rooming houses formerly used only during the summer season. With the advancement of the Hammel Public Housing Project these people moved into the Hammel Title I project site. Again, they moved into crumbling summer homes, and again, despite the promises of decent living conditions, in a city-subsidized project. In three years, a beach-front resort community was transformed into an area of disease-ridden, crime-breeding, overcrowded boarding houses.

Some years ago, a few real estate speculators saw promise in Hammels. They found a few hotelkeepers tired of their trade and a few homeowners willing to sell their beach houses at reasonable prices. The speculators bought these properties, installed stoves of ancient vintage, rickety furniture, sinks, heating, and a scattering of toilets and slapped sprinklers in the halls. At that point, they offered these rooms to the Welfare Department. For each room the city paid them up to $60 a month. Entire families were sent to cook, eat, sleep, live, and die in quarters that gave them less comfort than pigs in a sty.

> Slum Town condemns reliefers to idleness and breaks
> their spirit. They are isolated from the mainland of
> Queens where wage earners can get jobs. Parents
> and children lose the desire and ability to help them-
> selves in the immoral, unhealthy influence of the
> Slum Town. [8]

One third of all the tuberculosis in the Rockaways occurs in the teeming, garbage strewn 10-block area of
the Hammels Slum Town. There is 10 times as much
venereal disease in the Slum Town. The garbage-
littered streets show part of the reason why deaths and
disease have a field day in the Slum Town. Battered
old garbage cans line the streets, frothing over with
green and rotten scraps . . . beer cans . . . orange
peels . . . personal rubbish from the 2,000 families
in the teeming slum. [9]

When the Hammel Title I program was started, 1,800 families were involved; 1,200 were black. In an attempt to stop this
periodic migration of families from place to place into substandard
summer accommodations, a plan was advanced to construct the
Edgemere Houses in conjunction with the Hammel Title I project
for use as a relocation resource. But, in fact, this project, like
its predecessors in the Rockaways, brought in thousands of non-
Rockawayites, overtaxing schools, hospitals, and community
facilities.
The question arises: What happened to the 1,200 black
families from Hammel? Some moved out of the Rockaways while
others moved to an area similar to what they had left. This was
Arverne.

This is the way it is today for Arverne residents. They
live in old and decaying bungalows and walk along debris
strewn streets. Bold, scampering rats, bugs, uncollected garbage and packs of hungry dogs are everyday
sights. The area is composed primarily of summer
homes converted into rooming houses, many condemned
by the city. Many landlords neglect their properties
because urban renewal is supposedly on the way.
    The dark brown animal bites into the stuffing from
a broken chair. It then scuttles to the springs of an old
mattress and hunts for something to eat.
    Rats are a common sight in Arverne . . . and the
rats have a better time of it than the people.
    Garbage litters the area. Packs of wild dogs run
loose. Groups of teenagers congregate on street corners, ignoring the heat of the day and the filth that sur-
rounds them.
    Abandoned cars, their bodies stripped and tires
slashed, dot the curbs. [10]

The entire history of Arverne is a story of the indiscriminate construction of building public housing without solving any of the community's problems, of a lack of comprehensive planning, of a wandering people shunted from place to place from one ramshackle rooming house or bungalow to another, of overcrowding, unsanitary conditions and general blight, and it is a story of a municipality's inability to cope with the problems of individuals, minority groups, and the community.

SAMPLE INTERVIEW NO. 1

1. Arverne is a good place to live in now. In the projects, most people are in the same economic category.
2. Good: not much turnover in housing, due to middle-income residents. Bad: shopping facilities are few and the available ones are far enough away so that one cannot get there without a car. Even a candy store is a long walk. You need to walk ten blocks to get a match!
3. This is my real home. I am living here ten years. I moved from Edgemere to Arverne. Most people are working people—they are in and out—you don't get to know them.
4. I would move out, because rents go up very steep as income increases, but I wouldn't move out of the Rockaways.
5. When I moved here, I didn't know anyone, but many relatives have moved here since.
6. Most people are trying to find a decent place to live at a reasonable rent.
7. When I was on welfare, I was discriminated against. Now that I am working, the same people have a different attitude toward me. South Jamaica, where I lived before, was not as compact as it is now. The area was middle class. I moved to the Rockaways because my welfare worker sent me here. I moved to the Rockaways out of necessity. The area was not hustle-bustle when I moved here.
8. Property values are subject to bigotry—slumlords are charging Park Avenue prices and providing lousy housing. Tenants are paying champagne prices for apartments and getting beer-money service. The slum landlords are cleaning up. Poor people get no services, landlords allow buildings to fall apart, while reaping profits. And the field rats . . . it can be very bad out here.

―――――――――――――――

Interviewee was Margaret Haines, President, Parents' Association, District 27, Arverne Urban Renewal Office.

9. Right now, not much tension exists. There was some racial tension among children. Tension was not primarily among residents but outsiders on the beaches.

10. There are too many projects here. Edgemere was a beautiful place in 1966. They discriminated by family type, especially against one-parent families. I had to go through a social evaluation because my husband and I were separated. But they let down the barriers and allow everyone in the project now. It is like a small hell-hole. Projects have let their guards down, undesirables get into Edgemere. Projects lose their stable families and neighborhoods tend to decline. People are running to escape an unbearable situation. The Housing Authority should go back to its old ways.

11. The neighborhood was converted from summer bungalows to project areas. There was a need for decent, sound, winterized housing instead of converted bungalows, which are the dreams of the slum landlords.

12. Shopping
        groceries: out of the area
        clothing: out of the area
        appliances and furniture: out of the area
        parks: don't go there even though the park is right
           near my house
        clinics: in the area
        movies: don't go at all

13. Lack of good medical care is not a serious problem. There used to be a lack of facilities; it's getting better but is by no means a grade-A situation. A lot of this is due to the transformation of the community from summer to year-round. Aches and pains of a growing community are evident in Arverne.

14. I use Queens General Hospital. I almost died because they made me go to Queens General because I had no private doctor!

15. Yes.

16. Yes; no recreation in the winter time.

17. Yes.

18. Children go outside the area for roller skating, bowling, ice skating, to Flushing Meadows or Elmont—quite a distance. There are no nice parks or domes in the area. There are lots of teenagers on your hands that can cause lots of problems.

19. Streets out here are filthy. You always see lots of abandoned cars that remain in the streets for months.

20. Parking regulations have been started with alternate side of the street parking, and it is enforced. Streets are sometimes cleaned. This is still in the experimental stage.

21. Sometimes garbage is not picked up properly. If garbage is in a bag, in this area, the garbage man will not pick up the bag.

Garbage collectors will not even pick a broom up if garbage cans are knocked over.

22. There is a need for more day care centers. A mother can go back to work if there are more day care centers. Prices are prohibitive and many mothers cannot afford to go back to work, so they remain on welfare. Stupid jackasses are making decisions, not realizing their real effect. An increase in the number of day care centers and lower prices can help lower the welfare rolls.

23. Public transportation is very bad; such slow service! Only one Green Line Bus, old antique buses that were used elsewhere are shipped here. Green Line has no competition and gives lousy service. Bus service stops at 12:00 midnight. Trains are very bad. It takes 1 hour and 45 minutes to get to Manhattan. If you miss the train, you lose 45 minutes to an hour in traveling time. The ride is much better during morning hours. Expresses run in the morning and afternoon hours.

24. It is not safe for children to cross streets. There are policemen assigned to dangerous corners. All parents are concerned about policemen receiving a call, answering the call, and leaving the children. It is a very, very serious and dangerous condition.

25. The school [PS 105] now has the largest number of children in District 27. More children than some junior high schools. The school now has an annex—the sixth graders are moved elsewhere. There are over 1,400 children. PS 105 sits in the center of the peninsula and is getting clobbered; it is across from two large projects. In the western side of peninsula, population is decreasing because the children have grown up. In the schools near projects, enrollment has skyrocketed. Turnover in projects insures a constant flow of school-age children. The Board of Education let the cat out of the bag: instead of building schools before the children get there, they build after the children arrive. Many teachers are not as dedicated as they used to be, they are there only for their paychecks and give less than a damn for the children, especially those in the lower-income black segment of the population. They are teaching here only because they cannot get jobs elsewhere. They get tenure, and it is as hard as "hell" to get a tenured teacher out. There are children who come into school (ages seven and eight) who never went to school before (ex-residents of welfare hotels). Many nine-year-olds are put into first grade. No school is equipped to handle this problem. Teachers continue to promote these children. With the budget cuts, these children get short-changed. Ten percent of New York City children are hyperactive; the teachers cannot handle them, and the children are destroyed. PS 105 had four security guards, now it is down to one. Title I is helping to improve reading scores of children.

26. No, schools are not opened in the evening and during summers because of cutbacks in money.

27. The library doesn't have great facilities.

28. Food in this type of area is inferior. In Cedarhurst, prices for food are lower for meats and vegetables, and the quality is higher.

29. Three more theaters have been closed down since early 1960s.

30. There are many churches, not many storefront churches. Churches can help the stability of the community.

31. No, there wasn't much to cut! The services are at the same levels as they were when the area was a summer community, but the population has increased significantly.

32. Poor.

33. Sometimes storekeepers in the area overcharge. Managers can treat you like a piece of dirt. Storekeepers do not live here; they live in other parts of the city or suburbs.

34. The neighborhood has inadequate police protection. Police don't harass people.

35. No courts; the closest one is in Jamaica.

36. Schools, covered earlier.

37. Welfare workers no longer visit recipients. Two satellite offices need more staff; the population has increased.

38. Crime is a very serious problem here. You are a prisoner in your own house. Pocketbook snatching, house robberies are among the major crimes.

39. Not too many fires like there used to be. There were many abandoned buildings and many fires in them.

40. In certain parts of the area, there are hangouts for drug users.

41. The neighborhood is not extremely noisy.

42. No gang problems here for the last three or four years.

43. There is a problem. I don't let my children go out and play unless I can go and watch them.

44. High-rise buildings are crime havens. They can rob from one floor and hide on another floor.

45. Most stores have had burglary gates for the last six or seven years.

46. I've lived here 14 years, in Edgemere-Arverne.

47. Bad housing was very definitely a very serious problem. This is still so in many sections. I moved here because I was desperate for housing and had no choice.

48. Yes, $155.85.

49. The projects have month-to-month leases. There is no real control over your length of stay. Hand in your tax return at year end, and you will be told of your rent increases.

51. Yes, my rent is too high!

52. Yes, they do take advantage of the welfare tenants.

53. I have four rooms: two bedrooms, living room, and kitchen.

54. The bathroom in the apartment does not have a window, it has an air vent.

55. Yes, the elevator runs efficiently; elevators are safe, the house has only six floors. There is an intercom system in the building for security.

56. The rent is controlled by the New York City Housing Authority.

57. When I first moved to the Rockaways, I lived in a bungalow. There were many water rats and roaches. We used cans from tomatoes to prevent rats and roaches from entering the children's beds and cribs. We rarely received enough hot water. If I complained, sometimes I got action because I was a cooperative tenant and swept the hallways and sidewalk.

58. Landlords do not live in the neighborhood; they live in the suburbs.

59. There is a laundry room, but I don't use it because it is a hassle. I go outside of the area to wash my clothing.

60. There are tenant organizations in the projects, but they are not doing what they should.

61. Local neighborhood improvement groups exist. They concentrate on their own little areas, not the entire Rockaway peninsula.

62. No, I do not belong to any clubs.

63. They don't help the community; they help their own little areas.

64. No.

65. No.

SAMPLE INTERVIEW NO. 2

1. Of course, this neighborhood is a good place to live in. It has a lot of natural potential, proximity to the beaches. In the past five years, the ethnic background of the community has changed. The newer residents have no real ties and roots in the area. Newcomers—British West Indians, Haitians, Jamaicans, Puerto

---

Interviewee was Jules St. Prix, President, Arverne Civic League.

Ricans—settled in the eastern part of Arverne. The physical atmosphere of the area demonstrates this.

City services were different five years ago. In 1970 we had
three garbage pick-ups per week, early and efficient mail delivery.
When a lot of the old-timers left, mail service became inefficient.
I was forced to cancel my newspaper delivery. As a consequence
of the neighborhood change, sewer and snow removal services have
slackened. Mosquito spraying has been stopped. An abundance of
empty land, prone to mosquitoes, exists in Arverne. The land is
owned by the city and federal government.

2. Within city limits, this area presents the best quality of
life in terms of density of population. Good points: suburban life
within city limits, proximity (in distance) to Manhattan, best beach
around (on the Eastern seaboard) because of accessibility and small
crowd attendance. The transient population is estimated at more
than 1 million. However, you don't find many beer cans, or papers.
Houses are relatively new in the eastern half of the neighborhood.
Air here is fresh and not polluted. The community is fairly quiet.
Natural characteristics of the area reflect on people's character.
There is ethnic diversity and communication.

Bad points: lack of services and not solving the problems;
services are "patch up" services. Transportation is out of the
question. When you take the train, you never know when you will
get to the city. Long-term inequity of the double fare. Lack of
businesses and shopping in the area. Shopping does not exist with
respect to Arverne; no drug store, lack of doctors and dentists.
The influx of welfare recipients presents a burden on the present
population. This started with the construction of projects. Welfare
recipients were concentrated in these buildings. Five years ago,
I used to keep my doors unlocked. Large numbers of burglaries
are committed in this area now. This increases with the number of
welfare clients moving in. The influx of welfare recipients in large
numbers is detrimental to the economic situation of Arverne. This
even helps to destroy the limited number of businesses that are
left. The sewers flood in high tide. Houses are constructed without planning, many have flooded basements. The building department allowed buildings to be constructed without providing measures
for this. There is no sewer system that accommodates proper
drainage. Water remains for 52 hours after the rainfall. The
Highway Department is negligent, many potholes and cracked sidewalks. There is too much vacant land. Community Planning District No. 14 has no real input. Community groups have no real
power. There is a large concentration of nursing homes in this
area and they do not add to the economic base. There is no sufficient public ambulance service, which led to the existence of

voluntary ambulance service, which is not federally or city funded.
There are no centrally located places for city ambulances to park.

Noise from the airplanes overhead is unbearable. The
market value of houses in this area is affected by this extreme
noise. Muggings and robberies are bad, but not as bad as in other
areas in the city. There is a tremendous lack of movies, restaurants, and other places of amusement. The life style of the area
does not warrant movie theaters. Children don't have that need to
go to a park. Schools are not overcrowded. One school that was
built for 4,000 kids is one-quarter empty. The quality of education
is something else! P.S. 42 has the lowest reading level in the city
at the present time. Ten years ago it was one of the best in the city.

3. I think of this neighborhood as my real home and most
people in the area feel the same way.

4. I would not like to move.

5. I have many friends in this area, but no relatives.
Friends were made while I lived here.

6. People in this area have the same hates and loves of the
area as previously mentioned.

7. This area is more congenial than Crown Heights. People
share a common interest.

8. Property values change; they do not relate to growth;
growth is not related to general cost of living. The real value of
property has not changed. Rents have not risen significantly since
1970. As a matter of fact, rent in a community such as this is not
a big thing, since most people own their own homes and most
renters live in public housing.

9. There are not many tensions, especially considering the
racial and ethnic diversity. There is, however, some uneasiness
among residents. There are some tensions between old timers and
newcomers. Uneasiness is created by residents of surrounding
areas and the projects.

10. Yes, the public housing projects in this neighborhood
affected the quality of the area. There was a big program of building projects, experiments that were intended to fail. People were
not given the chance to own their own apartments. Buildings were
not planned for people to live in. Welfare brings in a tremendous
number of undesirables. Nobody is benefiting from this; the industrial complex is the only thing benefiting, not the people!

11. Pick up a lot of people, pack them in large houses, give
them some money: you instill illness in them and you entertain
present illnesses. People have no sentiment for the area, no
feelings of love for anyone or anything. Planning was vicious, not
for the good of the people. From what I heard, the area was good
before the projects came. It could get worse if the community
does not fight to maintain and increase services.

12. We do most of our shopping outside the area such as groceries, clothing, appliances and furniture, doctors and clinics, movies. The banking is done in the area. As for parks and playgrounds, people just don't go there.

13. Lack of good medical care is not a problem. Peninsula Hospital and South Shore Hospital are close by. Some people, however, have to go to Jamaica Hospital, which is not that close to Arverne.

14. Peninsula Hospital is supposed to have decent medical care. This hospital is geared toward any possible accidents occurring at Kennedy Airport. After the recent accident, the situation was a mess!

15. The lack of recreation is no great problem. People go fishing and boating.

16. There is a great lack of recreation for teenagers.

17. The recreation problem for children is a great one. My children don't use any recreational facilities.

18. The only recreational facilities we enjoy are the beaches and water.

19. The streets and sidewalks are in bad condition. Abandoned cars are a problem, and this has always been the case.

20. There are no parking regulations in the area, nor is there any street sweeping.

21. Garbage pick-up is not done properly. There are only two pick-ups per week and we never know when we will have them. Stray dogs are a problem and they affect the amount of garbage on the sidewalk.

22. There are not enough day care facilities in this neighborhood.

23. Public transportation certainly is a great problem in this area. Train stations are fairly safe and clean, but a train ride to Manhattan takes about two hours.

24. There were crossing guards before the freeze on city employees. Street lighting is fairly adequate.

25. Schools were not equipped to handle the influx of new students and this had a bad effect on the quality of education. The quality of the student has also changed. Many ex-residents of welfare hotels move to the projects and their children up to the age of eight never went to school. The high school is not at full capacity.

26. Public schools were opened during evening hours and during summer months.

27. Yes, yes, we have libraries but they are going to close because they are considered underutilized. There are only two libraries for a population of 100,000 people.

28. Neighborhood groceries have a poor quality of merchandise, especially bread and milk.

29. No movie theaters that I know of have been closed down.

30. There are many churches in the area and a few synagogues have closed down. Lately, there have been some storefront churches opening up. Church could be good if it involves itself actively in the real life of the community. The church is divorcing itself from the community.

31. Public services and facilities have definitely decreased over time: school, post office, sewers, sanitation.

32. The general quality of the public facilities is fair in this vicinity. Signs are in poor condition, street lights are adequate in some places, there is some litter on the streets and in the alleys.

33. Storekeepers overcharge in this area. They treat people badly only in an economic sense. Storekeepers are rarely area residents.

34. Police protection is inadequate, but the number of policemen for the population of this size is adequate. However, the police are inadequate in the performance of their duties in respect to abandoned cars, trespassers, responding to calls, stray dogs, and so on. Their attitude on the job is wrong. People are not really harassed, but they are being closed in. Police take a long time to respond to calls, but at 12:00 midnight police are going around with flashlights and checking cars.

35. There are no courts in the immediate area.

36. Schools are not that good. Teachers do not harass school children.

37. Welfare workers do not visit the area, clients go to the satellite offices.

38. Crime is not a serious problem for me and my family. I am not in fear of any particular crimes; although I can note significant changes from when I moved here.

39. There are some fires in this neighborhood, more than there were in the past.

40. Kitty Park is a hangout for drugs and drug users.

41. This neighborhood is not noisy.

42. We have no gang problems here.

43. Children play in the streets, and in the summertime on the beach.

44. High-rise buildings tend to perpetuate crime.

45. Most stores have burglary gates, but there aren't many stores to speak of.

46. I have lived in this neighborhood for five years, and five years in the same house.

47. Bad housing is not a problem in this area.

50. Local banks in the area do nothing for the people. They are not granting any mortgages.

52. Rents are predominately higher for welfare tenants; however, I am not certain of their situation.

57. No, I am a home owner and I don't suffer from rats, mice, holes in the wall or ceilings.

58. Landlords often live outside of the building and outside the area.

60. There are two tenants' associations that I know of. They don't have the problem of trying to improve housing conditions. The buildings are fairly new.

61. There are a few local neighborhood improvement groups in this area.

62. I am the president of the Arverne Community Team, and I also belong to the Rockaway Democratic Club and Arverne Renewal Planning and Development.

63. Clubs or organizations help the community in a sense that they are a part of the community; they represent life in the community in a collected and unified sense.

64. We have asked for no help from any of our community leaders.

65. We don't count on our political figures for any help of any kind.

NOTES

1. Long Island *Press*, 1954.

2. New York City Planning Commission, <u>New York City Master Plan</u>, 1969.

3. Richard Geist, "The Wreck of the Rockaways," <u>New York Affairs</u>, 1972.

4. Ibid.

5. Ibid.

6. Ibid. See also Rockaway Office of Neighborhood Government, <u>Report to the Community</u>, 1973.

7. Geist, "The Wreck of the Rockaways," op. cit.

8. From "The Slum-town," Long Island *Press*, March 27, 1954.

9. From "Filth in the Slum-town," Long Island *Press*, March 25, 1954.

10. From "Rats and Debris Have Taken Over the Streets of Arverne," Long Island *Press*, August 1, 1968.

12
THE CONTROL AREAS

SELECTION OF CONTROL AREAS

The method used in this study to define test areas was discussed earlier in the study. To review, test areas are defined as
having had a predominantly white population in 1950 that subsequently has changed to black. In the process of this racial transition,
the housing submarket structure of each test area has changed (accompanied by the realization of a class-monopoly rent).

The method used in this study defines control areas as similar
as possible to test areas (in terms of housing characteristics).
Comparisons can now be made between the trends in rents and
neighborhood quality in each. Three major problems have to be
solved: control areas must be determined; rents must be obtained;
a way must be found to compare housing and neighborhood quality.

The three control neighborhoods have been selected on the
basis of housing quality, land use, population, and other data, as
well as my own personal knowledge of the area. The major criterion in selecting control areas was to locate the neighborhoods
and census tracts within neighborhoods whose submarket structure
remained the same for the entire period (1950-70) and whose submarket structure (as defined in Chapter 2) is such that little class-
monopoly rents have been realized.

For purposes of this study, control areas have been selected
to conform with submarket 2, the white ethnic area. Housing and
neighborhood quality in the control areas have generally been better
than that of the test areas, although some of the test areas were
"white ethnic" areas in 1950. By examining combinations of different types of mechanisms that determine rents in neighborhoods, the
neighborhoods can be identified.

In the following section, brief neighborhood profiles for the control neighborhoods are presented. These areas are not analyzed in any detail; their function is to serve as a "control" in the empirical experiment.

CONTROL AREA NO. 1: HIGHLAND PARK, CYPRESS HILLS, CITY LINE

Highland Park, Cypress Hills, and City Line are north of Atlantic Avenue to the Queens border and east of Fountain Avenue (to the Queens line). This area is as desirable today as it was in the 1950s: "Highland Park has the most adequate transportation facilities, the most substantial housing, the highest median income, the largest percentage of single women over age 14, the most adults over 65, and the fewest children under 15 years old." Reminders of better days, these neighborhoods have been relatively unaffected by deterioration and continue to be attractive for white families of modest means. The area houses a predominantly Italian population.

Nearly 40 percent of the housing in this area is owner-occupied. The area contains a mixture of one- and two-family detached homes with small front or backyards and apartment houses. Apartments are generally large and rents are relatively low, especially when compared to the rents in neighboring deteriorated East New York (see Table 12.1). Structural fire rates are below the city average and vacant buildings are not in evidence. There are 97 vacant buildings in the area, 39 of which are in one census tract. Buildings are aging but well maintained.

Although the same police precinct services both this community and East New York, and statistics are not completed for Highland Park, et al., officials from the police department claim that the major portion of crime occurs in East New York. Juvenile delinquency in the Highland Park-City Line area is far below the borough average.

Residents of this area generally have lower rates of communicable diseases than their neighbors. This, in part, is probably due to a cleaner and thus healthier living environment.

With the exception of the Model Cities area, all publicly aided housing in the so-called East New York Area is, in fact, in the Highland Park-Cypress Hills-City Line area. Publicly aided housing is located south of Linden Boulevard and east of Fountain Avenue. The construction of public housing and urban renewal projects in these areas has tended to displace former site residents; many have been forced to crowd in small houses in the East New York core area. This has caused a rise in rents in East New York.

TABLE 12.1

Rents and Population Composition: Highland Park, 1950, 1960, 1970

Tract Number	1950			1960			1970		
	Total Population	Black Population	Rent ($)*	Total Population	Black Population	Rent ($)	Total Population	Black Population	Rent ($)
405	2,483	28	34.00	2,287	429	57.00	3,444	2,911	96.00
1140	1,161	1	28.00	1,210	35	47.00	1,069	507	79.00
11420	1,475	0	40.00	1,319	16	70.00	1,212	232	84.00
114202	2,252	7	47.00	1,966	6	73.00	2,268	277	83.00
1146	2,796	9	40.00	2,587	13	64.00	2,288	421	86.00
1148	3,028	8	42.00	2,549	33	52.00	2,385	836	84.00
1168	2,201	8	30.00	1,977	7	52.00	2,008	282	79.00
1170	2,337	21	31.00	1,931	6	58.00	1,398	227	80.00
117201	2,225	6	46.00	1,867	1	72.00	1,632	33	80.00
117202	2,969	0	43.00	2,981	0	64.00	2,906	86	83.00
1174	3,249	6	37.00	2,986	0	61.00	3,185	43	83.00
117601	2,158	0	41.00	1,951	2	58.00	1,834	66	81.00
117602	2,621	6	39.00	2,318	3	58.00	2,243	7	82.00
1178	1,302	0	40.00	1,249	12	57.00	1,247	37	80.00
118201	2,231	0	39.00	2,090	0	63.00	1,928	62	80.00
118202	2,384	7	41.00	2,162	0	62.00	2,146	84	81.00
1184	3,903	4	39.00	3,656	0	62.00	3,422	34	80.00
1186	1,125	2	40.00	2,109	0	66.00	2,107	50	81.00
1188	3,995	8	36.00	3,415	0	58.00	3,386	106	80.00
1190	3,699	10	35.00	1,518	0	64.00	1,449	107	80.00
1196	2,198	9	36.00	4,923	250	56.00	5,462	3,298	101.00
1200	2,177	2	40.00	1,538	8	64.00	1,690	198	110.00
1202	1,257	0	41.00	1,095	0	62.00	1,134	80	102.00
1220	743	0	38.00	1,023	2	62.00	950	161	90.00

*Rent is the consideration paid for a four-room apartment.

Source: U.S. Bureau of Census, 1970 Census Statistics for New York City (Washington, D.C.: U.S. Government Printing Office, 1971).

> They put up this urban renewal project on the site I was
> forced to leave. I went down to the office to apply for
> an apartment. Since I've lived in this area 15 years, I
> feel that I am qualified to live in this housing. But the
> Housing Authority couldn't care less about this fact.
> They bring in people from other areas to live in this
> housing. They don't want us Puerto Ricans as tenants—
> and this housing is supposedly for us! Now I live in
> a crummy apartment with no heat and rats.

The publicly aided housing in this area has increased overcrowding
in neighboring East New York; in addition, some of the prior site
residents displaced from the area (because they are competing for
space with so many others in a similar predicament) will be forced
to pay a higher price for shelter.

CONTROL AREA NO. 2: RIDGEWOOD-GLENDALE

Ridgewood straddles the Brooklyn-Queens boundary just beyond
the eastern end of Newtown Creek. The area became a community of
German farmers at the end of the nineteenth century. In the years
between 1900 and 1930 it gradually changed from farms and picnic
groves to closely packed rows of one-, two-, and even six-family
houses occupied by families of predominantly Germanic origin.

While most of Queens is being overturned by population shifts
and superhighways, Ridgewood remains essentially the same German-
American and Middle European community it has been for 60 years.
The bulk of Ridgewood, lying north of the Brooklyn-Queens line, has
changed little in appearance or population. Signs of economic decline, run-down houses and vacant stores, are not that evident here,
although there are some signs of this.

The politics of Ridgewood fit its temperament. Its civic groups
have given emphatic support to the philosophy of neighborhood schools,
and they have fought the involuntary bussing of pupils from mixed
white and black areas to all-white sections.

Ridgewood is a medium- to low-income community of small
retail merchants, craftsmen, mechanics, factory workers, and office employees. Tenancy of the two- to six-family apartments,
which line a crosshatching of blocks without interruption, is usually
of long duration, passed on from one generation to another or held
for new immigrant arrivals who have family or national ties with the
older residents. More often than not, the landlord lives in his own
building, preserving its well-kept appearance. Tenant turnover is
low, as are the rents.

Census figures in 1970 indicate that while the city percentage average income paid for gross rent was about 20 percent, many of Ridgewood's residents paid less than 13 percent (see Table 12.2). The Ridgewood area does not contain any public or publicly aided rental housing.

Parking is a problem in many areas of Ridgewood. The developers who built houses after World War I, unchecked by zoning laws, wedged the dwellings onto undersized lots. Many blocks are filled with the familiar row house, which doesn't include a garage. The detached houses left just a few feet for driveways; undersized foreign cars are the only ones that could pass through them.

Ridgewood has more than 500 retail stores. Myrtle Avenue is the principal business street. With the exception of supermarkets, furniture stores, and a few household supply stores, retail outlets are small, carrying a broad range of specialties. Delicatessens, meat shops, pastry shops, import stores, and bars and restaurants offering German cuisine and imported beer are neighborhood fixtures. Most of the retail outlets are owned and operated by Ridgewood residents, a fact that most residents feel contributes toward neighborhood stability.

A glance at the statistics of Ridgewood in 1970 reveals a community nearly 100 percent white German-American. Ridgewood has a better health and social welfare record and less crime and delinquency than most of Brooklyn and Queens. The 104th Precinct area, of which Ridgewood covers approximately 20 percent, ranked 66th in total crime and 64th in felonies in 1974, accounting for approximately .0063 of the city total. Juvenile delinquency rates are similarly low.

There are not many fires or vacant buildings in this area. Perhaps this, in large part, is due to the close-knit nature of the community and the fact that it is made up, to a large extent, of resident homeowners.

From the point of view of political power, the most significant characteristic of Ridgewood is the xenophobic tribalism of the majority of the area's residents. The capacity to make one's voice heard is not a diffusely scattered ability but rather a deep-seated aspect of life in the neighborhood.

CONTROL AREA NO. 3: RAVENSWOOD

Ravenswood, located in the westernmost part of Queens, owes its early development and years of growth to an extensive waterfront and proximity to Manhattan. In 1870 Ravenswood, Astoria, Hunters Point, Steinway, and Dutch Kills were consolidated with Long Island City.

TABLE 12.2

Rents and Population Composition: Ridgewood-Glendale, 1950, 1960, 1970

Tract Number	1950			1960			1970		
	Total Population	Black Population	Rent ($)*	Total Population	Black Population	Rent ($)	Total Population	Black Population	Rent ($)
535	1,543	8	25.93	1,341	0	47.00	1,103	0	74.00
539	905	1	32.77	1,183	1	53.00	3,584	37	81.00
545	3,555	1	25.20	3,420	0	51.00	3,700	0	74.00
547	3,913	5	28.11	3,562	1	54.00	3,711	60	77.00
549	4,535	1	26.73	4,120	0	58.00	4,157	61	77.00
551	4,661	4	26.79	4,216	0	62.00	4,417	0	79.00
553	2,333	1	34.68	2,052	0	55.00	2,043	0	77.00
555	2,111	7	28.16	1,820	1	55.00	1,720	16	79.00
557	3,940	1	32.75	3,457	0	58.00	3,046	0	82.00
559	1,239	1	31.24	1,073	0	54.00	934	21	79.00
583	3,486	2	36.81	3,246	0	58.00	3,101	0	88.00
585	4,099	4	34.57	3,804	1	57.00	3,421	0	86.00
591	5,307	6	26.20	5,044	1	51.00	5,090	0	78.00
593	3,965	3	41.30	3,561	0	61.00	3,728	76	82.00
595	3,032	3	40.02	3,817	1	60.00	3,877	0	89.00

*Rent is the consideration paid for a four-room apartment.

Source: U.S. Bureau of Census, 1970 Census Tract Statistics for New York City (Washington, D.C.: U.S. Government Printing Office, 1971).

TABLE 12.3

Rents and Population Composition: Ravenswood, 1950, 1960, 1970

Tract Number	1950			1960			1970		
	Total Population	Black Population	Rent ($)*	Total Population	Black Population	Rent ($)	Total Population	Black Population	Rent ($)
29	1,695	29	34.29	1,368	16	51.00	994	12	83.00
31	1,994	12	37.74	1,625	4	52.00	594	0	81.00
35	674	0	28.64	491	—	62.00	387	0	71.00
37	7	0	—	—	—	—	—	—	—
39	1,718	0	33.84	1,444	6	53.00	1,200	30	85.00
41	1,159	7	34.53	1,023	0	49.00	966	10	77.00
43	289	13	32.00	3,921	850	83.00	3,261	862	97.00
45	588	48	28.54	3,773	92	57.00	3,216	63	111.00
47	1,472	6	58.47	5,422	638	81.00	5,373	2,106	102.00
49	527	1	45.50	424	0	82.00	445	0	99.00
51	2,397	5	41.93	1,925	0	56.00	1,772	12	85.00
53	6,041	14	44.94	5,496	3	61.00	4,753	95	92.00

*Rent is the consideration paid for a four-room apartment.

Source: U.S. Bureau of Census, Census Tract Statistics for New York City (Washington, D.C.: U.S. Government Printing Office, 1971.

264

Industry has been established in the area since its settlement. During the latter part of the nineteenth century and the early twentieth century a variety of manufacturing firms settled in the area.

As a growing industrial area, Ravenswood attracted a heterogeneous population. Irish immigrants settled in the community, along with Italian, Slavic, Polish, and Canadian immigrants.

The population of Ravenswood did not increase between 1940 and 1970, although two public housing projects were built during the period. The new construction has changed the ethnic makeup of the area to a slight degree. There were approximately 1,200 blacks in the area by 1970, most of whom lived in the public housing census tracts.

Ravenswood has sound, low-priced housing, for low- and middle-income families (see Table 12.3). The buildings vary widely in size, age, and function, and include small houses, large apartments, one-story factories, large power plants, and multistory lofts. Housing in this district is generally sound and well-kept, but pockets of deterioration exist. There is sufficient variety in the homes and communities to attract a broad spectrum of moderate-income families seeking low rents.

The neighborhood has two public housing projects: Ravenswood Houses, a city public housing project of more than 2,100 apartments, and Queensbridge Houses, a federal public housing project consisting of a series of 26-story brick buildings constructed in 1942 to replace slums. Ravenswood is a low-income area. Crime and juvenile delinquency rates are well below the borough average. Fires are not common in this neighborhood.

Most of the educational facilities have sufficient space to accommodate enrollments; there are two libraries in the immediate area. While there are no voluntary or municipal hospitals in the area, there are two proprietary institutions within the larger Astoria-Long Island City area. Transportation facilities in the area are generally good, but many people are required to use a combination of subway and bus to travel in order to reach some destinations.

In sum, the area is both a pleasant residential community and an industrial section. The most serious problem here is the conflicts between residents and industry.

APPENDIX A:
METHODOLOGY AND DATA SOURCES

Six basic data sources have been employed for empirical analyses of this study. The methodology that follows presents the procedures of gathering and manipulating these data. This appendix proceeds from a discussion of data available for the city to show these varying bodies of data were refined via factor and regression analyses.

FIRE DATA

The fire data were obtained from New York City Fire Department records for the period 1960–73. These represented fires by occupancy and cause and consist of the following:

1960–68	1970–73
Structural	Structural
Residential	Nonstructural
Outside	Transportation
Vacant buildings	Emergencies
	False alarms

As instances of fire had to be assigned to census tracts, variable transformations that weighted data for fire districts and census tracts by population had to be performed.

CRIME DATA

The data on crime were obtained from the New York City Police Department Annual Reports of Crime and Related Activity (complaints)

(1960, 1965, 1970, 1974). This study was concerned with the more serious general police activities.

Crimes against the person (murder and negligent manslaughter, forcible rape, felonious assault, narcotics), crimes against property (robbery, burglary, larceny, auto theft), and total misdemeanors and total crime constitute this study's definition of crime.

As instances of crime had to be assigned to census tracts, variable transformations which weighted data for precincts and by census tracts by population were performed.

HEALTH DATA

The health data (vital statistics) were obtained from Bureau of Health, Statistics and Analysis reports for 1950, 1960, and 1970 for each health area. These represent deaths and communicable diseases and consist of the following:

Deaths due to:

			1970
Drug dependence			1970
Cirrhosis of the liver	1950	1960	1970
Suicide	1950	1960	1970
Homicide	1950	1960	1970
Tuberculosis	1950	1960	1970
Syphilis	1950	1960	1970

Communicable Diseases

Tuberculosis	1950	1960	1970
Syphilis	1950	1960	1970
Gonorrhea	1950	1960	1970
Infectious hepatitis			1970
Lead poisoning			1970

YOUTH-RELATED DATA

A group of variables were assembled on juvenile delinquency and youth-related statistics by health area. These data were obtained from Program, Planning and Budget Review, Youth Services Agency. Variable transformations were performed by weighting health area data by population within census tracts.

REAL ESTATE DATA

Real estate data were obtained from the New York City Department of Real Estate. It is from this source that a variable measuring neighborhood housing quality was assembled. Data collected by block (for all New York City blocks) indicated the number of buildings in each block that had been taken over by the city because of a three-year period in which the landlord did not pay property taxes. This, in effect, is a measurement of housing abandonment that, taken as axiomatic, is strongly associated with neighborhood housing quality.

CENSUS DATA

A substantial number of variables for this analysis have been extracted from the decennial censuses of population and housing. Variables from these sources fall under three categories: housing characteristics, population characteristics, and family characteristics, and are as follows:

Housing
    Total number of housing units
    Total number of owner-occupied housing units
    Percent owner-occupied housing units
    Total number of units built before 1929
    Percent of units built before 1929
    Number of structures with five or more units
    Percent of structures with five or more units
    Contract rent
    Median number of rooms
Population
    Total population
    Black population
    Percent black population
Families
    Total number of families
    Total number of female-headed families
    Percent female-headed families
    Percent of families below poverty level
    Median family income
    Total number of residents
    Total number of five plus years residents
    Percent of five plus years residents

VARIABLE TRANSFORMATIONS

This study focuses on the census tract as the unit of analysis. As a consequence, a series of variable transformations had to be performed since all data were not assembled on this basis. These transformations were necessary for all data on health, crime, juvenile delinquency, and youth-related statistics and fires. Census tract values were derived by assigning weights to each census tract, by total population (since the data is population-based data), and assessing the weights of variables accordingly. For example, to derive a census tract estimate of auto theft, one would calculate as follows:

Census Tract Auto Theft = Precinct Auto Theft

$$\frac{\text{Census Tract Population}}{\text{Precinct Population}}$$

Since the study neighborhoods are homogeneous, these transformed estimates are reliable measures.

APPENDIX B:
HISTORY OF FEDERAL
HOUSING PROGRAMS

Since 1934 the United States has established an array of housing programs of bewildering complexity. A history of federal policies for housing the urban poor would chronicle a succession of
programs, each, in its turn, oversold to the public only to become
sadly mired down in its operation, leaving the central dilemma—
millions of families trapped in squalid living conditions—as unre-
solved as ever. The causes of disappointment have varied with circumstances. In most cases, unanticipated costs, red tape, and
local political conflicts over building codes, tenant selection, lending practices, and site location have combined to frustrate congressional intent. In a few dramatic cases, exposés of windfall profits,
shoddy construction practices, and other forms of human venality
have culminated in outright congressional hostility.[1]

Housing programs have been enacted for a variety of purposes:
to create jobs, to clear slums, to improve the tax base of central
cities, and, supposedly, to help the poor. Some of these purposes
are contradictory. For instance, indiscriminate slum clearance
severely hurts poor families by restricting the supply of housing,
more specifically, by operating as a population removal device.

The primary purpose of housing programs should be to meet
the housing needs of today's urban poor. The existing arsenal of
federal housing programs shows serious deficiencies.

Furthermore, the basic purpose of many existing housing programs has not been to provide housing for the poor. In their earlier
years, slum clearance was the stated goal of the public housing and
urban renewal programs, even though this results in an overall reduction in the supply of restricted housing. Low-income families
are simply priced out of the market and many families face severe
problems in relocating. The most successful housing programs were
designed to help the middle class obtain mortgage financing.

270

Programs whose announced purpose is to provide housing for the poor are not effective. The subsidies provided under the Public Housing and Rent Supplements programs are not sufficient to allow the poorest families to live in such housing.

The history of federal housing activity dates primarily from the 1930s, but there were forerunners during and after World War I and even as early as the 1890s. This history is traced and analyzed in some detail in the following section.

HISTORY OF FEDERAL HOUSING ACTIVITY

Initial Efforts

Congress directed its attention to housing problems as early as the 1890s when it held the first hearings on slums and blight. These hearings and the writings of reformers like Jacob Riis helped to create a national awareness of housing problems.

The federal government became active in the housing field during World War I, having built close to 30,000 units for workers near major shipyards and munition plants.

Considerable congressional interest in housing arose following World War I. Bills were submitted, without success, to create a system of banks oriented to residential finance and to give special consideration to veterans. Substantial federal efforts to influence the production and financing of housing did not occur until the 1930s.

Home Finance

In the early 1930s, Congress and the executive branch found themselves faced with two overwhelming problems: the collapse of mortgage credit and the system of home finance that had been in use; and the need to generate jobs.

The Home Loan Bank System was created in 1932. The new Home Loan Bank Board was authorized to extend loans to its member savings and loan institutions through regional branches. In effect, the savings and loan associations were required to concentrate on residential financing. The board faced a financial crisis with limited jurisdiction and found itself plagued with opposition from other banking sources of mortgage funds. After the inauguration of President Franklin Roosevelt, a separate insurance system was created for savings and loan associations. Public confidence in the banking system was enhanced.

Another effective measure to support the mortgage market was the establishment in 1933 of the Home Owners Loan Corporation (HOLC), which had the power to buy mortgages threatened with foreclosure. Although established amid dire predictions of its financial future, HOLC at its peak held over 15 percent of the mortgage debt of the country and proved extremely effective in its role.[2] By the time of its end, some years after World War II, it had fully repaid the Treasury and its books showed a small profit.

Mortgage Insurance

A second major effort, in the area of mortgage instruments, was also highly successful. This was the National Housing Act of 1934, which established a system of mortgage insurance to be administered by the Federal Housing Administration. FHA brought about major changes in the practices used in financing housing.

The FHA mortgage insurance programs begun in 1934 were designed to reduce the risks of mortgage lenders in order to induce them to make credit available on more liberal terms. In return for a premium paid by the borrower, FHA insures the lender against risk of default.

Another development that helped the middle-class market was the creation of secondary market facilities in which government-insured mortgages could be bought and sold. The Federal National Mortgage Association (FNMA), originally incorporated in 1938, was chartered to perform this function.

Public Housing

In 1933 the Public Works Administration had offered loans to nonprofit and limited-dividend housing corporations for the construction of low-cost apartments. A program of direct federal construction of low-cost housing projects, primarily in already existing slum areas, was initiated in 1934. Some 60 projects were constructed, but the program ran into local opposition and eventually into legal obstacles. A change in technique became politically imperative, and the Public Housing Program was born with the passage of the U.S. Housing Act of 1937.

The salient feature of the public housing program is that the development, ownership, and management of projects are the responsibilities of local housing authorities. Rents in public housing projects are lowered by a combination of federal and local subsidies. Admission to and continued occupancy of public housing has been restricted to families of relatively low income. The families of fully employed blue-collar workers and semiskilled workers are intended to be eligible.

World War II and After

World War II brought with it the creation of the National Housing Agency. A second major development of the war years was the creation in 1944 of the Veterans' Mortgage guarantee program, administered by the Veterans Administration.

During the years 1946-50, housing production leaped from 1 million to 2 million units.[3] The growing pace of postwar housing activity brought pressure on interest rates and congressional efforts to maintain these rates at a low level. Simultaneously, Congress liberalized the basic FHA mortgage terms by authorizing a longer mortgage life and higher loan-to-value ratios. In response to the need for greater federal support if relatively low interest rates were to be maintained, Congress restructured the FNMA in 1948 and prohibited creation of the other federally chartered, privately funded National Mortgage Association that had been authorized during the 1930s.

The period immediately following World War II was a time of heated controversy over federal government housing policies. This issue was settled in the Landmark Housing Act of 1949. Although it authorized a public housing program of 135,000 units annually for six years, the 1949 act established a separate slum clearance and urban redevelopment program, which has since evolved into urban renewal. It was to be the responsibility of this program to clear slums and private areas and to provide sites for new moderate-cost housing as well as residential, commercial, or industrial facilities deemed necessary.

The 1950s

Although Congress had authorized large appropriations for public housing in the Housing Act of 1949, the program was curtailed in the early 1950s. This cutback was a result both of Korean conflict budget stringencies and successful efforts of the Appropriations Committee to reduce the number of new units as well as their design amenities.

The major housing legislation of the 1950s was the Housing Act of 1954. The law added conservation and rehabilitation programs to broaden the 1949 slum clearance and urban redevelopment program into a more comprehensive tool.

The Housing Act of 1954 also initiated the requirement that a local government develop a "workable program" for community improvement before it could be eligible for assistance under the public housing, urban renewal and, later, the 221(d)(3) programs. To be certified as having a workable program, a locality was required to develop a master plan, to adopt or update various codes governing building, zoning, and fire standards, and to muster relocation and financial resources.

Public housing was continued at its reduced Korean-conflict appropriation levels. The high density, minimum amenity projects that the act promoted are now looked upon by many as "horror" cases, concentration camps, or jails, demonstrating a lack of understanding that adequate housing means more than four walls, a roof, and a door. During the postwar years, public housing slowly lost many of its working-class residents and came to house large concentrations of poor families.

FNMA's responsibilities were divided in 1954 into three functions, all separately funded. These were its secondary market operations, its special assistance functions, and its management and liquidation operations. The secondary market function involves the trading of FHA- and VA-supported mortgages originated by private institutions. Special assistance involves the purchase of mortgages that cannot be marketed to private lenders because of noncompetitive interest or because of lack of market experience with the program or instrument. This function became important in later subsidy programs like 221(d)(3).

The 1954 act modified urban renewal to enable production of housing at reduced cost. FNMA special assistance was made available for insured loans to build middle-income housing.

The Housing Act of 1959 contained the first break in the pattern that restricted development and operation of subsidized projects to public owners. The section 202 program begun in that year authorized direct loans from the federal government, originally at a rate based on interest rates on outstanding federal debt, to nonprofit sponsors of rental projects for the elderly and handicapped.

The 1960s

The 221(d)(3) Below Market Interest Rate Program, established by the Housing Act of 1961, expanded opportunities for private development of subsidized housing. The program authorized FNMA to purchase mortgage loans made to limited dividend and cooperative, as well as nonprofit, entities at low interest rates based on the average interest paid on the outstanding federal debt.

The 1965 Housing Act acknowledged the decreasing utility of the borrowing power technique used in the 221(d)(3) and 202 programs and pegged the below-market interest rate at no higher than 3 percent.

The 1965 act also created two new subsidy techniques, one of which, rent supplements, became the subject of heated political controversy. The rent supplement program attempted to adjust housing subsidies to the needs of individual families, rather than simply to provide financial support of total project costs. Tenants were required to pay at least 25 percent of their income toward rent, and the federal government would make up the difference between that payment and the rental value of the units they occupied. The second new technique introduced in 1965 was the Section 23 leasing program, which enabled local public housing authorities to subsidize rents in existing rental units.

The cabinet-level Department of Housing and Urban Development was also created in 1965. The Model Cities Program, which attempts to coordinate government policies, both physical and social within a defined neighborhood, was established in 1966.

The Housing Act of 1968 culminated the strong movement toward use of housing subsidies in private dwellings. Its most important new feature was the Homeownership Program in Section 235. This program provided modest subsidies to enable lower-income families to purchase new and, in some cases, existing homes. The act also initiated a new rental program, Section 236, for families above the public housing income levels. This program was intended ultimately to replace both the 202 and 221(d)(3) programs since it provided a larger interest subsidy equal to the excess over an interest rate of 1 percent instead of 3 percent and since it had the advantage of correlating subsidy with tenant need. Both of these new programs relied almost exclusively on private developers. Both programs also relied totally on private mortgage financing supported by subsidies payable directly to the mortgage lender in contrast to the government's purchase of the mortgage in addition to the interest subsidy. The act of 1968 also made FHA mortgage insurance more easily available in declining urban areas and for families with imperfect credit histories. This, in part, probably was a cause of the tremendous number of FHA foreclosures in many New York City areas, for example, South Jamaica and East New York.

The Housing and Urban development Act of 1969 was regarded as innovative legislation for public housing. For the first time, federal annual contributions were authorized to be used for operating expenses as well as debt service. Considered even more important are the provisions of the Brooke amendment, making additional federal annual contributions of $75 million available for application against some of the most difficult problems facing public housing: rising rents for low-income tenants; growing insolvency among many local housing authorities; insufficient resources to provide adequate operating and maintenance services.[4] The Brooke amendment authorized the federal government to pay the difference between annual operating costs of public housing and 25 percent of tenants' income, allowing reduction of rents below actual operating costs so very low-income tenants will not have to pay over 25 percent of their incomes for rent. [5]

The 1970s

The Housing and Community Development Act of 1974 created Section 8 to replace the old Section 23 (leased public housing). The act also had a consolidating effect on a number of community development programs.

FEDERAL HOUSING SUBSIDY PROGRAMS

To date, there are a great many federal housing programs. Most are administered by the Department of Housing and Urban Development, but the Veterans Administration, the Farmers Home Administration, and the Department of Defense all have significant housing programs of their own. The major HUD housing subsidy programs are outlined below.

Public Housing

The public housing program, as it has traditionally operated, places responsibility for development, ownership, and management of subsidized rental projects in the hands of independent local government agencies called housing authorities. Rents in public housing are lowered through a number of subsidies, both federal and local. The cost of project development is financed with long-term tax-exempt local bonds. This tax exemption lowers direct debt retirement costs. The federal government makes annual contributions to the local housing authority that cover all costs of retiring the bonds. The federal government is also authorized to pay a local authority an additional $120 per year for the benefit of each family that is elderly, displaced, extremely poor, or contains four or more children. Lastly, public housing projects do not pay normal real estate taxes but instead pay lower amounts in lieu of taxes. Roughly one-half of all public housing units are occupied by blacks and Puerto Ricans and one-third by elderly persons.

The public housing program has been exclusively a rental program. Some recent efforts have been made to encourage ownership by tenants. For most of its history, congressional pressure has required that projects have few amenities. This has proved to be short sighted since many projects have been so distinctive in appearance that they have stigmatized the neighborhoods in which they are located and the tenants themselves.

202 and 221(d)(3) Below Market Interest Rate Programs

These two low-interest loan programs use the same subsidy technique. The 202 program begun in 1959 is administered by the Housing Assistance Administration. The subsidy used is a direct loan from HUD to sponsoring nonprofit corporations, at a flat 3 percent interest rate. Only elderly or handicapped persons are permitted to occupy these 202 projects. The permanent loans may have a term of up to 50 years and can cover up to 100 percent of the cost of a project.

The 221(d)(3) Below Market Interest Rate (BMIR) program, a considerably broader program than 202 in terms of eligible sponsors and eligible tenants, was begun in 1961. FNMA is now authorized to purchase 221(d)(3) mortgages bearing interest rates of 3 percent. Interim financing must be arranged with conventional private lenders at market interest rates. The maximum term for low-income mortgages is 40 years. The mortgage can cover up to 100 percent of replacement costs for nonprofit and cooperative sponsors and 90 percent for profit-oriented sponsors.

The majority of 221(d)(3) projects consists of newly constructed row houses and walk-up apartments. They are either rental projects or cooperatives. They must be located in communities that have workable programs, a requirement that has restricted the use of the 221(d)(3) program. Income limits for 221(d)(3) BMIR projects are usually several thousand dollars higher than the limit for admission to public housing in the same area.

Rent Supplement

The rent supplement program was offered by the administration in 1965 as a substitute for 221(d)(3). Under the rent supplement technique, the tenant family pays 25 percent of its income toward rent, while the federal government pays directly to the landlord the difference between economic rent levels and the tenants' contribution.

The rent supplement program attempts to shift the responsibility for building and operating low-rent housing projects from the local housing authorities to private groups, both profit and nonprofit. To be eligible for supplements, a family must have a low income, have few assets, and be a member of one of the following groups:

elderly, handicapped, displaced by government action or natural disaster, or now living in substandard housing. As a tenant's income rises, his subsidy is reduced. For this reason, a family whose income rises substantially after admission to a rent supplement project is not required to leave it.

HUD has been forced to impose regulations on this program that have made it increasingly unworkable. One regulation requires that in no instance may a tenant receive a supplement that exceeds 70 percent of the fair market rental of the unit. Other regulations that have proved to be very damaging to the program establish specific dollar limits on construction costs and on maximum fair market rentals. These low maximums inhibit production and force those who do build to produce rather austere projects.

The limits on maximum rents and construction costs have made the rent supplement program generally unworkable for new construction in major central cities outside the South and Southwest.

Section 236 Rental Housing Program

The 236 program, part of the Housing Act of 1968, was designed to replace eventually both 202 and 221(d)(3) programs. Like the rent supplement program, it relies on private developers—both nonprofit and profit oriented—of rental or cooperative housing. The subsidy technique is similar to that used in the rent supplement program: the tenant pays 25 percent of his income toward rent, and the federal government pays a supplement that makes up the difference between a tenant's payment and market rents. There is, however, a crucial difference. The maximum federal payment on a unit lowers the rent to the level that would be achieved had the project been financed with a 1 percent mortgage. Thus, the primary difference between 236 and the rent supplement program is that the subsidy under 236 is not as deep.

The maximum federal subsidy to a tenant per month would be about $50 to $60. This is not enough to reach the poorest families. To be eligible, a family's income must not exceed 135 percent of the limits for admission to public housing projects.

In many communities, particularly in higher-cost cities, the income spectrum that 236 can serve may have been narrowed so much that some builders will be reluctant to participate in the program for fear they will be unable to find enough eligible tenants willing to occupy the units. However, some relief is provided by a provision permitting 20 percent of the appropriations to be used for families whose incomes exceed the limits for admission, but whose incomes are still below 90 percent of the 221(d)(3) BMIR limits in that area.

Section 236 offers larger subsidies than those available under 202 and 221(d)(3) BMIR by providing the equivalent of 1 percent loans instead of 3 percent loans. In addition, it avoids the budgetary impact problems raised by direct loan programs and provides a technique for adjusting the amount of subsidy to a tenant's income. Lastly, the program is not subject to the Workable Program Requirement, which does apply to 221(d)(3).

Section 235—Homeownership

The homeownership program contained in the Housing Act of 1968 was a major landmark in the history of federal housing legislation. Prior to its enactment, all major subsidy programs were limited to rental units, with cooperative housing units permitted in a few instances.

Assistance under the new homeownership program generally has been restricted to new or substantially rehabilitated units. Private builders have planned the housing and have had it approved by FHA for inclusion in the program prior to the beginning of construction. When built, the houses were sold to eligible buyers who financed their purchases with FHA-insured market rate mortgages from private lenders. The subsidy technique used was similar to that in the Section 236 rental program. All families must devote at least 20 percent of their income to paying off the mortgage. As family income rises, the federal payments due to the lender consequently will be gradually reduced and eventually eliminated.

Rehabilitation Subsidies

All programs discussed earlier can be used to subsidize housing costs in rehabilitated dwellings. In addition to these programs, there are a number of relatively minor ones that can be used for rehabilitation. Two of these, the Section 312 loan program and Section 115 rehabilitation grant program, can be used only within limited Urban Renewal or Concentrated Code Enforcement areas. The Section 312 programs, enacted in 1964, provide direct 3 percent loans to homeowners, the proceeds of which can be used for rehabilitation and, if necessary, also for refinancing existing mortgages. The 312 program was the first to authorize federal housing loans at less than the average cost of federal borrowing.

The Section 115 rehabilitation grant program, also designed to support the urban renewal process, was begun in 1965. Only families who own and occupy their own homes and who have very low incomes are eligible for these grants.

A third rehabilitation subsidy program, Section 221(h), was enacted in 1966. This program is extremely limited in scope. Its main significance is that it provided a historical precedent for the homeownership program of 1968 into which it has submerged. Sponsors of 221(h) projects must be nonprofit organizations. These sponsors acquire and rehabilitate single-family units and then sell them to families whose incomes are below public housing income limits. The subsidy is often inadequate to enable these families to participate in the program.

RECENT ACTIVITIES

The Housing and Community Development Act of 1974 is omnibus legislation, the provisions of which alter significantly federal involvement in a wide range of housing and community development activities. The new law contains eight titles:

I   Community Development
II   Assisted Housing
III   Mortgage Credit Insurance
IV   Comprehensive Planning
V   Rural Housing
VI   Mobile Home Construction and Safety Guards
VII   Consumer Home Mortgage Insurance
VIII   Miscellaneous

The new law consolidates several existing categorical programs for community development into a new program of community development block grants. The primary objective of the title is the development of urban communities by providing decent housing and a suitable living environment and expanding economic opportunities for persons of low and moderate income.[6] This objective is to be achieved through elimination of slums and blight and detrimental living conditions, conservation and expansion of housing and housing opportunities, increased public services, improved use of land, increased neighborhood diversity, and preservation of property with special values.[7] Title I will supersede the following programs: open space, urban beautification, historic preservation grants, public facility loans, water and sewer and neighborhood facilities grants, urban renewal and NDP grants, Model Cities supplemental grants, and rehabilitation loans.

The new measure revises the law governing the low-rent public housing program, provides additional annual contributions to contract authority, and authorizes a new lower-income housing assistance program.

The measure continues the provision authorizing public housing agencies to fix, subject to approval by the secretary, income limits for occupancy and rents in traditional public housing. However, it deletes the requirements for a gap of at least 20 percent between the highest income limits for admission and the lowest unassisted rents and income limits for continued occupancy in projects.[8]

Family income is redefined. For families in units under the new lower-income housing assistance program, income is defined as total family income. For families in regular public housing, income, for purposes of the Brooke amendment limitation, continues to be adjusted in accordance with a statutorily prescribed formula that has been revised by eliminating double deductions for secondary wage earner spouses, clarifying deductions for dependents, eliminating deductions for heads of households or their spouses, and adding a deduction for foster child care payments made to a family. A requirement is added under which every family in regular public housing is required to contribute at least 5 percent of its gross income to rent. For families in the new program, the lowest possible contribution to rent is 15 percent of total family income, with the secretary authorized to establish a higher required contribution level. Also, the aggregate minimum rental required to be paid in any year by families in any project administered by a public housing agency receiving operating subsidies is to be an amount at least equal to 20 percent of the sum of the incomes of all such families.

At least 20 percent of families in any project placed under annual contributions in any fiscal year beginning after the effective date of the requirement are required to have incomes not in excess of 50 percent of area median income.

Homeownership for public housing tenant families will be facilitated by authorizing the sale of projects to tenants (under Section 8) and the continuation of up to debt service annual contributions with respect to units sold to tenants.

The law authorized a new lower-income housing assistance program that replaced existing authority for assistance with respect to low-income housing in private accommodations (Section 23). Major features of the new program (contained in Section 8 of the proposed revised U.S. Housing Act of 1937) are as follows:

Assistance will be provided on behalf of eligible families occupying new, substantially rehabilitated, or existing rental units through assistance payments contracts with owners (who may be private owners, cooperatives, or public housing agencies).[9] Eligible families are those who, at the time of initial renting of units, have total annual family incomes not in excess of 80 percent of area median income, with adjustments for smaller and larger families.

Assistance payments contracts will specify the maximum monthly rent that may be charged for each assisted unit. Maximum rents may not exceed by more than 10 percent a fair market rent established by the secretary periodically, but not less than annually, for existing or newly constructed rental units or various sizes and types suitable for occupancy by eligible families, except that maximum rents may exceed fair market rents by up to 20 percent where the secretary determines that special circumstances warrant or that such higher rents are necessary to implement an approved housing assistance plan.[10]

The amount of assistance provided with respect to a unit will be an amount equal to the difference between the established maximum rent for the unit and the occupant family's required contribution to rent. Aided families will be required to contribute not less than 15 nor more than 25 percent of their total family income to rent. At least 30 percent of the families assisted with annual contract authority allocations must be families with gross incomes not in excess of 50 percent of area median income.[11]

Maximum rent levels will be adjusted annually or more frequently to reflect changes in fair market rentals established for the area for similar sizes and types of dwelling units or, if the secretary determines, on the basis of a reasonable formula.[12]

Up to 100 percent of the units in a structure may be assisted, upon application of the owner or prospective owner. Assistance payments for any unit may run for a minimum period of one month. In the case of existing units, payments may be made for as long as 180 months. In the case of new or substantially rehabilitated units, payments may be made for up to 240 months.

Owners of new or substantially rehabilitated assisted units will assume all ownership, management, and maintenance responsibilities, including the selection of tenants and the termination of tenancy.

Newly constructed or substantially rehabilitated dwelling units to be assisted under the program are to be eligible for mortgage insurance under FHA programs.

Provisions relating to adjusted family income, minimum rents, and a requirement that at least 20 percent of the families in any project other than under the new program be very low-income families must be implemented on a single date. Provisions relating to debt service and operating subsidy authorizations also must be implemented on a single date.

The measure revises the Section 202 direct loan program for housing for the elderly and handicapped. Major changes include loans made at rate equal to Treasury borrowing rate plus adequate allowances for administrative costs and probable losses, eligibility for occupancy has been expanded to include developmentally disabled individuals, provisions for the assurance of a range of services for occupants. In addition, the secretary is required to consider the availability of assistance under the Section 8 program when determining Section 202 project feasibility and to assure the projects aided under both Section 202 and the Section 8 program serve both low- and moderate-income families in a mix appropriate for the area and viable project operation.

The new law makes a variety of changes in FHA authorities. Specific amendments include the following: basic single-family home mortgage limits are increased about 36 percent, mortgage limits are increased about 20 percent for the lower-income nonsubsidized Section 221(d)(2) program and for the subsidized homeownership Section 235 program.[13] Basic multifamily per-unit mortgage limits are increased about 30 percent, the per-unit mortgage limits are increased about 20 percent for the Sections 221(d)(3) and 236 multifamily lower-income subsidy rental programs. Overall maximum project mortgage dollar limits previously applicable are removed.

A new FHA coinsurance authority was established and contains the following major features: Use is optional with lenders, who must assume at least 10 percent of any loss, subject to a limitation on overall liability for catastrophic losses (expiration of authority, June 30, 1977); the aggregate principal amount of coinsured mortgages and loans may not exceed 20 percent of the aggregate dollar amount of all multifamily mortgages insured; the sharing of premiums between HUD and lenders is required to be on an actuarially sound basis. Construction under the demonstration program must be inspected to ascertain whether minimum standards applicable under the regular program are met.

Insurance authority for Section 235 homeownership is extended for two years. The amount of unused contract authority previously approved in appropriation acts is available for one year from enactment and then will lapse. Any additional contract authority is subject to approval in appropriation acts. Other amendments include: continuation of HUD's authority to use up to 30 percent of funds for existing units; income limits set at 80 percent of median income for the areas; authority to insure advances of mortgage proceeds with respect to property constructed or rehabilitated pursuant to a self-help program; and minimum down-payment requirements increased to 3 percent of value.

Insurance authority on the Section 236 rental program is extended for two years. HUD is expected to approve commitment of these additional funds where a community has identified its special housing needs and demonstrated that such needs cannot be met through the lower-income housing assistance program. Further amendments include: additional assistance for tenants who cannot pay the basic subsidized rental charge with 25 percent of their income;

authority for increased subsidies to meet higher operating costs resulting from increased taxes or utility costs; a requirement that at least 20 percent of funds be allocated to projects for elderly or handicapped; a requirement that at least 10 percent of funds be used for rehabilitation projects; provision for reducing tenant contributions toward rent from 25 percent of income to as low as 20 percent where utilities are billed separately; income limits set at 80 percent of median income for area; removal of 10 percent project limitation on number of nonelderly single persons who may be subsidized.

The new law revises Section 701 of the Housing Act of 1954 and amends Title VIII of the Housing and Urban Development Act of 1964. Major features of the revised Section 701 include the following: Grantees may be states, cities of 50,000 or more, urban counties, metropolitan areawide organizations, Indian tribal groups or bodies, or other governmental units or agencies having special planning needs. Activities that may be undertaken with grant money include those necessary to develop and carry out a comprehensive plan, to improve management capability to implement the plan, and to develop a policy planning evaluation capacity to determine needs and goals and develop and evaluate programs.

The new law also includes a new National Mobile Home Construction and Safety Standards Act of 1974 and a new Consumer Home Mortgage Assistance Act of 1974. The new law also makes a number of changes in existing rural housing law. Since none of these are directly applicable to the present study, the provisions of each will not be explained here.

TITLE VI

Title VI of the Civil Rights Act of 1964 USC 2000d to d-4 prohibits discrimination on the ground of race, color, or national origin in programs and activities receiving federal financial assistance. As of 1973, a series of additional amendments was adopted. The most important of these provisions involve prohibiting discrimination in the selection of sites for facilities of federally assisted programs, and requiring affirmative action to overcome the effects of past discrimination. [14]

More specifically, in determining the site or location of housing, accommodations, or facilities, an applicant or recipient cannot make selections with the purpose or effect of excluding individuals from, denying them the benefits of, or subjecting them to discrimination under any public housing program. This would include selection of a public housing site in an undesirable neighborhood or a racially segregated area. As Title VI goes on to state: a recipient under any program or activity may <u>not</u>, directly or through a contractual or other agreements, on the ground of race, color, or natural origin: Subject a person to segregation in any matter related to his receipt of housing, accommodations, facilities, services, financial aid, or other benefits under the program or activity.[15]

In administering a program where the recipient has previously discriminated against persons on the ground of race, color, or national origin, the recipient must take affirmative action to overcome the effects of prior discrimination.

CURRENT HOUSING POLICIES

The newest panacea for solving the nation's enduring slum problem is a national program of housing allowances. The theory is: Since the nonpoor are able to get decent housing without the need for government bureaucracy or subsidy, the government should give the poor direct cash assistance to spend on housing so that, as housing consumers, they will no longer be poor; it is expected that the slum problem will then dissolve.[16]

Proponents of this approach assume that the housing allowance will expand consumer choice with respect to housing type, location, and landlord. The recipient of direct cash assistance would be free to seek out housing any place in the housing market. In contrast, existing government subsidies limit the recipient to residency in public housing and FHA units.

Furthermore, it is assumed that landlords would now be furnished with enough revenue to provide necessary repairs and, as a result, would encourage landlords to maintain their buildings.

This follows from the assumption that abandonment of buildings in large cities is a function of the inability of the poor to pay the ongoing costs of owning and maintaining a building.

In addition, it is assumed that this program will be more administratively efficient. By giving cash subsidies directly to the poor and allowing them to seek out their own housing, there is no need for bureaucratic intermediaries like local housing authorities. Moreover, the direct cash assistance approach permits benefits to be given to persons who do not live in jurisdictions served by local housing authorities.

Apart from these assumed advantages to housing consumers, it is assumed that a housing allowance program will be less expensive than current approaches. The federal government has been in the low-income housing business since the 1930s and has spent, according to administrative calculations, almost $90 billion.

What Has Been Happening?

Some 14 million persons in the United States receive welfare payments.[17] The Department of Health, Education and Welfare found that at least one-half of all welfare recipients live in substandard housing.[18] Under the welfare program families receive a lump sum with a specified portion of that amount earmarked for housing.

A second public program that resembles housing allowances is leased public housing. Under the public housing program, local housing authorities have since 1965 been able to use federal subsidies they administer to lease units from private owners and sublease them to eligible low-income families. This program differs from the direct cash assistance approach in that the local housing authority acts as intermediary.

The evaluations of the leased housing program paint a disturbing picture of how low-income tenants fare in the private market. A 1972 audit report by HUD found widespread evidence that much of leased public housing was substandard. In addition to poor housing conditions, the HUD report found that local housing authories were paying private landlords rents in excess of prevailing market levels.[19]

Based on the serious shortcomings of the leased housing program, it seems inevitable that the low-income tenant armed with only his housing allowance will have little protection against landlords who charge excessive rents, fail to make repairs, or otherwise exert the power inherent in a monopoly market.

Finally, the failure of the homeownership program for lower income families made available under Section 235 of the 1968 Housing Act provides ample evidence of how the private sector behaves toward subsidized consumers. Under these programs of interest-rate subsidies, moderate-income families have been able to purchase new, existing, or rehabilitated homes. A raft of exposés by the House Banking and Currency Committee, the General Accounting Office, and the Civil Rights Commission[20] have uncovered scandals in these programs in so many cities, which led HUD to take the unprecedented step of suspending Section 235 for a time. House prices were sharply inflated, with realtors purchasing older, dilapidated homes at panic-sale prices in areas undergoing racial transition, then reselling them again at huge profits. Many of the existing houses "have no resale value, and even minimal repairs will place such a burden on the homeowner's income that the congressional purpose of affording decent, safe, and sanitary housing for low- and moderate-income individuals not only has been thwarted but amounts to sheer fraud."[21]

HUD has had to repossess approximately 250,000 homes and has now become the nation's biggest slumlord. This experience shows clearly the behavior of the real estate industry's fast-buck artists in the market and the inability of moderate-income consumers to exert an effective countervailing force.

What Are We Getting Now and How Will This Change?

Five major defects in the housing market, apart from inadequate incomes, stand out as serious barriers to attaining decent living conditions for all Americans. These are not enough existing housing, substandard conditions prevalent in the low-income housing sector, widespread discrimination, rising and uncontrolled rents, and the pattern of legal relationships between landlords and tenants. There is a severe shortage of housing in the low and moderate rent categories in many areas of the United States. Urban renewal, highways, and other public programs that annually demolish tens of thousands of units, as well as demolitions by private owners seeking more profitable uses for their property, add constantly to this shortage. The housing allowance program, confined to use for existing units, will do nothing to add to the total supply of housing and can, therefore, be effective only in those areas where there is an abnormally high vacancy rate for low- and moderate-income housing.

The past several decades have seen a marked decline in housing conditions in a great many inner-city and rural areas. Landlords in these areas for the most part have not kept up their properties, nor have they had to. The short supply of available housing has created a monopoly market for landlords, and local housing code officials have been unable to enforce minimum housing standards. The few landlords who desire to maintain decent conditions were often deterred by deterioration in the surrounding neighborhood— created by a neglect by fellow landlords and the city's failure to provide proper levels of municipal services—and by the red-lining practices of banks and insurance companies, which effectively cut whole areas off from badly needed renovation capital. The cumulative result of these years of neglect will not be obliterated simply by giving current housing consumers more rent money to spend.

An example of how landlords will respond to the added rent revenue made through housing allowances is provided by New York City's maximum base rental (MBR) program. An analysis of the impact of MBR by the New York State Study Commission for New York City revealed the following:

HDA inspected buildings with violations on the books; of the 36,000 certifications which landlords reported as free of violations, 17,000 were found, upon

> inspection, to be false. . . . If HDA inspections of
> violations showed that almost half of the certifications
> were false, it could well be imagined what an inquiry
> into "essential services" might produce.[22]

Given the final form of the MBR program and its subsequent administration, it is obvious that it has become primarily a mechanism for increasing rents paid.

In the housing market, some money talks louder than other. Merely having the ability to pay the rent or sale price does not guarantee that the housing consumer will get what he wants to buy. Federal, state, and local fair housing laws, landmark court decisions, and various affirmative action programs haven't had an effect on the housing problem.

The implications of this discriminatory market for the housing allowance program are clear. Landlords will covertly charge a premium to housing allowance recipients for the privilege of being accepted as tenants. Realtors and agents will steer minority families to older, racially changing neighborhoods that offer the possibility of profitable blockbusting. Despite increased rent rolls, landlords will refuse to invest in major repairs because the influx of poor and minority tenants make the market a monopoly market. Lenders will continue to red-line these neighborhoods when considering repair loans and refinancing.

The widespread shortage of low- and moderate-income housing has led to unprecedented rent rises over the past few years. In the current market, with landlords free to charge what the traffic will bear, the poor are being badly squeezed. With a tight housing supply and rampant discrimination in the rental of available units, the response of landlords will be to inflate rents as much as possible.

In most parts of the United States, tenants are legally vulnerable to the caprice of their landlords regarding the condition of the housing they lease and the terms and rules of tenancy. In the absence of a written lease (and most low-income tenants have no such protection), a landlord may raise the rent without limitation and on short notice. Landlords may evict a tenant without a lease for no stated reason with only 30 days' notice. The tenant is not permitted to raise as a defense against eviction the dilapidated condition of the premises.

NOTES

1. Arthur Solomon, Housing the Urban Poor (Cambridge, Mass.: MIT-Harvard Joint Center for Urban Studies, 1974), p. 1.

2. Report of the President's Committee on Urban Housing, A Decent Home (Washington, D.C.: U.S. Government Printing Office, 1968), p. 55.

3. Ibid., p. 56.

4. See H. Wolman, "How Is Federal Housing Policy Made," Journal of Housing, April 1969, p. 189.

5. Ibid.

6. Department of Housing and Urban Development, Summary of the Housing and Community Development Act of 1974, August 1974, p. 1.

7. Ibid.

8. Ibid., p. 6.

9. Ibid., p. 7.

10. Ibid., p. 8.

11. Ibid.

12. Ibid.

13. Ibid., p. 10.

14. Department of Housing and Urban Development, Nondiscrimination in Federally Assisted Programs—Title VI of the Civil Rights Act of 1964, July 1973, p. i.

15. Ibid., pp. 2-3.

16. C. Hartman and D. Keating, "The Housing Delusion," Journal of Social Policy, January 1974, p. 31.

17. Ibid., p. 32.

18. Department of Health, Education and Welfare, The Role of Public Welfare in Housing (Washington, D.C.: U.S. Government Printing Office, 1969).

19. Department of Housing and Urban Development, Office of Audit, "HUD Monitoring of Local Authority Management of Section 23 Leased Housing Program," Region 1, July 1972.

20. Reports on the Section 235 home ownership program are: U.S. Congress, House Committee on Banking and Currency, Investigation and Hearings of Abuses in Federal Low and Moderate Income Housing Programs: Staff Report and Recommendations, 91st Cong., 2d sess., December 1970; Committee on Government Operations, Defaults on FHA Insured Home Mortgages—Detroit, Michigan, 92d Cong., 2d sess., June 20, 1972, H. Rept. 92-1152; and U.S. Commission on Civil Rights, Home Ownership for Lower Income Families: A Report on the Racial and Ethnic Impact of the Section 235 Program (Washington, D.C.: U.S. Government Printing Office, June 1971).

21. Department of Housing and Urban Development, Office of Audit, op. cit.

22. New York State Study Commission, The Management of the Maximum Base Rental Program by the Housing and Development Administration of New York City from June, 1970 to October, 1972, pp. 37, 70, and 81.

BIBLIOGRAPHY

HOUSING

Abrams, Charles. Forbidden Neighbors. New York: Harper, 1955.

Adams, Ian, William Cameron, Brian Hill, and Peter Pena. The Real Poverty Report. Alberta, Canada: M. G. Hurtig, 1971.

Aiken, Michael, and Robert Alford. "Community Structure and Innovation: The Case of Public Housing." American Political Science Review 64 (September 1970): 843.

Altshuler, Alan. The City Planning Process: A Political Analysis. Ithaca, N.Y.: Cornell University Press, 1965.

_____. Community Control. New York: Western Publishing Company, 1970.

Anderson, Martin. The Federal Bulldozer: A Critical Analysis of Urban Renewal 1949-62. Cambridge, Mass.: MIT Press, 1964.

Bailey, Martin J. "Effects of Race and Other Demographic Features on the Values of Single Family Houses." Land Economics, May 1966, pp. 215-20.

_____. "Note on the Economics of Residential Zoning and Urban Renewal." Land Economics, August 1959, pp. 288-90.

Banfield, Edward. The Unheavenly City. Boston: Little, Brown, 1968.

Banfield, Edward, ed. Urban Government: A Reader in Administration and Politics. New York: The Free Press, 1969.

Becker, Gary. The Economics of Discrimination. Chicago: University of Chicago Press, 1957.

Beehler, G., Jr. "Colored Occupancy Raises Values." Review of the Society of Residential Appraisers 1, no. 9 (September 1945).

Bellush, Jewel, and Stephen David, eds. Race and Politics in New York. New York: Praeger, 1972.

Blalock, Hubert. "Economic Discrimination and Negro Increase." American Sociological Review 22 (1969): 584.

Blank, David, and Louis Winnick. "The Structure of the Housing Market." Quarterly Journal of Economics 67 (May 1953): 181.

Bookchin, Murray. "The Myth of City Planning." Liberation 18, no. 2 (1973): 24.

Bradburn, Sudman, Grockel, and Noel. Side by Side (Integrated Neighborhoods in America). Chicago: Quadrangle Books, 1971.

Burghardt, Stephen, ed. Tenants and the Urban Housing Crisis. Dexter, Mich.: The New Press, 1972.

Carey, George. "Density, Crowding, Stress and the Ghetto." American Behavioral Scientist, 1970, p. 495.

Carmichael, Stokely, and Charles V. Hamilton. Black Power: The Politics of Liberation in America. New York: Vintage Books, 1967.

Casstevens, Thomas. Politics, House and Race Relations. Berkeley: University of California Press, 1967.

Clark, Tom C., and Philip B. Pearlman. Prejudice and Property: An Historic Brief against Racial Covenants. Washington, D.C.: Public Affairs Press, 1948.

Collard, D. "Price and Prejudice in the Housing Market." Economic Journal, June 1973.

Commission on Race and Housing. Where Shall We Live? Berkeley: University of California Press, 1958.

Cox, Oliver. Class, Caste and Race. New York: Monthly Review Press, 1959.

Crecine, J. P. Financing the Metropolis. Beverly Hills, Calif.: Sage Publications, 1970.

Dear, M. "The Neighborhood Impact of Mental Health Facility Siting." Regional Science Research Institute Discussion Paper, Series G.P.O., Philadelphia.

DeVise, P., et al. "Slum Medicine: Chicago's Apartheid Health System." Chicago: Community and Family Study Center, University of Chicago, Report No. 6, 1969.

Donnison, D. V. The Government of Housing. Penguin Books, 1967.

Downs, Anthony. "An Economic Analysis of Property Values and Race." Land Economics, 1960, pp. 181-88.

_____. Urban Problems and Prospects. Chicago: Markham, 1970.

Duhl, L. J., and R. L. Leopold, eds. Mental Health and Urban Social Policy. San Francisco: Jossey-Bass, 1968.

Duncan, Beverly, and Phillip Hauser. Housing and Metropolis Chicago. Glencoe, Ill.: The Free Press, 1960.

Duncan, Otis. The Negro Population of Chicago: A Study of Residential Succession. Chicago: University of Chicago Press, 1957.

Dyckman, John, et al. Community Facilities: Social Values and Goals in Planning for Education, Health and Recreation. Berkeley: Institute of Urban and Regional Development, University of California, 1967.

Edel, Matthew, and Jerome Rothenberg, eds. Readings in Urban Economics. New York: Macmillan, 1972.

Eiberson, Harold. Sources for the Study of the New York Area. New York: City College Press, 1960.

Farley, Reynolds. "The Changing Distribution of Negroes within Metropolitan Areas: The Emergence of Black Suburbs." American Journal of Sociology 75 (January 1970).

Fisher, E. Principles of Real Estate Practice. New York: Macmillan, 1923.

_____. Urban Real Estate Markets. Washington, D.C.: National Bureau of Economic Research, 1951.

Fisher, R. Twenty Years of Public Housing. New York: Harper, 1959.

Forman, Robert. Black Ghettos, White Ghettos and Slums. Englewood Cliffs, N.J.: Prentice-Hall, 1971.

Fowler, Gary. "Residential Distribution of Urban Appalachians." Unpublished paper, Columbus, Ohio, 1974.

Freedman, Leonard. Public Housing: The Politics of Poverty. New York: Holt, Rinehart and Winston, 1969.

Friedman, Lawrence. Government and Slum Housing. Chicago: Rand McNally, 1968.

Goodman, Robert. After the Planners. New York: Simon and Schuster, 1971.

Gordon, D. M., ed. Problems in Political Economy: An Urban Perspective. Lexington, Mass.: D. C. Heath, 1971.

Goro, Herb. The Block. New York: Random House, 1970.

Graves, Clifford. "The Planning Agency and the Black Community." Planning 1971. Chicago: American Society of Planning Officials, 1971.

Grigsby, W. G. Housing Markets and Public Policy. Philadelphia: University of Pennsylvania Press, 1963.

Gutman, Robert, ed. People and Buildings. New York: Basic Books, 1972.

Harberger, Arnold. The Demand for Durable Goods. Chicago: University of Chicago Press, 1960.

Harris, R. N. S., G. S. Tolley, and C. Harrel. "The Residential Site Choice." Review of Economics and Statistics 50 (May 1968): 241.

Hartman, Chester. "The Limitations of Public Housing: Relocation Choices in a Working Class Community." Journal of the American Institute of Planners 29 (November 1963): 283.

Harvey, David. Social Justice and the City. Baltimore: Johns Hopkins University Press, 1973.

Harvey, David, and Lata Chaterjee. "Absolute Rent and the Structuring of Space by Governmental and Financial Institutions." Unpublished paper, Baltimore: Johns Hopkins University, 1974.

Haugen, Robert A., and A. James Heins. "A Market Separation Theory of Rent Differentials in Metropolitan Areas." Quarterly Journal of Economics, November 1969, pp. 62-66.

Hauser, Phillip. The Study of Population. Chicago: University of Chicago Press, 1959.

Helper, Rose. Racial Policies and Practices of Real Estate Brokers. Minneapolis: University of Minnesota Press, 1967.

Hill, Herbert. Demographic Change and Racial Ghettos: The Crisis of American Cities. Detroit: University of Detroit, 1966.

Hill, William. "Racial Restrictive Housing Covenants." Opportunity, March 1946.

Hirshen, Al, and Vivian Brown. "Too Poor for Public Housing: Roger Starr's Poverty Preferences." Social Policy, May/June 1972, p. 28.

Hoyt, Homer. The Structure and Growth of Residential Neighborhoods in American Cities. Washington, D.C.: FHA, 1939.

Hunter, David R. The Slums. New York: The Free Press, 1964.

Jacobs, Jane. The Death and Life of Great American Cities. New York: Random House, 1961.

Kain, John. Race and Poverty. Englewood Cliffs, N.J.: Prentice-Hall, 1969.

Kain, John, and John Quigley. "Housing Market Discrimination, Home Ownership and Savings Behavior." American Economic Review, March 1972.

Kriesberg, Louis. "Neighborhood Setting and the Isolation of Public Housing Tenants." Journal of the American Institute of Planners 34 (January 1968): 43.

Kristoff, Frank. "Housing, Policy Goals and the Turnover of Housing." Journal of the American Institute of Planners 31 (August 1965): 232.

Lansing, John B., and Nancy Barth. Residential Location and Urban Mobility: A Multivariate Analysis. Ann Arbor: Survey Research Center of Institute for Social Research at the University of Michigan, 1964.

Lansing, John B., and Robert Marans. "Evaluation of Neighborhood Quality." Journal of the American Institute of Planners 35 (May 1969): 195.

Larner, Jeremy, and Irving Howe. Poverty: Views from the Left. New York: William Morrow, 1965.

Laurenti, Luigi. "Effects of Non-White Purchases on Market Prices of Residences." The Appraisal Journal, June 1952.

_____. Property Values and Race. Berkeley: University of California Press, 1960.

Ledbetter, William, Jr. "Public Housing—A Social Experiment Seeks Acceptance." Law and Contemporary Problems 32 (Summer 1967): 490.

Lee, T. "Urban Neighborhoods as a Socio-Spatial Schema." Journal of Human Relations 21, no. 3 (1972): 241-68.

LeGates, Richard T. "Can the Social Welfare Bureaucracies Control Their Programs: The Case of HUD and Urban Renewal." Working Paper No. 176. Berkeley: Institute of Urban and Regional Development, University of California, 1972.

Lempert, Richard, and Kyoshi Ideka. "Evictions from Public Housing: Effects of Independent Review." American Sociological Review, October 1970, p. 852.

Lipsky, Michael. Protest in City Politics: Rent Strikes, Housing and the Power of the Poor. Chicago: Rand-McNally, 1969.

Long, Herman, and Charles Johnson. People vs. Property: Race Restrictive Covenants in Housing. Nashville, Tenn. Fisk University Press, 1947.

Loring, William. "Housing Characteristics and Social Disorganization." Social Problems, 1967.

Lowry, Ira, Judy Gueron, and Karen Eisenstadt. Welfare Housing in New York City. New York: Rand Institute, 1972.

Luttrel, Jordan. "The Public Housing Administration and Discrimination in Federally Assisted Low Rent Housing." Michigan Law Review 64 (March 1966): 87.

Lym, Glenn R. "Effect of a Public Housing Project on a Neighborhood: Case Study of Oakland, California." Land Economics 43 (November 1967): 451.

Marcus, M. "Racial Composition and Home Price Changes." Journal of American Institute of Planners 34, no. 5 (September 1968).

Margolis, Julius, ed. The Public Economy of Urban Communities. Resources for the Future, Inc. Baltimore: Johns Hopkins University Press, 1965.

May, Arthur. The Valuation of Residential Real Estate. Englewood Cliffs, N.J.: Prentice-Hall, 1942.

Mayhew, Leon H. Law and Equal Opportunity: A Study of the Massachusetts Commission against Discrimination. Cambridge, Mass.: Harvard University Press, 1968.

McEntire, Davis. Residence and Race. Berkeley: University of California Press, 1960.

McGraw, B. T. "Desegregation and Open Occupancy Trends in Housing." Journal of Human Relations, Autumn 1954.

McKenna, Joseph, and Herbert Werner. The Housing Market in Integrating Areas. St. Louis Center of Community and Metropolitan Studies, University of Missouri, 1969.

Meyerson, Martin, and Edward Banfield. Politics, Planning and Public Interest: The Case of Public Housing in Chicago. New York: The Free Press, 1955.

Mitchell, Robert E. "Some Social Implications of High Density Housing." American Sociological Review 36 (February 1971): 18.

Molotch, Harvey. "Racial Change in a Transition Community." American Sociological Review 24 (December 1969): 873.

Moore, William, Jr. The Vertical Ghetto: Everyday Life in an Urban Project. New York: Random House, 1969.

Mulvihill, Robert. "Problems in the Management of Public Housing." Temple Law Quarterly 35 (1962): 163.

Muth, Richard F. Cities and Housing. Chicago: University of Chicago Press, 1969.

Myrdal, Gunnar. An American Dilemma. New York: Harper & Row, 1962.

National Advisory Commission on Civil Disorders. Report of the National Advisory Commission on Civil Disorders. Washington, D.C.: U.S. Government Printing Office, 1968.

National Committee against Discrimination in Housing. How the Federal Government Builds Ghettos. New York: 1967.

_____. The Impact of Housing Patterns on Job Opportunities. New York: 1968.

Newman, Oscar. Defensible Space. New York: Macmillan, 1973.

Page, A. N., and W. R. Seyfried, eds. Urban Analysis: Readings in Housing and Urban Development. Glenview, Ill.: Scott, Foresman, 1970.

Parker, Elsie Smith. "Both Sides of the Color Line." The Appraisal Journal 1, no. 3 (July 1943).

Pascal, A. H. The Economics of Housing Segregation: Memorandum RM-5510 RC. Santa Monica, Calif.: The Rand Corporation, 1967.

Peattie, Lisa Redfield. "Public Housing: Urban Slums under Public Management." In Race, Change and Urban Society, edited by P. Orleans and W. Ellis. New York: Sage Publications, 1971.

Perloff, Harvey S., and Lowdon Wingo, Jr., eds. Issues in Urban Economics. Baltimore: Johns Hopkins University Press, 1968.

Phares, Donald. "Racial Change and Housing Values: Transition in an Inner Suburb." Social Science Quarterly 52 (December 1971): 560.

Pynoos, Jon, Robert Schafer, and Chester Hartman, eds. Housing Urban America. Chicago: Aldine, 1974.

"Racial Discrimination in Public Housing Site Selection." Stanford Law Review 23 (1970): 63.

Rainwater, Lee. Behind Ghetto Walls: Black Family Life in a Federal Slum. Chicago: Aldine, 1970.

_____. "The Social Effects of the Physical Environment." Journal of the American Institute of Planners, May 1961, p. 127.

Rapkin, Chester, and William G. Grigsby. The Demand for Housing in Racially Mixed Areas. Berkeley: University of California Press, 1960.

Ridker, Ronald, and John Henning. "The Determinants of Residential Property Values with the Special Reference to Air Pollution." Review of Economics and Statistics, May 1967, pp. 246-57.

Robinson, Corrienne. "Relationship between Conditions of Dwelling and Rentals by Race." Journal of Land and Public Utility Economics, August 1946.

Ross, William. "A Proposed Methodology for Comparing Federally Assisted Housing Programs." American Economic Review, May 1967, p. 91.

Ryan, William. Blaming the Victim. New York: Pantheon, 1971.

Shank, Alan, ed. Political Power and the Urban Crisis. Boston: Holbrook Press, 1973.

Shietinger, E. F. "Racial Succession and Changing Property Values." Land Economics, November 1954, pp. 201-8.

Shuman, Sara. "Differential Rents for White and Negro Families." Journal of Housing, August 1964.

Social Science Panel. Freedom of Choice in Housing. Washington, D.C.: National Academy of Sciences, 1972.

Speigel, Hans, and Stephen Mittenthal. Neighborhood Power and
Control: Implications for Urban Renewal Planning. Institute of
Urban Environment, School of Architecture, Columbia University,
New York, 1968.

Spengler, J. J. "Population Pressure, Housing and Habitat." Law
and Contemporary Problems, 1967.

Sterner, Richard. The Negro's Share. New York: Harper &
Bros., 1943.

Sternlieb, George, and J. B. Indik. "Housing Vacancy Analysis."
Land Economics, February 1969.

Stokols, Daniel. "On the Distinction between Density and Crowding:
Some Implications for Future Research." Psychological Review
79 (May 1972): 275.

Sutermeister, Oscar. "Inadequacies and Inconsistencies in the
Definition of Substandard Housing." Housing Code Standards:
Three Critical Studies. Research Report No. 19. Washington,
D.C.: National Commission on Urban Problems, 1970.

Suttles, Gerald. The Social Construction of Communities. Chicago:
University of Chicago Press, 1972.

_____. The Social Order of the Slum. Chicago: University of
Chicago Press, 1968.

Taggart, Robert, III. Low Income Housing: A Critique of Federal
Aid. Baltimore: Johns Hopkins University Press, 1970.

Taueber, Karl E., and Alma F. Taueber. Negroes in Cities: Residential Segregation and Neighborhood Change. Chicago: Aldine,
1965.

U.S. Bureau of the Census. Measuring the Quality of Housing: An
Appraisal of Census Statistics and Methods. Washington, D.C.:
U.S. Government Printing Office, 1967.

_____. The Methods and Material of Demography. Washington,
D.C.: U.S. Government Printing Office, 1969.

U.S. Department of Housing and Urban Development, F.H.A. Techniques of Housing Market Analysis. Washington, D.C.: U.S.
Government Printing Office, 1970.

U.S. Department of Housing and Urban Development, Department of Justice, Office of Economic Opportunity. Legal Tools for Better Housing. Report on a National Conference on Legal Rights of Tenants. Washington, D.C.: U.S. Government Printing Office, 1967.

U.S. Housing and Home Finance Agency. Open Occupancy in Public Housing. Washington, D.C.: U.S. Government Printing Office, 1968.

University of Kentucky. An Economic Analysis of Migration from Rural Eastern Kentucky. Contract #NIH-70-2198, National Institute of Health.

Vietorisz, Thomas, and Bennett Harrison. The Economic Development of Harlem. New York: Praeger, 1970.

vonFurstenburg, George M. "Distribution of Federally Assisted Rental Housing." Journal of the American Institute of Planners 37 (September 1971): 326.

vonFurstenburg, George, Bennett Harrison, and A. Horowitz, eds. Patterns of Racial Discrimination. Vol. 1: Housing. Lexington, Mass.: D. C. Heath, 1974.

Watkins, Alfred. "City Age and the Typology of Subemployment." Document No. 9. Research Center for Economic Planning. New York, 1975.

Weaver, Robert. The Negro Ghetto. New York: Harcourt, Brace, 1948.

Welfare Council of New York City. Census Tract Data on Population and Housing. New York, 1940.

Wilkinson, R., and Gulliver. "The Impact of Non-Whites on Housing Prices." Race, no. 12 (June 1971).

Willie, Charles, Morton Wagenfeld, and Lee Cary. "Patterns of Rent Payment among Problem Families." Social Casework, October 1964.

Wilner, D. M. The Housing Environment and Family Life. Baltimore: Johns Hopkins University Press, 1962.

Wingo, Lowdon. Cities and Space: The Future Use of Urban Land. Baltimore: Johns Hopkins University Press, 1963.

Wolman, Harold. Politics of Federal Housing. New York: Dodd, Mead, 1971.

Wolpert, J., and R. Ginsberg. "The Transition to Interdependence in Locational Problems." In Behavioral Problems in Geography, edited by K. R. Cox and R. Ginsberg. Evanston, Ill.: Northwestern University Press, 1969.

Woodruff, Thomas. "Migration and the Labor Markets for Appalachian Workers." RCEP Working Paper No. 4, June 1974.

Yancey, William. "Architecture, Interactions and Social Control: The Case of a Large Scale Public Housing Project." Environment and Behavior 3 (March 1971): 3.

Yin, Robert, ed. The City in the Seventies. Itasca, Ill.: F. E. Peacock, 1972.

NEW YORK CITY STUDY NEIGHBORHOODS

Berubee, Maurice, and Marilyn Gittel. Confrontation at Ocean Hill-Brownsville. New York: Praeger, 1969.

"Crown Heights and Williamsburg—A Comparison of Two Hasidic Communities in Brooklyn." Protestant Council of Greater New York, 1969.

Friedman, Nathalie, and Naomi Golding. Neighborhood Variation: The Implications for Administrative Decentralization: An Analysis of Subcommunities in Brooklyn Community Planning District 5 (East New York). New York: Bureau of Applied Social Research, Columbia University, 1974.

_____. Urban Residents and Neighborhood Government: A Profile of the Public in Seven Urban Neighborhoods of New York City. New York: Bureau of Applied Social Research, Columbia University, 1973.

Geist, Richard. "Wreck of the Rockaways." New York Affairs 11, no. 2 (1974): 90.

Glauber, Rae. All Neighborhoods Change—Brownsville. New York: N.P., 1961.

Goell, Milton. Brownsville Must Have Public Housing. New York: Brooklyn Committee for Better Housing, 1940.

_____. East New York Must Have Public Housing. New York: Brooklyn Committee for Better Housing, 1941.

Hoberman and Wasserman. South Jamaica Community Development Study. New York: Hoberman and Wasserman Architects, 1971.

Housing and Development Administration. "Planning for a Target Area—East New York." New York, 1967.

Human Resources Administration. The Plan for Community Social Services, East New York, HRA District No. 13. New York, 1972.

Kaufman, R. "A Housing Market Analysis of the Rockaway Peninsula." New York: Housing and Development Administration, 1969.

Landesman, Alter. Brownsville—The Birth, Life and Passing of a Jewish Community in New York. New York: Bloch Publishing Company, 1971.

New York City Planning Department. New York City Master Plan, 1969.

_____. "Public and Publicly Aided Housing 1927-1973." New York: Department of City Planning, 1975.

Office of Neighborhood Government, City Planning Department, Housing and Development Administration. "CHAMP STRATEGY, CHAMP FACTS—Crown Heights." New York, 1972.

Protestant Council of Greater New York. East New York and Neighboring Communities. New York, 1973.

State Study Commission for New York City. Urban Renewal in Brownsville. New York, 1973.

SOCIAL INDICATORS AND
NEIGHBORHOOD QUALITY

American Statistical Association. "Social Indicators for Small Areas." Washington, D.C.: U.S. Department of Commerce, Social and Economic Statistics Administration, 1972.

Bauer, R., ed. Social Indicators. Cambridge, Mass.: MIT Press, 1966.

Carlisle, Elaine. "The Uses of Small Area Social Indicators." In Social Indicators and Social Policy, edited by Andrew Schonfield and Stella Shaw. London: Heinemann, 1972.

Donnison, David, and David Eversley. London—Urban Problems, Patterns and Policies. Beverly Hills, Calif.: Sage Publications, 1973.

Fried, Joseph. Housing Crisis U.S.A. New York: Praeger, 1971.

Halpern, Irving, John Stanislaus, and Bernard Botein. Slums and Crime—A Statistical Study of the Distribution of Adult and Juvenile Delinquents in the Boroughs of Manhattan and Brooklyn. New York: New York City Housing Authority, 1934.

Hughes, James. Urban Indicators, Metropolitan Evolution and Public Policy. New Brunswick, N.J.: Center for Urban Policy Research, Rutgers University, 1972.

Insel, Paul, and Rudolf Moos. Health and the Social Environment: Issues in Social Ecology. Lexington, Mass.: Lexington Books, 1974.

Katz, Alfred, and Fean Felton. Health and the Community. New York: The Free Press, 1965.

Lambert, John. Crime, Police and Race Relations. London: Oxford University Press, 1970.

Marcuse, Peter. "Social Indicators and Housing Policy." Urban Affairs Quarterly, December 1971.

Mays, John. Crime and Social Structure. London: Faber and Faber, 1963.

Monti, Lorna. Social Indicators for Austin, Texas: A Cluster Analysis. Bureau of Business Research, Graduate School of Business, University of Texas, Austin, 1975.

Norris, J. N. "Uses of Epidemiology." New Society, December, 1970.

Schonfield, Andrew, and Stella Shaw. Social Indicators and Social Policy. London: Heinemann, 1972.

Shulman, Harry. A Study of Problem Boys and Their Brothers—A Report of the Subcommission on Causes and Effects of Crime. New York: New York State Crime Commission, 1929.

Somers, Anne R. Health Care in Transition. Chicago: Hospital Research and Education Trust, 1971.

Thrasher, Frederick. The Gang. Chicago: University of Chicago Press, 1929.

U.S. Department of Health, Education and Welfare. Toward a Social Report. Washington, D.C.: U.S. Government Printing Office, 1972.

Wilner, Daniel. The Housing Environment and Family Life: Longitudinal Study of the Effects of Housing on Morbidity and Mental Health. Baltimore: Johns Hopkins University Press, 1962.

Yin, Robert. Policy Uses of Urban Indicators. New York: The Rand Corporation, 1972.

ABOUT THE AUTHOR

DIANE GOLD received a BSBA from Babson College. She received an M.A. in Sociology from New York University. She completed an M.A. and Ph.D. in Economics at the New School for Social Research. Dr. Gold is currently an Assistant Professor of Accountancy at Bernard Baruch College of the City University of New York. She is currently doing research on municipal services and public transportation systems.